HAROLD WILSON AND THE 'BIG SIX'

CW01091165

By the same author

(as Mike Lloyd-Jones)

Just Complaints

The Fortunate Island

The Tackle and Bait

HAROLD WILSON AND THE 'BIG SIX'

Michael Lloyd-Jones

HOWL BOOKS

ISBN-9798846376960

First published in 2022 by Howl Books

CONTENTS

1

Cabinet-Making for Beginners

Harold Wilson's government came to power in October 1964 with a knife-edge margin of only four seats (at the time an unprecedently small majority). Opinion polls earlier in the year had predicted a substantial Labour victory but over the summer the gap had narrowed. Nonetheless the final polls before the day of the election (from both NOP and Gallup) had suggested that Labour would win with a double-figure majority.

But while Wilson may have arrived in Downing Street with a less than convincing victory, his qualifications for office were undeniable. A brilliant academic career at Oxford had been followed by ground-breaking work as an assistant to William Beveridge, before becoming, during the second world war, Head of Statistics at the Ministry of Fuel and Power. Within days of his entry to Parliament in the Labour landslide of 1945 he had been appointed by Attlee as Parliamentary Secretary to the Minister of Works, a clear signal that he was immediately recognised as a significant political talent. In 1947 he was appointed as President of the Board of Trade – making him, at 31, the youngest member of the cabinet. It was this post and its consequent work on deregulation of war-

time restrictions that gave him the opportunity to become at least something of a public 'personality', when he was able to appear on cinema newsreels announcing, with an early demonstration of a flair for phrase-making, that he was igniting a "bonfire of controls".

He had resigned from Attlee's cabinet in a walkout with Aneurin Bevan over the imposition of prescription charges, but after the Conservatives came back into power, in 1951, Wilson had returned to the fold and served as Shadow Chancellor and then Shadow Foreign Secretary under Hugh Gaitskell. In short, his résumé for the post of Prime Minister was glittering. Professor Peter Hennessey has concluded that "No one was better prepared on paper for No 10 than Harold Wilson."

Given his record and achievements it would have been easy to suppose that when Wilson finally came to power, he would dominate his government, casting all others around him into comparative shade. Before the election Conservatives had tried to dismiss him as a 'one-man band'. But the reality was that when he formed his Cabinet it was packed with figures who were, or would become, rival giants - figures who might not be his equal in terms of tactical skill but could easily compete with him in terms of brainpower and charisma.

But if Wilson assumed that a collaboration of major talents around the cabinet table - with all its possibilities for an effective pooling of knowledge, expertise and insight - would ensure political success, he was to be proved wrong. Despite repeated attempts to revise a negative retrospective judgment, the Wilson government

of 1964-70 has gone down in political history as at best a disappointment and at worst as a largely sorry and sometimes sordid record of failure. And instead of harnessing dynamic synergy (an almost Wilsonian phrase in itself), the drawing together of a group with such powerful egos bred tensions, rivalries and suspicions.

Wilson arrived in Downing Street with his cabinet appointments already mapped-out and determined, according to the recollection of his then Private Secretary, to complete the appointments at greater speed than that achieved by any of his predecessors. The names of his first six and most senior Ministers were sent to the Palace within hours of him being formally invited by the Queen to form a government. Whilst this speediness clearly indicates that his appointments had been planned in advance, the haste in their announcement is likely to have been prompted by an eye to image-making - a determination to be seen to be living up to a pledge he had made a few months earlier: "We are going to have to tackle all these problems pretty well at once. What we are going to need is something like what President Kennedy had after years of stagnation – the programme of 100 days of dynamic action."[1]

In making his choices Wilson was under no illusion that he had a completely free hand. Amongst his first and most senior appointments it was inevitable that he would include George Brown and James Callaghan – his two opponents in the leadership contest of just eighteen months before. Wilson was acutely conscious that his victory in the leadership contest had not been a walkover and that he was far from a unanimous choice of his backbenchers. Wilson had topped the first leadership ballot with 115 votes, but his opponents Brown and Callaghan had attracted 129 votes between them. In the final run-off ballot against Brown, after Callaghan had been eliminated after finishing in third place, the final vote had given him a 41-vote lead over his nearest rival, George Brown, a decisive victory but not a totally emphatic one. So, Wilson had clear evidence that he had not been overwhelmingly endorsed by his party – a fact that would have been no surprise, because in his career he had managed to breed mistrust on both his left and his right wings.

Beyond these personal issues Wilson was also hyper-sensitive to what he saw as the lessons of his party's history and in particular to the dangers of party division. For Wilson, his memory of the Labour's party's previous splits (between Ramsay Macdonald and the party in 1931 and more recently between Hugh Gaitskell and Aneurin Bevan) was a preoccupation that became not just a guide to his actions but a determiner of them. Over time his concern to 'keep the party together' would develop into something approaching an obsession.

So, in his selection of cabinet colleagues Wilson was conscious that he was constrained not just by the personalities who had been his rivals for leadership, but also by a need to show balance between the wings of his party. For example, his appointment of the left-wing trade union leader Frank Cousins as Minister of Technology was counter-balanced by his choice of right-wing trade union leader Ray Gunter as Minister of Labour. A further constraint was the obligation to draw his ministerial team from the mixed bag that had made up the Labour shadow cabinet.

Months before the election Wilson had confided to Tony Benn that his first Cabinet would have to be a compromise: "My real cabinet will be made in 1966 – just as Clem's was in 1947."[2] But there was never to be a 'real' cabinet – not in the sense of a group of men and women picked and melded to be of one mind with their leader. Events and crises – some of them prompted by events outside of the government's control but some very much of its own making – meant that Wilson would never feel strong enough to exercise a free hand in the choice of his colleagues. In fact, as time passed he felt increasingly vulnerable and was repeatedly suspicious of what he recognised – or misinterpreted – as efforts to dislodge and replace him.

Partly in consequence – and partly because of a natural tendency – Wilson ensured that his cabinet was kept suitably distanced from decisions in which he believed they should not interfere. His tactics included extensive use of Cabinet committees, including eventually the creation of an 'inner-cabinet', and tactical destabilisation through the frequent reshuffling of his Ministers – for example during the nearly six years in government Wilson had three different Home Secretaries, four Secretaries of State for Education and three Ministers of Transport.

This determination to keep his Cabinet at arms-length was not something which Wilson stumbled into as time went by, but a tactic which was overt from the very start. In his memoir of his 1964-70 administration Wilson recalled: "One of the first decisions to be taken by the new Cabinet was the endorsement of the economic proposals put before it by the three of us who had met on that first Saturday morning. There was no disposition to argue."

The reality behind this picture of collective consultation and unanimous Cabinet agreement is very different. Richard Crossman recorded that same meeting for his diary: "During this period – Monday to Thursday – of my first week there have been two Cabinet meetings. The first was a mere formality only concerned with the economic crisis and, honestly, we were told as little about it as the National Executive of the Party is ever told. It really was an absolute farce to have George Brown saying, 'Naturally you won't want to be told, for fear of the information leaking how serious the situation is. You won't want to be told what methods we shall take but we shall take them.'"[3]

In fact, two days before that first meeting of the full Cabinet there had been the first meeting of the Economic Affairs sub-committee. The members of this committee were assembled not for discussion but to be presented by Wilson with a *fait accompli*. He informed the members of the committee that he, George Brown and James Callaghan had already met and reached the crucial decision that there would be no change to the exchange rate.

Over time Wilson moved further and further away from cabinet-based decision-making and relied more and more on behind-the-scenes manoeuvring to establish his will.

Given the frustration this caused his colleagues it was hardly surprising that his tactics stimulated genuine distrust within the Cabinet which in turn fuelled more suspicion in Wilson's mind and increased his tendency to act in ways that stimulated further resentment.

Perhaps it would have suited Wilson to have filled his Cabinet with ministers who would prove capable at the level of their own department but would be willingly passive non-participants in the wider business of government.   But what gives Wilson's cabinet its particular significance and makes its story so full of lasting drama is that it was dominated not by nonentities but by ministers of great ability and with big personalities to match. The heft exercised by these characters ensured that their successes, failures, ambitions, frustrations and rivalries played out not quietly but as high drama.

Past attempts to examine and analyse Wilson's first government have, however, been mainly focused on the dominating role of the Prime Minister. This singularity of focus is understandable but has had the effect of imposing a particularly 'Wilsonian' view of the administration. This study aims to redress the balance and sets out to explore and illustrate the drama of this first Wilson government through biographical studies of the personalities, action and influence of a 'Big Six' - the most significant figures around Wilson's cabinet table: George Brown, Richard Crossman, James Callaghan, Barbara Castle, Denis Healey and Roy Jenkins.

These ministers form a diverse group. They came from different wings of the party and from different socioeconomic backgrounds - for example, while Richard Crossman's father had been a barrister, George Brown's father had been variously a lorry driver and a salesman. Unlike the prominent members of most previous cabinets they did not share a similar academic background – Castle, Crossman, Healey and Jenkins had all gone to Oxford, but Brown and Callaghan had not been to university at all. As a group they were frequently at odds amongst themselves. They were not even all in the Cabinet for the entire length of the administration. Roy Jenkins did not join the Cabinet until the end of 1965 and George Brown, though there from the beginning, had resigned by 1968.

One thing they all had in common, with the exception of Wilson, was a complete lack of any previous experience in government. – none of them had ever run a government department. More critically still, not one of them was emotionally prepared for the shock that followed from the immediate revelation of the true state of the government's finances and none of them, Wilson included, was intellectually prepared to handle the desperate economic crisis that they faced from their first day in office.

And yet, for all their inexperience, their disagreements and their rivalries, these ministers still formed a formidable team. Professor Noel Annan, in his survey of *Our Age*, rated the Wilson cabinet of 1964-70 amongst the most talented of the twentieth century.

They were all formidable politicians – bright, confident and fiercely combative. Each of them was a 'big beast' - a variety of politician largely absent from political life over the last twenty-five years – and the story of their characters, alliances and conflicts enables us to perceive the Wilson administration as a far more textured and nuanced thing than the conventional narrative of a group helpless in the hands of a master-puppeteer.

The 'Big Six' featured here may seem a very partial selection. Readers may puzzle at the exclusion of some notable figures – Tony Crosland, for example. But Crosland, despite his legendary status as the author of *The Future of Socialism*, cut a curiously weak figure in the Wilson government. He was a man of ideas rather than a practical actor and his deliberately-cultivated air of louche detachment kept him out of the mainstream – which perfectly suited Wilson, who knew well that at the time of his run-off against Brown for the Labour leadership, Crosland had characterised it as a contest "between a drunk and a crook".

The portraits that follow are not drawn exclusively from these ministers' time in cabinet. I have tried to trace out their backgrounds and their evolution as politicians, to explain how they came to be chosen by Wilson and to describe the experiences they had to draw on once in office. And because it seems unnecessarily short-sighted to draw a concluding line in 1970, I have at least lightly sketched-out their subsequent years. The back stories and the descriptions of the subsequent careers are in most cases only briefly described, but in one or two cases a more extended study is indicated. It would be impossible, for example, to make sense of Richard Crossman's behaviour and working relationships in office without knowledge of his previous time in Parliament and earlier – and short-sighted not to review the multi-faceted career of Roy Jenkins beyond 1970.

Conventional accounts of the 1964-70 government understandably place Wilson in the foreground. This study deliberate reverses that perspective to concentrate the initial focus on the stories of six of his leading colleagues. Of course Wilson features throughout each of the studies, but it is only in the last chapter that he gets singly-focused attention. This allows for a broader, more balanced study of the work of the Wilson government and enables its achievements – and its failings – to be more evenly evaluated than when it is all viewed through a lens primarily if not exclusively trained on Harold Wilson.

This is not a history of the 1964-70 government but a political character study. The dominant theme of this book is an examination of how, at the most senior level of government, the characteristics of individual politicians – their backgrounds, temperament and outlook - impacted on practical politics and external events.

2

George Brown:
Drunk with Power

The ups and downs of George Brown's career were physical as well as metaphorical. The man, whose formidable abilities and talents brought him to the heights of government office, was also a hopeless drunk, whose alcoholism would eventually precipitate a fall that was on occasions quite literal. A man of ordinary abilities, so evidently in the grip of a destructive dependency, could never have progressed. But although the effects of his alcoholism were frequently and publicly displayed, George Brown rose and continued to rise, His friends and colleagues stuck to Brown and continued to admire him, because, despite everything, he could be unmatched in his brilliance.

George Brown was born in Lambeth, just a few weeks after the start of the First World War, on September 2nd,1914. His family occupied two rooms in the Peabody Buildings in Lambeth, a housing development created by the American philanthropist and housing campaigner, George Peabody. Over the coming years his family moved, first to another Peabody block in Southwark and then to a London County Council flat in Streatham. When he left school, he found employment as a clerk in a business in Cheapside, a part of the City of London. He lost this job after just a year but was able to then find work for the John Lewis Partnership. His first job there was menial work in the company's fur store, but George attracted notice from the management and he was soon working as a junior salesman in the fur department of the Oxford Street store, earning commission on every fur he was able to sell.

Brown had become interested in politics while still at school and while working for John Lewis he became increasingly active in the Labour Party and in the Labour League of Youth. Soon after he got married, he left John Lewis and went to work for the Transport and General Workers Union and it was this move which, although financially disadvantageous because it meant losing his generous income from fur sales, was to provide him with a springboard from which he could enter national politics.

Although determinedly socialist, Brown was from the start instinctively on the right wing of the Labour Party. It was this position that provided the opportunity with which he attracted notice from the party's leadership, when he involved himself directly in the decision to expel the maverick Labour MP, Stafford Cripps, from the party.

Cripps had antagonised the leadership of his party by campaigning on two separate but related issues. Firstly, he had argued for the Labour Party to make common cause with the Communist Party to form what he called a 'United Front'. Secondly, he had campaigned for an alliance between socialists and capitalists which could confront the menace of fascism. This movement he, rather confusingly, termed a 'Popular Front'.

It was the notion of a 'Popular Front' that provided the party with a *casus belli*. Cripps had put up a paper supporting his idea to the National Executive, which duly rejected it. Cripps then sought to go around the Executive by circulating his paper to the local Labour Party branches and to Labour MPs. The National Executive tried to stop him from promoting the 'Popular Front' in this way and when he refused they agreed to expel him from the party. The National Executive's decision came up for debate at the party conference in May 1939 and it was there that George Brown got a chance to make a name for himself with a speech from the rostrum.

Brown was attending the conference as a constituency delegate for his local party, St Albans. He had, almost by chance, an opportunity to speak on the motion to expel Cripps and although his speech was described by his biographer as "emotional, excitable and, frankly, rather muddled", it was almost rapturously received. Brown had, even at this early stage, the seeds of a gift for the kind of naturally-stirring, almost tub-thumping, oratory that would make him in the future a platform favourite. His speech to the Stockport conference even included the use of a rallying form of fraternal address - "Brothers!" - that was to become almost a trademark feature in his speeches.

The impression that Brown made with his speech was sufficient to bring his name to mind when, after the war, a new Labour candidate was being sought for Belper, a constituency in the south of Derbyshire. The offer of candidature was dependent on Brown getting sponsorship from the Transport and General Workers Union. After some initial difficulty Brown eventually got the Union's agreement. At the previous general election, which because of the hiatus of war had been ten years earlier, the Conservative candidate had scraped-in by just over 800 votes. In the post-war Labour landslide George Brown romped home with a majority of just under 9000.

It had been a delay of six years before Brown's attention-catching speech at conference had paid its dividend, but within days of entering Parliament he benefited from something even further back in his past. While living as a teenager in Southwark he had helped to campaign for George Isaacs, the local Labour candidate. After Clement Attlee appointed Isaacs as Minister of Labour and National Service, Isaacs invited Brown to become his parliamentary private secretary.

To have been appointed as a PPS at the first opportunity was in itself a huge boost to Brown's fortunes. But, as luck had it, the position unexpectedly opened-up to offer far more responsibility and scope than a PPS would ever normally have. The task facing Isaacs as Minister of Labour and National Service was enormous. The demobilisation of around three million men and their return to the workplace was a huge programme to manage. In order to cope, Isaacs looked for a way of reducing the burden. His responsibilities also included the absorption of displaced persons from the chaos left in Europe at the end of the war and Isaacs saw an opportunity to slim down his workload by effectively delegating some of this work to his PPS. So Brown, at a stroke, although nominally still just a parliamentary private secretary, became a de facto junior minister, albeit unpaid.

Brown's luck continued. He had caught the eye of Hugh Dalton, a Labour veteran and, at the start of Attlee's government, Chancellor of the Exchequer. Dalton liked to gather around himself young MPs whom he regarded as showing promise and, as he recorded in his diary, these protégés would enjoy both his encouragement and his behind-the-scenes activities to advance their careers: "We must get our good young men on. I am always hammering at the PM on this."[1] Brown became one of those protégés and when another of them, Hugh Gaitskell, was, in May 1946, promoted from Dalton's PPS to the post of a junior minister in the Ministry of Fuel and Power, Dalton then invited Brown to take Gaitskell's place.

To have gone in less than a year from entrant backbencher to PPS to the Chancellor of the Exchequer was striking progress. It inevitably meant that Brown had to get used to the unofficial role of a proper parliamentary private secretary – essentially feeding back to Dalton titbits of information, gossip and rumour that Brown could pick up around the House and elsewhere. After his backroom role at the Ministry of Labour and National Service this might have seemed a step away from the direct machinery of government, but at least there was no loss of salary involved. Unfortunately for Brown working for Dalton in this way also drew him into a doomed plot against the Prime Minister.

Dalton was a born plotter and intriguer and a compulsive schemer. Roy Jenkins, with characteristic biographical flair, neatly pinned to the page Dalton's compulsion: "Some politicians try to intrigue in success, which is natural if not admirable. Others, and Dalton was not alone in this, try to do so in failure, which is perverse. Dalton found it difficult not to do so in all circumstances...".[2]

Brown's ear for backroom gossip provided music for Dalton's ears. In July 1947 Dalton recorded in his diary that Brown had told him that "all the boys all talked, during the all-night sitting this week on the Transport Bill, about the lack of leadership. Most were in favour of substituting Bevin for Attlee".[3] This played exactly into one of Dalton's schemes – to get Attlee replaced as Prime Minister by Ernest Bevin, so that he (Dalton) could step into Bevin's current position as Foreign Secretary, a post that Dalton coveted as a swansong to round-off his long career in politics.

Dalton tried to draw Bevin into his plot, during a long car journey together, returning from the Durham Miners' Gala and, incautiously from Brown's point of view, disclosed that Dalton had been assured by his PPS that many Labour MPs were in favour of Bevin displacing Attlee in Number 10. Bevin was non-committal at the time, but he later confronted Brown, telling him that he had never trusted him and now never wanted to see him again. Brown was not surprised soon after to be summoned to a meeting with the Prime Minister. But instead of the dressing-down he expected to receive, he was astonished to hear Attlee offer him his first step up the ministerial ladder - Parliamentary Secretary in the Ministry of Agriculture.

It had been a narrow squeak for Brown, whose biographer surmises that Attlee had decided that he was a troublemaker whose mischief needed to be sublimated by being kept occupied by government business. The Ministry of Agriculture at the time was certainly a good place to guarantee occupation for its ministers and officials. There was an urgent post-war need to improve the country's self-sufficiency by maximising food production, including a major Agricultural Bill to guarantee prices and regularise the market. The remit of the ministry was vast and Brown found himself dealing with a huge range of topics, including farm machinery, crop estimates, tractor tyre production, grazing land and poultry keeping.

This work continued to keep Brown occupied through and beyond the 1950 General Election in which he retained his seat (with an increased majority) and returned to his place at the Ministry of Agriculture. But although the Labour government was returned to power, it was with a tiny majority of just five. In May 1950 Herbert Morrison temporarily became acting Prime Minister while Attlee had to be hospitalised with a duodenal ulcer and it was during this interval that Brown was offered the post of Minister of Works.

As at his previous ministry the remit of the Ministry of Works was vast in scope. In the first months in post

Brown found himself dealing with an almost endless list of topics and while some of them related to major issues such as brick production, the greater bulk of the work involved wading through a mass of minor responsibilities, some of them almost comic, such as the issuing of towels to civil servants and the provision of lavatories in public houses. Perhaps it was the triviality of much of the Ministry's work that tempted Brown to stage a showdown with the Yeomen of the Guard, the men who staffed the Tower of London, in a row over Sunday opening. In itself the substance of the dispute was as petty as much of the rest of the Ministry's work, but by refusing to back down and manoeuvring the beefeaters into accepting defeat, Brown did achieve a victory that was personally satisfying and demonstrated that he was capable of resolute leadership.

These were heady days for George Brown, but it was not to last. In October 1951 Attlee, whose government was beset with difficulties that included a serious economic problem, called a general election. Brown was returned again at Belper, but Labour lost overall and Churchill returned to Number 10. This was in itself a serious setback to Brown (not least because it meant that financially he was £4000 a year worse off) but, to make matters worse, Attlee did not offer him a shadow spokesman post and so he was reduced to an entirely backbench role – a significant psychological wounding for a man who had until now received some kind of preferment almost from his first days in Parliament. It was for Brown almost like beginning all over again. To add to the hurt, he stood for election to the shadow cabinet in 1954, but failed to get enough votes to gain a place.

This did not mean that Brown was without significance in the party. He was appointed a member of the British delegation to the Council of Europe's Consultative Assembly (he was to become over time a passionate supporter of European integration) and was elected Chairman of the trade union group of MPs. This chairmanship provided a significant position from which to continue to make his mark and by 1956 Richard Crossman acknowledged Brown as "one of the coming forces, since he's far the ablest young trade unionist in the House".[4]

Brown's position remained firmly on the right of his party and this inevitably put him in contention with Aneurin Bevan, whose figurehead position on the party's left, made him a natural target for Brown's antipathy. It also made Brown a natural ally for Hugh Gaitskell, who detested Bevan and would eventually come into almost open warfare with him and his supporters. These alliances helped to keep Brown on the right side of history.

Brown stood again for election to the Shadow Cabinet in 1955, this time successfully. Attlee made him shadow spokesman on the work of the Ministry of Supply, a co-ordinating department that had been of vital importance during the war but was now in its twilight years. Within months, Attlee announced that he was going to step down as party leader and it was Hugh Gaitskell who succeeded him in the consequent leadership election. When Gaitskell naturally resigned from his role as Party Treasurer, Brown saw his chance and decided to stand for election in Gaitskell's place. He had the support of his local party and the backing of a substantial block of trade union votes, but when the contest was held it was Aneurin Bevan who won, though Brown came a respectable second, demonstrating that he was now established as a significant figure in the party.

The failure to become Party Treasurer was on the face of it a setback. But Brown was nonetheless full of self-confidence in his future and that, combined with a natural outspokenness that was intensified by alcohol, gave increasing rise to displays of ill-temper and belligerence. This was clearly on display in May 1956 when he attacked, to his face, the Russian leader, Nikita Khrushchev, who was visiting the UK on a goodwill visit. At a dinner the Labour Party's National Executive held in the Russian visitors' honour, Brown had taken immediate exception to remarks Khrushchev made criticising Britain's contribution to the war. In response, Brown openly abused Khrushchev for what he had said - and the Russians more generally for having originally entered into a pact with Hitler in 1939.

Brown's attitude towards Khrushchev was one with which most of the National Executive, with the exception of the most left-leaning, probably agreed, but its tone and directness caused some embarrassment. Luckily this incident did not stand in Brown's way to promotion and may even have done him some good, because the following year Gaitskell moved Brown from his post shadowing the Ministry of Supply and made him the spokesman on defence - a front-line role that was to become a hotseat as the row developed within the Labour party over the issue of Britain's independent nuclear deterrent.

Brown's growing popularity in the party stemmed from a recognition that though emotionally erratic, he was at least passionate in his beliefs and ready to stand up for a fight. This could be seen by others as an asset – provided it was on your side he was fighting. The trouble was that it was not always certain whose side he was on. He had become a close ally of Gaitskell, but deviated from his leader's firm stand on opposition to nuclear disarmament, advocating instead a curious half-state that seemed to be both before and against at the same time. Similarly, he broke away from Gaitskell's line opposing entry to the Common Market (a prospect which Gaitskell denounced as a breach with a thousand years of history). Brown was firmly pro-Europe and tried in vain to convince Gaitskell to be of the same mind. But these differences were easily set aside when, after Aneurin Bevan died in 1960, creating a vacancy for the post of deputy leader of the party, Brown ran successfully for the post, comfortably defeating James Callaghan and Fred Lee in the race. At this point Brown saw himself as almost at the top of the tree and his sense of this commanding position was confirmed when, in November 1962, he successfully overcame a challenge for the deputy's post from Harold Wilson (who had mounted a failed challenge to Gaitskell for the leader's job just two years before). Brown beat Wilson by 133 votes to 103, a result which not only gave

Brown inevitable satisfaction but also gave him what turned out to be a false sense of invulnerability.

It was only two months later that Gaitskell suddenly died. It seemed to Brown inevitable that he would succeed Gaitskell as leader, with Number 10 as his potential prize at the next election, due in 1964. At this moment Brown believed his moment had come. But it turned out that the path to leadership was not to be an automatic crowning of the next-in-line. There was to be a leadership election and he would be once again facing his rival, Harold Wilson. Even so, Brown felt confident – it was only a matter of months since he had decisively beaten Wilson for the deputy leadership and it seemed to Brown inconceivable that MPs who had preferred him for the deputy's post would not continue their support into his bid for leadership. It turned out that Brown had miscalculated on three points.

The first miscalculation was Brown's reckoning that Wilson's alliance with the left was regarded by many as being largely a badge of convenience and that he could not therefore rely on support from that side of that party. But Brown's difficulty here was that he was undeniably of the right. Therefore, whether Wilson had really been genuinely at heart a man of the left was beside the point – given the choice, the left had nowhere else to put their votes but behind Wilson. Brown's disadvantage on this front was compounded by the fact that no other leftist candidate entered for the election.

The second miscalculation was that it would be a straight contest – Brown vs Wilson. But the entry of a third candidate – James Callaghan – was a real setback for Brown, particularly as Callaghan was also undoubtedly of the right, meaning that potentially the votes on that side of the party might be split. Callaghan probably suspected that he had no chance of beating both Brown and Wilson, but he may have thought it useful to put down a marker for his future career. It is also certain that he received some secret encouragement to run from Wilson supporters, whose real aim was the opportunity to split-off some of Brown's votes.

The third miscalculation was that Brown's personal weakness – his drinking problem and his consequent emotional instability – would not affect voting choices. Brown – insofar as he recognised that he had a problem – judged that if people would overlook this aspect of him to vote for him as deputy leader, then they would similarly discount it at a leadership election. He was wrong. What was deemed excusable in their deputy was far more off-putting in their choice of leader, with the possibility of their choice becoming the next Prime Minister.

Brown compounded the difficulties he now faced in this election by aggressive canvassing that alienated some potential support. His campaign was marked by personal abuse, arm-twisting and rumours that offers of advancement were being made to buy support. These campaign blunders were made worse when Brown divisively declared that if he won, he would not have Wilson as his deputy.

Wilson by contrast conducted his campaign with deftness and subtlety, avoiding any direct canvassing himself. The behaviour of the two leading candidates could not have presented a more marked contrast. It was Wilson who suddenly seemed the leader-in-waiting and Brown who seemed the lost cause. In the event Wilson came first in the three-way ballot and comfortably beat Brown in the final run-off between the two of them.

Brown was devastated by his defeat – it was, apart from failing to gain a place in the elections for shadow cabinet places in 1956, the first significant rebuff he had received since first entering Parliament. In any event, Brown was never a man to accept defeat gracefully. He was consumed with a seething resentment at what he saw as the treachery of those who had voted for Wilson and this blended into a personal hatred for his new leader. An additional factor in all this was that Brown had a particular contempt for 'intellectuals' and to find himself, a self-made man, beaten by a former Oxford don was acutely painful.

Wilson made an immediate gesture to Brown, announcing that he wished him to stay on as deputy leader. This overture reinforced the image for which Wilson was striving – he projected himself as a healer. Brown's response was abruptly to retreat to Scotland where, in bitter isolation, he avoided making any response to Wilson at all. This disappearing-act confirmed the impression which had driven many to vote for Wilson – Brown was not a healer but a self-centred factionalist.

Predictably, Brown's wounds never healed but, eventually, after days of seething, Brown returned to London and agreed to continue as the party's deputy leader. But opportunities for further grievance were afforded by the fact that, in his absence, the post of Shadow Foreign Secretary, which Brown had coveted, had been allocated to Patrick Gordon Walker. Brown had to content himself with the offer of shadow spokesman on home affairs.

For the next months, Brown and Wilson became if not on easy terms, at least able to work together without open offence being given or taken. And then, late in the year, events brought Brown's drink problems into the most public view. On November 23rd President Kennedy was assassinated and Brown was one of a number of figures invited to contribute to a tribute on television that evening.

Brown arrived at the studio already well-oiled and highly emotional. He was shown into one of the hospitality suites where he found ample opportunity to take on more fuel. Also waiting in the room to take part in the programme were a group of others, including the American actor Eli Wallach. For reasons only known in George's now extremely befuddled mind, he decided to pick a quarrel with Wallach, accusing him of being conceited and, bizarrely, finding fault with him as an actor because he had never appeared in a play by Ted Willis (the creator of the television series *Dixon of Dock Green*). Wallach was so provoked by Brown's behaviour that he had to be restrained from physically attacking him.

When Brown finally got into the studio, he found that he was being interviewed by Kenneth Harris, a man to whom Brown had already taken a dislike in the past. Harris had hardly posed his first question before Brown was belligerently pitching-in and apparently trying to divert his tribute to Kennedy into an argument with his interviewer. Brown's contribution, rambling and incoherent as well as antagonistic, left no doubt in viewers' minds that he was drunk.

It was Brown's good fortune that although his condition was unmistakable, it was capable of an innocent explanation. Brown had, after all, met Kennedy on several occasions and could at least claim to have known him directly. Kennedy's death had caused widespread national shock and grief, and the average viewer, seeing Brown's condition, could have excused it as an understandable weakness in someone coping with a loss that was almost personal. What the average viewer could not know was that Brown was not just drunk on this particular occasion, but commonly drunk, on an everyday basis.

Sure enough, Brown's behaviour seemed to escape public comment, but it had not gone unnoticed by Wilson who decided to haul him over the coals. And once news of Wilson's intention was leaked to the press, then suddenly Brown's television fiasco started to be mentioned as having provoked the leader of the opposition into disciplining his deputy. Brown immediately counter-briefed, managing to create the suspicion that Wilson was victimising him and, after making a semi-apology at a parliamentary party meeting, Brown was able effectively to neutralise Wilson's threat. So, the year ended in a stalemate and the two men, their differences set aside for the sake of appearances, now devoted their energy to campaigning in the run-up to the general election.

Early in the new year Wilson started the unofficial campaign with a series of set speeches, intended to map out the new ideas that he intended to bring to government. In the second of those speeches, in January in Swansea, he previewed his idea for a new approach to economic planning: "We have been thinking," he declared, "in terms of a Minister of economic planning". This was the germ of the idea that was to eventually appear as a Department of Economic Affairs, with George Brown as its head. In his subsequent account of his 1964-70 government, Wilson explained the creation of the DEA as the result of a decision he had made long before the election that "Britain could hope to win economic security only by a fundamental reconstruction and modernisation of industry under the direction of a department at least as powerful as the Treasury. This new department would be concerned with real resources, with economic planning, with strengthening our ability to export and to save imports, with increasing productivity, and our competitiveness in domestic and export markets."

Although this idea was spun by Wilson as part of his modernising approach to the challenges of government, the reality was, as so often the way with his ideas, a case of old wine in new bottles. The true origin of Wilson's new thinking was to be found back in Attlee's days, when in 1947 he had created a Ministry of Economic Affairs, headed up by Stafford Cripps. The risk for Wilson in recycling this idea was that it inevitably created the perfect conditions for a power struggle, as his DEA and the Treasury fought for the upper economic hand. But throughout his time as Prime Minister one of Wilson's strategies for handling perceived rivals was to organise matters so that instead of forming alliances against him, they were kept busy fighting each other. So, by putting Brown in charge of the new DEA and sending Callaghan to the Treasury, Wilson was able to ensure his two rivals were inevitably in competition not with him, but with each other.

On the morning after the General Election, before the final results were in, Brown appeared on the BBC's election coverage programme, where he was interviewed by Robin Day. Brown, a little earlier in the programme, had been described by one of the presenters, Professor Bob Mackenzie, as a "voluble, hard-hitting figure – unpredictable in many ways". As soon as Brown's interview began it was clear that he was in an aggressive mood. When Day pressed him on the question of the smallness of Labour's predicted majority, Brown swept the question aside, saying, repeatedly, "We shall govern". By the end of the day Brown was facing up to a question much more serious than the issue of the government majority. At a meeting in Downing Street, he joined Wilson and Callaghan to consider the revelation, just made to the incoming government, that it was already facing an economic crisis, with a balance of payments deficit predicted to reach an eye-watering £800 million.[*]

---

[*] This projected deficit of £800 million is the equivalent of more than £14 billion at today's values.

Since the mid-1950s, successive Chancellors of the Exchequer had struggled to reconcile two competing priorities – unemployment and the balance of payments. Their problem was that these two issues presented as the twin horns of a dilemma. If measures were introduced that would reduce unemployment, then the economy consequently heated-up, increasing the demand for goods and putting upward pressure on imports, with damaging consequences for the balance of payments. If, on the other hand, deflationary measures were introduced with the aim of reducing imports, the result was a contraction in the economy that resulted in a growth in unemployment. Faced with this economic form of a devil's alternative, each Chancellor had opted to work on each priority in rotation. The switch between the priorities became such a routine part of a Chancellor's approach, that it even acquired its own terminology – it became known as the strategy of 'stop-go'.

And stop-go might have continued to be the economic set-menu right up until the 1964 Election, had not the last of the Conservative chancellors, Reginald Maudling, decided that he had devised the solution to squaring the circle. Maudling was a clever man, economically literate, and at the time of his Chancellorship at the height of his powers, only years later would alcoholism destroy him physically and financial corruption ruin him politically. It was because of his undoubted economic competence that no serious questions were asked when he developed his solution to the perennial game of 'stop-go'.

His strategy was to make a 'dash for growth' – replacing

alternating episodes of stop and go with relentless acceleration. Maudling had convinced himself that the 'stop' element of stop and go was part of the problem, not part of the solution. He decided that vigorous and uninterrupted expansion – lower taxes and increased government spending - would generate self-sustaining growth that would not only keep unemployment low, but would also benignly create the means to pay for the inevitable growth in imports. He was wrong – it was a political gamble rather than an economic theory - but his experiment conveniently ensured advantage for his government. His policy certainly promoted a feel-good mood in the country and this contributed to a significant drop in Labour's standing in the opinion polls, in the run-up to the general election. So, Maudling's policy had the effect of both reducing Labour's majority to a knife-edge and handing them the biggest and most immediate of the new government's problems.

During the election campaign, Wilson had claimed that the Conservatives were not being honest about the true state of the nation's finances, but he was still shocked by the scale of the trading deficit as it was presented to him within hours of entering Downing Street. On the Saturday after taking office, he, Brown and Callaghan met to discuss the crisis and how to tackle it. The obvious solution was devaluation, which would serve to boost exports, which would become cheaper for overseas customers and, simultaneously, inhibit imports, which would become more expensive. The view of Treasury officials was broadly against devaluation, but their advice was not needed. The three key players, Wilson, Callaghan and Brown, met on their own and each of them was, for different reasons, against the option of devaluation.

Callaghan's argument was basically a matter of principle – in particular that to devalue would be a betrayal of trust with those Commonwealth countries that held the so-called 'sterling balances'. Devaluation would at a stroke reduce the value of these balances, meaning that the countries owed that money – Egypt, India and Malaya, for example – would eventually only receive a repayment that had been discounted by the fall in the pound's value. Callaghan was disturbed at this prospect of the UK in effect defaulting on its overseas debts and so argued against devaluation on what were essentially moral grounds. And morality was pretty much the only ground on which Callaghan could stand. He had no academic training in economics and his only preparation had been to attend some seminars arranged for him at Nuffield College.

George Brown's position as Secretary of State for Economic Affairs, with its responsibility for preparing a National Plan, was predicated on a programme of expansion and so he might have been expected to favour devaluation as a means of harnessing resources for growth, rather than seeing those resources being eaten up by a large trade deficit. But Brown also came down against devaluation, for reasons similar to Callaghan's, but focused closer to home. Brown was in his working-class-hero mode and convinced that devaluation would be a betrayal of his class because it would mean a reduction in the value of workers' pay.

Wilson was also firmly against devaluation. Years later he explained that devaluation could not have been an option, because the two previous devaluations – in 1931 and 1949 – had both taken place under a Labour Prime Minister. If the government of 1964 had gone down the same road, he reasoned, then people would henceforth have said that Labour was the party of devaluation. This explanation is revealing. Any proper defence of the decision not to devalue ought to be based on economic arguments for that decision. Wilson chose instead, at least with hindsight, to defend his decision on the grounds of party-political advantage.

Even though both Brown and Callaghan came out against devaluation, it would still have been possible for Wilson to have insisted on it. His potential ability to swing the decision that way was due to more than his ultimate authority. Although neither of the other two liked or trusted Wilson, they did have confidence in his ability as an economist. His academic record, with an early fellowship at Oxford in Economics, led both Brown and Callaghan to believe that Wilson would best know which way the decision on devaluation should go. But their confidence was misplaced, as the subsequent course of the government would demonstrate.

The work of the new Department for Economic Affairs began amidst extraordinary difficulties. A vacant set of offices had been reserved in advance of the election, but there was no furniture, no equipment, no office supplies, no secretaries or typists and – according to one account –

without even soap in the cloakrooms. Despite the surrounding chaos Brown took up his work with enormous enthusiasm and energy. He had two main responsibilities – the introduction of measures to control prices and incomes and the preparation of a National Plan. It was through work on the first of these priorities that he was able to achieve a rapid and impressive early win, demonstrating that despite his aggressively combative nature, he could be capable of conducting impressively skilful negotiations. Within weeks he persuaded the Trades Union Congress, the Association of British Chambers of Commerce, the Federation of British Industries and the National Association of British Manufacturers to agree jointly to a *Statement of Intent on Productivity, Prices and Incomes*.

The notable achievement of this Statement was that it recorded the TUC's acceptance of the concept that wage increases should be in line with 'national output' – in other words an acceptance that economic growth and price stability could be dependent on some control of incomes. This was a positive step, but short on precision. It was a sufficient basis, however, for Brown to proceed to set-up a National Board for Prices and Incomes, headed by Aubrey Jones, who resigned as a Conservative MP in order to take up the post.

The NBPI's role was advisory, dealing only with cases referred to it by the government, and confined to coming to a view on whether any proposed increase in prices or wages was in the national interest. Its ability to reach any such view was, however, dependent on some measure of what the 'national interest' might be and, in April, Brown was able to publish a *Prices and Incomes Policy*, which indicated that, with certain exceptions, wage increases should be kept to a limit of between 3 and 3.5 percent.

Meanwhile, Brown had also been working with his advisers to produce a National Plan of nearly 500 pages, which was masterminded by the Director-General of the DEA, Donald McDougall. The Plan was published in the middle of September 1965 and set a target for growth of 25% between 1964 and 1970 – averaging-out at just under 4% per year. It purported to give full expression to the government's economic strategy over the next five years, with identified priorities, implications for national income and expenditure and an industry-by-industry analysis of projected production, labour needs and contribution to the balance of payments.

It was a highly elaborate piece of work, but the detail of the plan, propped up by impressive tables and charts, was built on assumptions that were not so much projections as wishful thinking – for example, it was presumed that over the period of the plan the growth in exports would be 5% annually (compared to the previous ten-year average of just 3%) and imports would fall to an annual growth of only 4% (down from the 5% average over the past ten years). These fanciful projections had the effect of, at a stroke, eliminating the balance of payments deficit.

A centrepiece of the plan was the projection of future production across all the major industries, demonstrating how the 25% growth target was to be met by 1970. But these figures had been blatantly massaged to produce the desired end-result. The companies' forecasts had been collected by questionnaires that were accompanied by guidance which explained that if the collated figures did not produce the projection required by the Plan, then companies would need to adjust their projections so as to fit. This was euphemistically described as a process of "mutual adjustment".[5]

By the spring of 1966, Wilson decided to call another General Election, with hopes this time of winning a secure majority and, despite any concerns about Brown's steadiness, he was given a leading part in the campaign. A BBC film about the 1966 campaign, *The Hecklers*, captures Brown dealing well with a persistent heckler: "I saw you at the beginning of the week," Brown called out to him, "and you have been with me ever since. What the hell are you using for transport? Helicopters?" His National Plan was foregrounded across the campaign and mentioned eleven times in the party manifesto. The result of the campaign, a majority of 96, was a gratifying boost of confidence to the party. But glad confident morning was soon to pass.

Little more than three months after the election, on July 6th, Brown wrote a Minute to the Prime Minister, regarding a meeting he was shortly to address, followed by a press conference: "The question of the 25 per cent growth target is bound to be raised. I am proposing to deal with it in my statement by saying that developments during the past year, especially in the external field, have imposed additional difficulties on us by prolonging the period of slow growth in the early years of the Plan, and that therefore the achievement of all our targets within the period we set ourselves now seems less likely than it did last year."

Brown's reference to "developments during the past year" was a delicate way of pointing to the fact that since coming into office in 1964 the government had been in an almost continuous struggle to contain a sterling crisis. The large deficit in the balance of payments, accompanied by significant outflows of capital, had triggered a series of emergency measures by the Chancellor and the Bank of England, including the drawing-down of huge loans from an international rescue fund, the selling of gold, the repeated raising of bank rate, import surcharges, tax rate increases and a credit squeeze.

These measures had exacerbated the tension between the DEA and the Treasury, which even in better times would have been expected to be marked by territorial friction. But Callaghan's desperate attempts to get sterling under control had infuriated Brown, whose National Plan was inevitably running out of credibility. Having turned his face firmly against devaluation as at least a partial solution to the balance of payments deficit, Brown seems to have overlooked that other ways would have to be found to tackle the problem. Whenever Callaghan was compelled to tighten his squeeze further, Brown was quick to object to what he dismissed as "deflationary shackles". These differences were not without consequence. When, for example, Callaghan was proposing an increase in Bank Rate of 1%, Brown put up such a prolonged resistance that by the time it could be implemented the rise in the rate needed to be increased to 2%.

The arguments were not discreet behind-the-scenes affairs. Leaks to the press ensured a regular flow of stories in the papers about one row after another. Each man shared his grievances in confidence with Wilson, who listened patiently and then, because it suited him to keep the two in a state of enmity, promptly leaked to each what the other had been saying about him. In the case of Brown, there was a particularly Wilsonian twist to the way he did this. Wilson made sure that it was at an evening meeting that he passed on to Brown what Callaghan had been saying about him - by this stage in the day Wilson could be sure Brown would be drunk, so ensuring that Callaghan's remarks would have an even more inflammatory effect.

The weeks after the election had seen an intensification of the government's economic plight and a point was reached when it created an unexpected possibility for rapprochement between Brown and Callaghan. Both men came, separately, to the conclusion that devaluation was essential. Eventually the two formed an unofficial pact on this issue and Callaghan went to see Wilson with the news that he now favoured devaluation and that Brown was of like mind. This presented Wilson with a two-pronged problem. He still regarded devaluation as a price too high to be worth paying and he viewed an alliance between Brown and Callaghan as something he did not want at any price.

Wilson, as was his way, came up with an artful solution.

He pushed Callaghan to accept, as an alternative to devaluation, a further package of cuts, and, to sweeten his deal, he offered to handle the announcement of those cuts himself – offering the possibility that this would deflect the thrust of any criticism to Number Ten and away from a Chancellor who was already deeply wounded in action. Callaghan agreed and that was the end of his truce with Brown.

On July 19th, Richard Crossman, at that stage Minister of Housing, met with Wilson and pressed the case for devaluation. Wilson, with Callaghan's agreement now in his pocket, continued to resist the idea – though he dangled the idea that he might be open to the possibility in the following year. It was clear to Wilson that, in order to square Crossman and other supporters of devaluation, he would have to bring the matter to Cabinet and at a meeting later that day it met to consider the arguments for and against. The vote eventually went Wilson's way, but Brown, who had for days been threatening resignation if devaluation was rejected, clearly signalled, at the end of the meeting, that he did not accept that the matter was now settled. The Cabinet met again the next day and agreed Wilson's package of cuts, far more extensive and severe than had been expected. The scale of these measures – and their implications for the economy - made publicly unmistakeable what most observers had for some time already known privately: the many hundreds of pages in Brown's National Plan were just so much economic litter.

That the National Plan was inherently unrealisable in its

aims and unworkable or irrelevant in its details was well-known to many of his cabinet colleagues who had recognised from the first that Brown's plan was at best whistling in the dark and at worst an attempt at a confidence trick. It would have been no surprise either to the officials across all the ministries and departments who had contributed to the action points within the plan – they knew that what had been offered to Brown were lists of things that were to be done in any case, regardless of a National Plan, and actions that had, in most cases, no bearing whatsoever on the achievement of a growth target of 25% by the end of the decade. The hollow nature of the Plan had from early days helped officials at the Treasury to overcome their fear of their functions being usurped by the DEA. They recognised that the Plan would eventually collapse-in on itself and that economic management would once again be their unchallenged territory.

Brown left the Cabinet meeting that had just agreed the Wilson/Callaghan package of cuts with a determination to distance himself from the measures. When he failed to appear on the front bench alongside Wilson during the Prime Minister's announcement of the new package, rumour spread amongst Labour Members that Brown had resigned or would do so imminently. William Rodgers, the Labour MP for Stockton-on-Tees, promptly organised a letter asking Brown to remain, which, very quickly, gathered the signatures of around a hundred MPs. This gesture of support sufficiently mollified Brown for him, later that evening, to appear outside Number 10 and declare that although there had been a disagreement (which he did not specify) he had decided to stay on as Secretary of State at the Department of Economic Affairs.

There was still work for him to do there. The new austerity measures included a statutory freeze on incomes and since the control of wages and prices was part of his department's remit, Brown now had to set about devising the necessary controls. Brown had continued to work hard on this area, up to and well beyond his early success in getting the agreement of the critical parties to his Statement of Intent. But despite this agreement and the setting up of the National Board for Prices and Incomes, there had been no sign of an easing-up in unions' expectations. In fact, the unions had signed-up for something they had no intention of complying with. Jack Jones, the General Secretary of the Transport and General Workers Union dismissed it as "just a bloody gimmick."[*]

By June 1965, Brown had to inform his Cabinet colleagues that the average rate of wage increases was rising and that, at a time when the norm was supposed to be in the range 3-3.5%, the increase in the current year was predicted to be even higher than the 8% recorded for the previous year. An attempt was made to toughen the current policy by requiring a three-month standstill on any wage or price increases referred by the government to the Prices and Incomes Board, but by the time of the July package of cuts it was obvious that no voluntary agreement was going to keep wage settlements within the

[*] Many years later it was revealed that at this time Jack Jones was a paid agent of the KGB.

required range (a range which Callaghan in any case thought too high, because unjustified by productivity). A Bill was prepared to impose a statutory prices and incomes policy and, in the face of opposition not just from the Conservatives but also from some angry Labour members, the measure was, after exhausting parliamentary sessions that included two all-night sittings, put onto the statute book.

So far as Brown was concerned this drew a final line under his work at the DEA and he accepted Wilson's offer of a move to the post of Foreign Secretary – a role for which Brown was spectacularly unfitted,[*] especially so because the daily engagements which are an essential part of this role would include banquets, receptions and cocktail parties which combined maximum opportunities for drinking with large-scale scope for insulting behaviour. Within days of his start in this new role, Barbara Castle observed Brown "rolling around distressingly sozzled"[6] at a reception during the Commonwealth Prime Ministers' Conference.

It will be remembered that Brown had, in 1963, hopes of becoming shadow foreign secretary and, while at the DEA, he was determined to take a continuing interest in foreign issues. In particular, he made a point of being involved in work on European relationships and also with the attempts to manage a response to Rhodesia's Unilateral Declaration of Independence. But, despite his

---

[*] "...the tactless George is left with the foreigners!" Cecil King, The Cecil King Diary 1965-70

background of active involvement in such matters, Brown's acceptance of the post of Foreign Secretary was less than enthusiastic. Asked by Barbara Castle if he was pleased with his new job, he told her "I hate it. I didn't want it. It was an order: this or go. He (Wilson) said he couldn't keep me at DEA after my little bit of business over resigning. Two years ago, when I wanted it, I couldn't have it. Now I don't want it I've no choice."[7]

Brown's installation as Foreign Secretary did, however, fit very comfortably into one of his particular passions – Europe. After Wilson decided early that autumn to enter into discussions with a view to applying for entry to the Common Market, he and Brown set off in the new year on a tour of the relevant European capitals to sound-out their reactions. Wilson's explanation for the composition of this two-man mission was that it would ensure a balanced judgment – he himself, he pointed out, was known to be sceptical about entry to the Common Market, while Brown was a long-established European enthusiast. Brown's evaluation of the teaming was very different. "It would have been logical for such a tour to be made by the Foreign Secretary alone," he recorded in his autobiography, "In the special circumstances of the time it might have been logical for the Prime Minister to make a round of visits to the Common Market capitals. For us both to go introduced that element of tension which so often touched the relations between the Foreign Office and Downing Street during Harold Wilson's government."[8] The "element of tension" no doubt included, on Wilson's part, an anxiety about what his

Foreign Secretary might say or do next. Brown's indiscretions in Europe could range from what the Foreign Office's Permanent Under-Secretary would later describe as "a bonhomie which goes beyond the personal"[9] to, at the other extreme, downright rudeness.

The tension between Wilson and Brown over international affairs extended far beyond the issue of Europe. The war in Vietnam had forced the Wilson government into a precarious balancing act, as it sought to placate the strong anti-war feelings within and beyond the Labour Party while at the same time remaining 'on side' with the Johnson administration, on which it depended for support for sterling. Part of Wilson's strategy in this situation was to attempt to represent his government as a potential peace-broker and, in particular, to use what he imagined was his significant influence with the Russians to use pressure or persuasion to bring the Hanoi government to some kind of negotiated settlement.

In February 1967 a visit to the UK by the Russian leader seemed to Wilson and Brown to offer an opportunity to involve the Soviets in mediation. They believed they had President Johnson's agreement to put forward a plan in which the traditional ceasefire held during the Vietnamese New Year would be extended by the US in return for an assurance that there would be an end to Viet Cong infiltration of the South. This offer was communicated to the Russians, with the open support of a US diplomat, Chester Cooper, who was in London acting as the President's representative. But it turned out that Cooper was not in the loop so far as the current position in the

White House was concerned. Johnson was infuriated when he was told about the specific terms of the offer that Wilson and Brown were presuming to make.

It all turned on a matter of a few words. Wilson and Brown's letter to Kosygin referred to the condition that infiltration "will stop". Johnson insisted that this was too loose and that any offer of a ceasefire or of talks depended on the condition that infiltration "has stopped".[10] The slight difference in wording between Johnson's line and what the Russians had been given to understand was significant, but it was a highly nuanced difference and Wilson and Brown could easily have been forgiven for not having spotted any ambiguity in advance, particularly since they had been assured by Chester Cooper that what they were putting forward to Kosygin represented the official Washington position. But it is an indication of the strained relationship between the Prime Minister and his Foreign Secretary that, when the misunderstanding became apparent, the two men turned not on Cooper, but on each other. "Wilson and Brown just went at each other, it was just terrible," Cooper recalled a few years later. "Brown accused Wilson of being too premature; and that time and time again during these discussions Wilson didn't inform Brown as to what was going on; Brown on at least three occasions that night resigned as Foreign Minister."[11]

In his time at the Foreign Office, Brown was repeatedly wrong-footed by Wilson over issues which not only frustrated the Foreign Secretary but also left him feeling unfairly exposed, even double-crossed. For example, late in 1967, the issue of arms sales to South Africa (a commitment made by the previous Conservative government, then inherited by Labour and never formally repudiated) escalated from a long-standing simmering point to an explosion. Brown, together with the Minister of Defence, Denis Healey, took the view that sales of weapons for the purposes of external defence should go ahead, partly because it was in the national interest that any Russian presence in the Indian Ocean should be counter-balanced and partly because the export of these arms would help with the balance of payments. Additionally, Brown saw the possibility of using the sales as a potential lever to persuade the South African government to put pressure on the illegal Rhodesian government in Salisbury. Wilson seemed to be in agreement with the overall approach and Brown therefore sent a communiqué, passed to the South African government through the UK's Ambassador, the purpose of which was to encourage that country to believe that a sale of arms might be agreed.

When news of this reached the ears of Labour MPs, there was an eruption of protest which Wilson handled by appearing to place the blame on Brown for presumptively encouraging the possibility of these sales, despite official government opposition. When the row blew up, Brown was in Brussels where a fog-bound airport delayed his return to London to defend himself. He eventually arrived in time to join a Cabinet meeting convened to discuss the affair – Healey subsequently described that occasion as "the most unpleasant meeting I have ever attended".[12]

Barbara Castle, a fervent opponent of the arms sales, agreed: "I have never known a higher or more bitter level of debate."[13] Wilson argued that he had never encouraged Brown to suggest to South Africa that there could be any arms sales. Brown countered by claiming to have a letter in which the Prime Minister had done exactly that. Healey then read out an extract from the record of a committee meeting which made it plain that Wilson had agreed to the idea of sales in principle. The division in the Cabinet was fierce and closely divided until, finally, Crossman, who opposed Brown and had been stoking up the backbench anger over South Africa, was able to bring the angry argument to an end by suggesting the final decision should be delayed for a few days. The interval was used by both Brown and Wilson to provide off-the-record briefings to the press to support their opposing positions, but Crossman's delay gave Wilson enough time to engineer victory and within a few days he announced to Parliament that South Africa would not be sold any arms. Brown subsequently wrote of the affair: "I came to the conclusion that the Prime Minister was capable of working in a way that made effective co-operation almost impossible."[14]

It was inevitable that the final breach could not be long postponed. It came just a few months later. The devaluation in November 1967 (described here in later chapters) had seemed to offer the opportunity for a breathing-space for the economy, until a further financial threat emerged, which actually had its origins not in the UK but in the US. One of the creations of the post-war

Bretton Woods Agreement had been the London Gold Pool, where reserves of gold were held on behalf of a mix of American and European banks. The purpose of the pool was to protect a fixed gold/dollar exchange rate. For most of the years after its creation the Pool worked effectively, with gold being sold from or bought for the Pool as needed to maintain the exchange rate. But by early 1968 it was clear that a growing shift out of dollars into gold threatened the continued operation of the Pool. The threat was not just to the US dollar – a British concern was that sterling holdings were being increasingly converted to dollars so that they could be exchanged in turn for gold. By mid-March the sales of sterling were so great as to raise the possibility that a further devaluation would be required.

Eventually it became clear that the Pool arrangement could not be sustained and late on the evening of 14 March 1968 the US government made a formal request to Britain to effectively suspend the Pool by announcing that it would not open on the following day. It was agreed in London to achieve this by means of declaring the next day a Bank Holiday, a decision that would have the advantage of closing not only the Pool, but the Foreign Exchange as well. The only difficulty was that the decision to declare the Bank Holiday could be taken only by a meeting of at least four Privy Councillors in the presence of the Queen. A meeting was duly arranged for shortly after midnight.

In all of this, Wilson was faced with a dilemma. As the most senior cabinet minister, Brown would expect to be involved in such decisions and as a Privy Councillor would be expected to be at the late-night meeting at the Palace. According to Wilson's own account he had tried to contact Brown earlier in the evening, when the crisis seemed to be coming to a head but was unable to put him in the picture because the Foreign Secretary could not be tracked down. Although this inevitably laid up difficulties for later, the Foreign Secretary's mysterious unavailability suited Wilson for now, because he was well aware that any involvement of Brown was unlikely to be helpful – in Wilson's mind was the probability that by this late hour Brown was most likely to be drunk, or well on the way to being so – and it seems that, despite Wilson's claim of an extensive search for Brown, the effort was half-hearted at best. Certainly Brown was in the House of Commons, sitting on the front bench, for at least part of the evening and he was certainly there at ten o'clock because Barbara Castle has left an account of how during a House vote at that time he had walked behind her through the division lobby, attempting to unbutton the back of her blouse as they passed through.[15]

Soon after, rumours began to circulate amongst Members about the plan to call the next day a Bank Holiday. Around about eleven o'clock, Brown telephoned Wilson in a furious temper over the news. What seemed to have infuriated Brown was not the decision to close the Gold Pool – he actually was in agreement with it – but the fact that he had not been informed about the crisis as it developed that evening and had not been involved in the decision that had then been reached. A final and bitter insult, as Brown perceived it, was that the Privy Council meeting had been organised without notifying him and that another and very junior member of the Council had been called in as a replacement. After the phone call Brown then invited to his room those members of the Cabinet he could locate in the House and vented his anger to them.

In the early hours of the morning Brown arrived at Number Ten, in a highly emotional and embittered state. He was joined by a number of Cabinet ministers who had also come directly from the House of Commons, having at that stage only heard Brown's side of the story. Brown accused Wilson of deliberately engineering his exclusion from that evening's discussions, to which Wilson responded with a flat denial, insisting that a great deal of effort had been fruitlessly expended trying to locate him. The row developed explosively until, according to one account, Brown stood up and walked threateningly over to Wilson, almost giving the appearance that the two men were about to come to blows. But, after more shouting from Brown, he left the room, slamming the door after him.

When, well-on into the night, Roy Jenkins, went to the House, as Chancellor of the Exchequer, to make a statement about the reasons for the Bank Holiday decision, Brown was to be seen sitting on the backbenches, telling anyone who would listen that he had resigned. But when the Cabinet met next morning, *sans* Brown, Wilson was not able to confirm the Foreign Secretary's departure. The Prime Minister was right to be cautious about the current state of play. Brown had threatened to resign on so many occasions that it was by no means certain that this time was going to be the genuine article.

Throughout the day Brown remained at home, clearly hoping that Wilson would extend a last-minute olive branch that would provide a pretext to avoid an irrevocable step. But no peace offer was made and, late in the afternoon, Brown wrote a letter to the Prime Minister. This letter was significantly ambiguous, expressing the belief that "I think it better that we should part company." Its lack of a specific statement of resignation was a cautionary note to Wilson that Brown might still be in two minds. To give his Foreign Secretary more time, Wilson deliberately delayed his response, a delay that served to encourage Brown to think that there might still be a way of hanging on. It was not until later in the evening that Wilson sent a reply noting Brown's resignation. Within hours it was announced that Michael Stewart had been appointed as Foreign Secretary.

In the end it was all something of an anti-climax. After all the years of turbulence and argument, Brown had left the government for reasons that failed to indicate a clear and substantial disagreement with government policy – in fact for reasons that seemed to be more about his own sense of self-importance. There was to be no comeback; Brown never again held government office, though he did retain his position as Deputy Leader of the party. He had served in the Wilson government for just under three and a half years; he walked out of it aged only fifty-three.

Brown did have a working life beyond his Cabinet years.

He campaigned furiously for Labour in the 1970 General Election; his biographer records that during that campaign he travelled thousands of miles and addressed hundreds of meetings. But he lost his own seat at Belper; a reflection not of personal rejection, but the consequence of demographic changes in the constituency. With Labour now out of power, Brown was rewarded in Wilson's resignation honours with a peerage and became Lord George-Brown.

Brown earned his living thereafter through a variety of undertakings: he turned his hand to journalism and became a regular contributor to papers including the *News of the World*. He also collaborated with a ghost-writer who wrote Brown's autobiography. A friendly industrialist, Lord Kearton, gave him a post as Industrial Relations Adviser at his textiles company, Courtaulds. Brown even undertook, under mysterious sponsorship, a tour of countries in the Middle East. During the mid-seventies he became a Director of First Fortune Holdings, a financial services group, where he met, or became reacquainted with, the woman who was his secretary there – Maggie Haimes. In 1982 Brown would leave his wife and set up home with her.

During the seventies he became increasingly disillusioned with the state of the Labour Party and was a strident critic of the strikes and industrial unrest. In 1976 he resigned from membership of the party, but, characteristically, later that evening was photographed lying in a street gutter – he subsequently excused this on the grounds that the flash of photographers' cameras had caused him to lose his balance. It was inevitable that at some stage the relentless alcohol abuse would catch up with him and it finally did on June 2 1985; he died in Truro Hospital.

Throughout his time in the Cabinet, the two sides of Brown's personality – his dynamic intelligence and his alcohol-dependent excitability – fought with each other, sometimes in full public view. But for his addiction to alcohol it could have been a very different story. That he was an exceptionally bright and acute analyst of political issues is plainly recorded by his close colleagues in government. Crossman, in one of many tributes to Brown to be found in his diary, observed: "There's no one more talented in the whole Cabinet, or nicer or more loyal or more basically constructive".[16] Barbara Castle admitted repeatedly feeling that Brown had "some of the best qualities of all of us."[17]

Brown's officials also recognised his abilities. Eric Roll, his Permanent Secretary at the Department of Economic Affairs, paid tribute both to Brown's "extraordinary energy and his determination never to accept an unsatisfactory situation without attempting to remedy it".[18] Another official at the DEA, Sir Donald McDougall, also praised him, although admitting, in coded language, that "on occasions his effectiveness declined as the day progressed."[19] Sir Nicholas Fenn, who worked closely with Brown at the Foreign Office, praised Brown's capacity for work, describing him as a "workaholic".[20]

It was the assignment to Brown of the specially-created

Department of Economic Affairs that ensured that this combination of talent and energy would not be expended productively but frittered away on a project that was doomed to failure. The separation of the DEA and the Treasury – in theory bridged by a 'concordat' dividing responsibilities and spheres of influence – inevitably set up mutual suspicion and hostility, exacerbated by the fact that Callaghan and Brown had been recent rivals for the party leadership.

That the National Plan was a waste of resources and political energy is obvious with hindsight, but Wilson's enthusiastic embrace of the idea of economic planning was not for its time eccentric. It is difficult now to appreciate the powerful attraction there once was in the idea of central economic planning - *dirigisme* on such a major scale is now seen as inherently mistaken But, particularly in Europe, in the aftermath of the Second World War, a rash of countries had become devotees of the concept of state planning. The French Government produced a series of national plans, the first appearing in 1945. The Labour Party manifesto of 1945 had promised that "Labour will plan from the ground up – giving an appropriate place to constructive enterprise and private endeavour in the national plan", and in due course there emerged a *Long-Term Programme of the United Kingdom* – though the production of this plan owed less to the fulfilment of a manifesto promise, than to the need to provide material to support the government's application for Marshall Aid.[21] The Conservative government had, in 1961, created the National Economic Development

Council, intended to map a path towards more stable growth. In the same year, an influential book, *The Stagnant Society*, written by the Financial Times journalist, Michael Shanks, had argued for a "master plan for economic growth over five-year periods". By 1962, the United Nations Economic Bulletin for Europe recorded fourteen countries that either had long-term economic plans in place or were in the process of preparing them.

So Wilson had not sounded in any way unorthodox or revolutionary when he had made planning a repeated refrain in his series of policy speeches around the country, in the run-up to the 1964 General Election. "We believe in planning," he said in Birmingham. In Swansea he declared the need for an "effective national plan". In Edinburgh he promised "steady purposive planning year in and year out...planning with teeth". And so it went on. There could be no going back. Once Labour was in power there had to be a National Plan and, because the vision of planning had been so recklessly oversold, its tone had to be unambiguously buoyant, promising expansion and growth.

Brown duly produced a plan that did not just promise growth, it quantified the promise. The target of 25% growth by 1970 was pie-in-the-sky, and experts knew it. Treasury advisers had warned that many of its projections were fanciful; James Callaghan later admitted that "when they examined the Department of Economic Affairs figures the Treasury's calculations showed that they did not add up to a consistent whole".[22] When the Plan was being discussed in Cabinet in August 1965, Anthony

Crosland pointed out that the assumptions in it about increases in production were not just unrealistic, they were plain wrong.[23]

The National Plan was economically unsound and its creation was a matter of political necessity only. It was all bound to backfire eventually, but the backfire effect went beyond just the damage of disillusionment when the Plan had eventually to be abandoned. More seriously, one of its unforeseen consequences was that the brave optimism of the Plan gave the impression to more realistic observers that the government simply had not grasped the gravity of the economic situation and was consequently not seriously-minded about tackling it. The Plan may have been written to convince the voting public that their government was now on course to a better future, but it came with the risk that overseas investors and financial speculators would interpret its wishful-thinking as a warning to shift out of sterling into something safer.

There is no evidence that Brown ever recognised his Plan as misguided or judged its creation a waste of effort. He clearly saw the disjunction between its expansionist vision and the deflationary reality of the government's measures to cope with the economic crisis – but in his mind it was the latter that was out of step. Brown was understandably committed to growth, but showed no sign of grasping that expansionary measures required not only investment but also – and critically - the confidence of the market.

Given the ambitious scale that was required of the Plan – and given its high stakes politically – George Brown was probably the only man in the Cabinet with the energy and political nerve to pull it off. After making such a song-and-dance about planning, Wilson's reputation was inextricably linked to the production of a National Plan and the bigger and flashier the better. The Prime Minister was well aware that the policies being pursued by his government were completely orthogonal to the aims and thrust of Brown's plan, but his political instincts told him that the Plan was proof-positive of his government's good intentions and if those intentions had been thwarted by the market, then voters would probably sympathy with the government rather than the market (the "gnomes of Zurich" as Brown skilfully demonised them).

A personal bonus for Wilson in all this was that his two rivals were totally preoccupied – Brown titanically absorbed in both the preparation of the Plan and in negotiations with the Unions to secure their acceptance of pay restraints and Callaghan meanwhile continually at risk of a nervous breakdown in the boiler-house of the Treasury. Any energy that either of his rivals had left was usefully absorbed in quarrelling with each other.

In the end the man who was the greater risk, Brown, blew himself up – just as everyone who knew him had recognised would be the inevitable end. His acceptance of the Foreign Secretaryship sealed his fate. The involvement in international relationships created a minefield in which Brown was certain eventually to self-destruct. But even in this last pock-marked stage of his political career, Brown was able to demonstrate that, despite the multiple occasions of tempestuous and offensive behaviour, he was still capable of a great success. In the aftermath of the Six-Day War between Israel and its Arab neighbours, Brown, through skilful diplomacy, was able to secure the unanimous agreement of the United Nations Security Council to Resolution 242, an achievement which to this day still stands as the internationally-recognised basis of any peace settlement in the Middle East.

But Brown's part in establishing this resolution is a rare example of his securing a policy success while serving in the Wilson government. But paradoxically he is entitled to be judged a political success. He was, for all his faults and failings, a popular figure – in fact his personal problems may have increased his popularity. He was a 'character' and his appeal to the public is reflected in the very prominent role he was given in Labour's campaigns. Even after his resignation – when he had been out of government office for years – he was one of Labour's most popular, and most effective, platform speakers.

Another of Brown's particular assets – so far as Wilson was concerned – was that he provided political cover. Brown was, of course, resolutely on the right wing of the party – but his background as a trade union official, his ability to negotiate with the union leaders and his production of a National Plan, could all give the impression that his socialism was on the distinctly left side of the movement. This was, for the Prime Minister, a useful personal asset. Brown's presence within the government - his position as effectively Deputy Prime Minister – helped Wilson to sail under false colours, maintaining the support of the left-wing of his party, no matter what. This was no comfort to Brown - the last thing he would have wanted to do was to be used as a prop to bolster Wilson's image.

Brown chose to title his autobiography *In My Way*, understood as a reference to the well-known song, lines from which appear in the book. But, consciously or not, his choice of title seems to hint at something deeper. Amongst other weaknesses, Brown suffered from serial resentment. He never let any slight pass unremarked or become forgotten. Many of the slights were in any case imaginary. His capacity to hold and nurture a grudge was apparently infinite. It is hard not to escape the inference that the words *In My Way* appealed to him because they tapped into his conviction that his progress and ultimately his success had been blocked - hindered and obstructed. Up until the votes were counted in the leadership election after Gaitskell's death, Brown had been convinced that he was certain of the ultimate triumph. Then suddenly he was faced by Wilson's victory. From that day onwards there was only one way in which Brown could view Wilson – as the man who got "in my way".

3

Richard Crossman:
The Politics of Disruption

In the months leading up to the 1964 General Election, Richard Crossman had been Labour's shadow spokesman for Education and Science. So when, on the first Saturday after the election, he responded to a summons to Downing Street, he was disconcerted to learn that what he was being offered was the post of Minister for Housing and Local Government.

It was not what he had expected, but Crossman was in no position to demur or bargain for something more to his taste because, since entering the House of Commons in 1945, he had been kept at arms-length by the two previous party leaders, had spent the best part of twenty years on the backbenches and had only been able to enter the shadow cabinet after Wilson's election as Leader.

Crossman's surprise at being assigned to Housing and Local Government was still clear on his first day at the Ministry. The daunting and formidable Permanent Secretary there, Dame Evelyn Sharp, recalled that Crossman's first words to her were "I don't know what I've been put here for". To avoid any implication that these words might indicate diffidence on the new

Minister's part, he then proceeded to discharge a warning shot across Dame Evelyn's bows. He made clear to her, she later recalled, his "complete lack of confidence in civil servants" and "a conviction that their purpose in life was to obstruct Ministers".[1]

If Dame Evelyn found this offensive (and of course she did) that was no more than a case of Richard Crossman starting as he had always carried on. He was by conviction and temperament a compulsive up-turner of apple carts, priding himself on his possession of what he described as "the priceless bump of irreverence".[2]

Richard Howard Stafford Crossman was born in 1907 into a modestly affluent home, solidly comfortable but not grand. His father was a barrister but had only been able to qualify after a legacy had provided him with the funds to give up school teaching and study for the bar. His practice was moderately successful (he was sufficiently well-regarded to be appointed in his later years as a judge), but his career was never especially lucrative.

In 1920, Richard Crossman, who from childhood was known by friends and family alike as 'Dick', won a scholarship to Winchester. As it happened his family was related to one of the school founders and, up until 1857, such descending children had been automatically entitled to a scholarship, qualifying as 'founder's kin'. Dick's father took great pride in being part of this heritage, but it may be that the son did not make too much of this family connection, because the past tradition of open-door scholarships for all those qualifying through an ancestral link had encouraged the currency within the school of the expression 'thick as a founder'.

In the event no one was ever going to consider Dick Crossman 'thick'. He distinguished himself as one of the school's brightest pupils (completely eclipsing the undistinguished school career of his near-contemporary at Winchester, Hugh Gaitskell). Dick became first a prefect and then Head Boy. A splendid school career was followed by a scholarship to New College, Oxford where Dick gained a stunning Double First and was immediately offered a fellowship. His academic success was unquestionable testament to Dick's brilliance – but in his case 'brilliance' was a particularly apt description, because his brainpower was matched by an addiction to staging demonstrations of intellectual fireworks.

In a cabinet outstanding for the number of high intelligences within it, Crossman and Wilson were probably the brightest and in times of sheer brainpower pretty-evenly matched. Both men were capable of mastering complex subjects without great effort, both had extremely retentive memories and could absorb and recall large amounts of information at will. But otherwise their minds worked in very different ways. Crossman was fascinated by the exploration of ideas and arguments for the sheer intellectual pleasure of it. His mind was ingeniously fertile, Wilson was a pragmatist to his fingertips, attracted to ingenuity only as a means to an end. Wilson was by conviction a fixer; Crossman was a compulsive disruptor.

Early in the war Crossman found the ideal avenue in

which to pursue his talent for disruption – a post in the Political Warfare Executive. The PWE was created to develop methods of psychological warfare that could be used to undermine Germany's morale and its war effort in general. Its mission was to make mischief and Crossman was originally recruited because of his fluency in German and his first-hand knowledge of its people (acquired during a gap year spent in Germany between his College finals and taking up his teaching post there – not to mention whatever insights he gained from a short-lived and disastrous marriage to a German woman he met while staying in Berlin).

Crossman's path into the Political Warfare Executive had opened-up after he had been invited by the BBC to deliver talks about life in Germany. The initial invitation developed into an opportunity to range more widely in his choice of topics and included a series of talks on Plato, which Crossman subsequently expanded into a highly successful book *Plato Today*. By 1940 he was a natural choice when the BBC was looking for a fluent German speaker to give broadcast talks aimed directly at listeners in Germany.

From propaganda broadcasts aimed at German workers it was a natural progression to be recruited into the PWE where he became head of the German section, responsible for organising daily propaganda broadcasts to Germany. Perhaps inevitably Crossman's tendency to disregard convention, and his determination that he knew best, led to tensions and difficulties with others. Even Hugh Dalton, a senior figure in the Labour party and the man who had put Dick in charge of PWE's German operations, confided to his diary in September 1941 that Crossman was "loyal to his own career, but only incidentally to anything or anyone else."[3]

In the last stages of the war Crossman was posted to Algiers as Director of Psychological Warfare at Allied Forces Headquarters, the base from which Operation Torch, the allied invasion of North Africa, was being planned. It is clear that while Crossman's career was favourably regarded by many of the people he worked with (including Harold Macmillan) others found him unreliable. At the end of the war, PWE's boss, Sir Robert Bruce Lockhart passed a not wholly complimentary judgement on Crossman's work for the organisation: "In British eyes Mr Crossman is somewhat lacking in team spirit, and on more than one occasion has led him not only to take unjustifiable risks but to defy regulations. If he doesn't win a prize for good conduct, he certainly deserves a commendation for distinguished service."

With the war over, Crossman was able to return to his ambitions for a life in politics. He had become a Councillor in Oxford in 1934, eventually becoming the leader of the Labour group. In 1937 he had been adopted as the Labour Party candidate in a by-election campaign in West Birmingham, up against a Conservative opponent running as the National Government candidate. Crossman fought a good campaign and, in a seat which had previously been held (with a substantial majority of over six thousand) by Austen Chamberlain, son of the famous Joe Chamberlain and brother of Neville, the current prime minister, Dick lost by less than three thousand votes.

Crossman had made such a good impression in his campaign that the following year he was selected as the Labour Party's prospective parliamentary candidate for Coventry East, a safe seat that Crossman would have been confidently expected to win at the next general election, due to be held in 1940. The outbreak of war, however, and the consequent postponement of parliamentary elections meant that he did not fight the seat until the General Election was held in July 1945, when he won the seat with a majority of nearly nineteen thousand and entered the House of Commons as one of the 259 new members in the Labour landslide.

Though Crossman's background – outstanding academic achievement, junior fellowship at Oxford at an almost unprecedentedly early age, leading city councillor and key wartime positions – might have been expected to help to catch Attlee's eye, the parliamentary odds were stacked against him. With so many long-standing Labour colleagues to draw on, Attlee inevitably made almost all but two of his appointments from the ranks of those with previous parliamentary experience - Harold Wilson and Hilary Marquand were the only ones from the new intake to be offered posts.

Unfortunately for Crossman it happened that there was an additional obstacle to his gaining the favour of the new Prime Minister. Crossman's father was a staunch Conservative but had for years counted Clement Attlee, a near neighbour, as a friend of the family. The Attlees were regular visitors to the Crossman home, particularly on Sunday afternoons, when Attlee enjoyed playing tennis on the court in the Crossman's garden. This had given Attlee plenty of opportunities to form a judgment of Dick both as a child and as a young man, and his opinion was, to say the least, distinctly unfavourable. "Plenty of brains. Character's the trouble," was Attlee's typically terse judgment.[4] This opinion was shaped partly by what he heard about Dick from his father and partly by direct observation of what Attlee judged to be extreme bumptiousness on Dick's part and complete disrespect for his parents.

Attlee was, on at least one occasion, able to use his friendship with the family to put Crossman firmly in his place. Dick had taken the opportunity to deliver to Attlee an extended exposition of his views on post-war reconstruction in Germany. Attlee waited until he had finished and then said simply, "I saw your mother last week. She is looking very well."

To make matters worse, when Crossman was offered a job – as a member of an Anglo-American Committee of Inquiry on Palestine - it led to a bitter dispute between himself and the Foreign Secretary, Ernest Bevin. Even before he began work on the Inquiry Crossman had become convinced that the solution to the problem of Palestine was partition – with a separate state each for the Arabs and the Jews. This cut directly across Bevin's conviction that the best solution was that Palestine should be an Arab state, but with the right of Jews to settle there.

This difference of opinion, further inflamed by a book

(*Palestine Mission*) rushed out by Crossman on the back of the inquiry's report, hardened into outright hostility, with Bevin developing an intense dislike and distrust of Crossman who, in return, accused Bevin of anti-Semitism. Years later Crossman had not softened this judgement: "Clement Attlee and Ernest Bevin plotted to destroy the Jews in Palestine and then encouraged the Arabs to murder the lot."[5]

Out of favour with both the Prime Minister and the Foreign Secretary, Crossman made no efforts to mend fences. In fact, in November 1946, six months after the Palestine report, Crossman together with Michael Foot formed the 'Keep Left' group, a factional caucus which issued pamphlets, gave speeches and organised meetings that concentrated criticism on Bevin in particular and the Labour government in general, for what it regarded as uncritical support for the United States. Unsurprisingly this group was regarded with extreme suspicion by Labour loyalists and Crossman and Foot were variously condemned by some of their fellow MPs as "long-haired intellectuals" and even "Communist lickspittles."[6]

The 'Keep Left' group remained, however, very much a fringe grouping until January 1951 when Aneurin Bevan walked out of the government in a row about the imposition of prescription charges. Bevan's departure was accompanied by two other members of the government – Harold Wilson (President of the Board of Trade) and John Freeman (Parliamentary Secretary at the Ministry of Supply). These three then started to attend meetings of the 'Keep Left' group which thereafter came to be referred to as the 'Bevanites'. This group then more than doubled in size from its 'Keep Left' origins and, by some accounts, eventually totalled as many as fifty supporters. The Labour loyalists reacted to the growth of the Bevanites with suspicion and hostility.

At the party's conference in October 1952, six members of the group – including Crossman and Wilson – captured seats on the Labour Party's National Executive, ousting in the process two distinguished party veterans, Hugh Dalton and Herbert Morrison, a humiliation from which neither man ever recovered. Unfortunately for Crossman the shine was almost immediately taken off his success. Typically, his bumptiousness led him to make incautious remarks the following day from the rostrum which led to him being roundly booed by conference.

Inevitably the group's success in the National Executive elections fuelled intense hostility from the right-wing traditionalists in the Party who were convinced that the Bevanites were subversively destructive. Attlee referred obliquely to them as a "party within a party" and Hugh Gaitskell, in a passionate speech at Stalybridge, condemned what he characterised as "mob rule" by "frustrated journalists".

In fact, all this suspicion and hostility was an overblown reaction to what was essentially no more than windy posturing. A fact which Crossman was well aware of, as he had noted in his diary for December 1951: "The fact is that Bevanism and the Bevanites seem much more important, well-organized and Machiavellian to the rest of the Labour Party, and indeed to the USA, than they do to us who are in the Group and who know that we are not organized, that Aneurin can never be persuaded to have any consistent or coherent strategy and that we have not even got to the beginning of a coherent, constructive policy."[7]

But while Crossman understood that the Group essentially represented no real threat to the traditional right wing of the party, he welcomed the way suspicion and condemnation added lustre to his reputation as a politician. Crossman was not at this time a prominent parliamentarian – he was not one of those skilful speakers able to gain attention by brilliant speeches in the House or sufficiently steeped in parliamentary procedure to be able to use its rules to make eye-catching interventions. But being a key member of the Bevanite group meant that he was definitely someone of note. Specifically of note as a trouble-maker.

The other means by which Crossman made sure of a public profile was though his journalism. He had been a deputy editor of the *New Statesman* since 1937 and written a monthly piece for the *Sunday Pictorial* since 1946 but in 1954 he landed a high-profile contract to write twice-weekly for the *Daily Mirror*. Crossman was a gifted writer, able to vary his style according to his audience. His ability to write swiftly and clearly was something that would eventually stand him in great stead when he became a Minister – and cause great frustration to his civil servants who were used to ministers who depended on them to put thoughts and ideas into writing.

At the end of December 1955, Clement Attlee retired

and Hugh Gaitskell replaced him as leader. Gaitskell, despite his resentment of the Bevanites, was prepared to make some conciliatory moves towards them and as early as February 1956 he went so far as to offer Bevan a job as Shadow Colonial Secretary. He had additionally put out some conciliatory feelers towards Crossman and involved him in discussions on foreign affairs. But no offer of an opposition post was ever forthcoming and in any event Gaitskell's olive branch was accompanied by a firm warning about future conduct. At the same time as tempting him with the possibility of being part of an informal committee on foreign affairs, Gaitskell was explicit about setting out the conditions of any rapprochement: "If we are to take you seriously as a politician," Gaitskell warned Crossman, "you've got to behave responsibly in future."[8]

At the General Election in 1959, Crossman held his seat with a slightly increased majority but Labour lost 19 seats overall, meaning that the Conservatives had, in an electoral first, won a third consecutive victory while at the same time increasing their majority. Crossman judged that Labour's campaign overall had been "splendid" but that "Gaitskell's whole tactic and leadership were wrong".[9] In particular, Crossman criticised Gaitskell for making a campaign pledge not to raise existing taxes and Crossman's antipathy towards his leader increased when he discovered that Gaitskell had decided that the way forward for the party depended on its dropping its commitment to nationalisation.

As the years in opposition went by, it was obvious that

Gaitskell was not inclined to invite Crossman onto the front bench and that even if Labour were to win the next General Election it was by no means certain that Gaitskell would offer Crossman so much as a minor role in Government. That next election was due in 1964, by which time Crossman would have been in Parliament for almost twenty years. At this stage it seemed quite likely that Crossman's parliamentary career would never amount to anything more than a succession of frustrating years on the backbenches. Crossman's disillusionment and lack of expectation is reflected in the fact that his political diary which he had kept since 1951 petered out in 1961.

Then in January 1963 Gaitskell died. His death was unexpected, not just on account of his age (he was just 56) but also because reports had played down the seriousness of his illness. Crossman immediately recognised that this event could trigger a change in his political fortunes. Within a few days of Gaitskell's funeral, Crossman recommenced his diary-writing and his first recorded entry clearly reflects a sense of optimism affected by Gaitskell's death: "Today I start my diary once more because it looks as though, quite unpredictably, my political life is beginning again."[10]

From the moment of Gaitskell's death, it was inevitable that there would be at least two contenders for the succession to the Labour leadership: George Brown who was deputy leader and Harold Wilson who had run unsuccessfully against Gaitskell for the leadership in 1960 (and, just a few months before, against Brown for the deputy's job).

There was no doubt in Crossman's mind about which candidate he would support. Crossman and Wilson had generally been on good terms – friendly, though not close – ever since Wilson had joined Bevan in the walkout from Attlee's cabinet. Crossman had some cause to question the authenticity of Wilson's alignment with the Bevanite left-wing of the party, but he had no doubts at all about Brown's commitment to the right. So, Wilson it had to be.

Once Wilson had been elected as Gaitskell's successor, Crossman finally achieved front-bench status as the opposition spokesman on science and higher education. Crossman threw himself into working across the full width of this brief, but it was the aspect of science which particularly interested Wilson. He had for a number of years frequently made reference to science in his speeches. At the Labour Party Conference in Scarborough in 1960, for example, he had declared to delegates, "Socialism must be harnessed to science and science to socialism". At the very start of his campaign to succeed to the leadership on Gaitskell's death, Wilson had already decided that science would be one of his central motifs and it duly found a place in his first television broadcast as the new party leader in February 1963.

Now Crossman's background was not remotely scientific; he was a classicist and fond of reminding others of this at any opportunity. In a parliamentary debate on science in July 1963 Crossman defiantly announced, "I must declare not an interest in science, but an ignorance of science." To remedy the gaps in his knowledge

Crossman made it a central part of his new role to consult with scientists and other academics to develop ideas that would develop this aspect of Labour's policy.

By August he had prepared a policy statement, duly published as *Labour and the Scientific Revolution*. The theme of this statement was thrust dramatically centre-stage when Wilson, casting around for a subject for his first speech to the party conference as leader in September, was, almost at the last-minute, persuaded by his assistant Marcia Williams to build his speech around some of Crossman's themes. The speech made a huge sensation and was rapturously received both within conference and beyond it. "We are re-defining and we are re-stating our socialism in terms of the scientific revolution", Wilson declared, in an echo of his speech four years earlier, and when he went on to talk of the "white heat" of this revolution he delivered a phrase with which his reputation would become indelibly associated.

As it was to turn out, all of Wilson's commitment to improved government intervention in and support for science and technology would eventually come to nothing. A charitable explanation is that the weight of economic crisis and the pressure of other events pushed the science agenda out of play. But some critics conclude that Wilson's commitment to science was never that real – more hot air than white heat. Professor Vernon Bogdanor has dismissed it as nothing more than an "obscure and clouded vision".[11] It was Wilson who had made such a fanfare of science and so the weight of disillusionment has to rest with him, but so far as

Crossman's contribution to the song and dance is concerned, the lack of follow-through is a portent of what was to become a series of failed Crossman projects.

Although Crossman was completely unprepared for his role as Minister of Housing and Local Government, there was at least no need for him to cast around seeking a mission. The Labour Party Manifesto, *The New Britain*, contained a number of commitments on housing and land, of which three were key: the repeal of the 1957 Rent Act, an increase in house-building and the creation of a Land Commission. Alongside these, Crossman soon found himself involved directly in planning decisions – decisions which traditionally had been handled easily within the department by the minister simply signing off on his officials' recommendation. This was an area in which Crossman was to take an increasingly direct involvement – much to the consternation of the civil servants.

Crossman chose to make the repeal of the Rent Act his most immediate priority. This Rent Act had been introduced in 1957 as a well-intentioned measure designed to increase the availability of housing for rent. The principal stimulus for this increase was the removal of controls which had prevented landlords from increasing the rents of higher-value homes. Protection was maintained for homes of a lower value, but only for the duration of the current tenancy – all new tenancies were to be free of rent control. In practice the Act had consequences which impacted at both ends of the market.

The loophole whereby any new tenancies were free

from rent control provided unscrupulous landlords with the incentive to drive out existing tenants and impose higher rents for their successors. One landlord in particular, Peter Rachman, was to become notorious for the brutal techniques he used to force out existing tenants and although he was only one example of this corrupt practice, it came to be so associated with his name that any activity of this kind came to be known as 'Rachmanism'. In a speech in the House of Commons as Leader of the Opposition, Harold Wilson after analysing what he called the "disease of Rachmanism" had made clear what his party believed to be the solution: "We say: repeal the Rent Act and replace it with a measure fairer to the tenant."[12]

Repealing the Rent Act might be one thing, replacing it with a fairer measure was another. Crossman opted for a two-step process. The first measure was to introduce a bill that would improve protection from eviction. As we have already seen, Crossman had antagonised his Permanent Secretary, Dame Evelyn Sharp, on his very first day in the Ministry. But in preparation of new anti-eviction proposals he provoked a row with her that was completely explosive. Judging that the provisions of the bill had been inadequately drafted, he tried to get hold of a department lawyer to establish how it could be tightened-up. It happened to be a Sunday and on being told that no department lawyer was available and, furthermore, that the Attorney General was not available either, Crossman turned for advice to Arnold Goodman, a well-known solicitor in private practice. Goodman duly provided ideas and the following day, Crossman took these points into the Ministry, so that the draft bill could be amended in line with what Goodman had suggested.

It was the involvement of an outside advisor that provoked Dame Evelyn to fury. She told him that his involvement of Goodman was "intolerable" and that she had "never been so insulted in her life".[13] Crossman held his ground and told her that she had to get used to his bringing-in outside advisors. True to his word, Crossman gradually developed a network of outside experts who he believed would give him the insights and the knowledge he needed. Dame Evelyn had no choice but to back down, but her resentment would not have been eased when the story of the affair was leaked to the political commentator Alan Watkins, who duly reported it with the claim that Dame Evelyn had had to be "subdued" by Crossman.[14]

The drafting and eventual passing into law of a protection from eviction measure gave Crossman the breathing space to develop a full replacement for the 1957 Rent Act. This commitment was to legislate for 'fair rents', but defining this concept in statute was to prove extremely tricky. A further complication was the decision to rule that 'fairness' could not take account of any scarcity of available property and must assume that supply and demand were in equilibrium. The idea of calibrating rent against rate values was explored but discarded.

The eventual solution, which passed into law as the Rent Act 1965, was to set up a system of local independent rent assessors charged with determining the 'fair rent' for any property referred to them for adjudication, with a right of appeal by either side to rent assessment committees. Crossman's measure was not, however, without some unforeseen, negative consequences. The insistence that rent officers must not take scarcity into account when reaching their judgements effectively defied the law of supply and demand and inevitably distorted the market by reducing the accommodation available for rent in areas where there was already a shortage to start with. A further weakness was the exclusion of furnished accommodation from the 'fair rent' process – an omission that Crossman himself would come to recognise as a mistake. Even Anthony Howard, a generally sympathetic biographer of Crossman, admits that the general effect of the legislation was to "dry up the supply of rented properties".[15]

For all that, it was generally recognised that the immediate intention of the Act – to determine some independent means of arriving at fairness – was fulfilled, even if the process had the characteristics of 'palm tree justice', with the judgements arrived at being essentially pragmatic and arbitrary. Even after the fall of the Labour government in 1970, the Conservative Julian Amery, by then Edward Heath's Minister for Housing and Construction, was ready to pay tribute to Crossman's legislation, acknowledging that "by and large the system of rent regulations introduced by the last government is working well. I pay tribute to them for it."[16]

At the same time as working on reform of the old Rent Act, Crossman was also addressing another major priority, his house-building programme. The Labour Party manifesto had promised to increase the rate of building for both rental and purchase but had carefully avoided committing itself to any particular figure: "While we regard 400,000 houses as a reasonable target, we do not intend to have an election auction on housing figures."

Just before Christmas 1964, Crossman met with Wilson and proposed a local authority house-building target of 135000 for the coming year. Completion of public sector housing over the last five years had averaged just 104000 homes annually, so Crossman's target was already ambitious. Wilson, however, immediately asked for an increase to 150000, which Crossman was happy to accept.

A building target is free, but making this programme a reality required money and at this point Crossman found himself faced with strong opposition from James Callaghan who as Chancellor of the Exchequer nominally held the purse-strings. Callaghan was by this stage having to face a financial situation in which the deficit was ballooning, there was a run on sterling and every day seemed to bring fresh bad news. In fact, the nearest thing to pass for good news was the agreement of another loan or line of credit to stave off disaster. Only a few days before Wilson had asked Crossman to increase his target for new council-home building, the Treasury had needed to draw down a credit of 1000 million dollars from the International Monetary Fund after it had run-through, in just three months, more than five hundred million pounds credit, mostly from the Federal Reserve Bank of New York.

The extent of Britain's dependence on almost day-today borrowing on this scale was understandably giving Callaghan sleepless nights. "It was like swimming in a heavy sea," he later recorded. "As soon as we emerged from the buffeting of one wave, another would hit us before we could catch our breath."[17]

So when Crossman proposed the expansion of the house-building programme to meet his new target, Callaghan exploded in, according to Crossman's diary, "a long, violent harangue".[18] Callaghan refused point-blank to fund the increase needed for Crossman's proposal. George Brown, however, made it clear that he was in favour of finding the money, which meant that the Chancellor and the Secretary of State for Economic Affairs were openly in disagreement. The matter was in effect decided when Wilson weighed-in and it became obvious that he was throwing his support in favour of expanding the programme. The decision was deferred for two weeks but when it came back to Cabinet, Wilson made it clear that Crossman's plans were to go ahead.

The big idea on which Wilson, Brown and Crossman relied to force the plan through was that costs could be reduced through the use of industrialised building methods, a process sometimes known as system-building, in which the main structures of buildings were pre-fabricated concrete sections, manufactured off-site and then bolted together at the construction site.

But, despite the savings system-building offered in terms of cost and time to build, in practice local authority housing completions were to climb only gradually and the best figure that Crossman was able to achieve was in his last year at the Ministry, when just under 143000 homes were completed. By 1967 completions actually reached the target and just beyond it, only to fall back again in each succeeding year of the government's life to a final figure in 1970 of 134000.

The use of system-building, which had been key to the agreement to the targets, eventually proved to be a dark chapter in the history of post-war housing. Crossman had, just a few days before originally agreeing the target with Wilson, been given a presentation on the processes of industrialised building and left the meeting feeling "warmed and excited".[19]

There turned out to be good reasons for being neither warmed nor excited. The problems of the current lack of understanding of and experience with system-building became apparent in horrific fashion on the 22nd May 1968 when a gas explosion in a flat in a system-built tower block called Ronan Point was followed by a catastrophic collapse of part of the building, leaving four people dead and seventeen injured. The subsequent enquiry found major flaws both in the design assumptions of the building and in its construction.

Crossman's own department did not escape the report's blame: "It is unfortunate that just when many large building firms, with the support of some architects, were advocating continental system building, engineers in this country were largely lukewarm or uninformed. It was in these unpropitious circumstances that the Ministry of Housing and Local Government, who themselves did not have qualified engineering staff to advise them, launched their industrialised building drive."[20]

A further weakness in the reliance on system-building was that the economic savings it promised were crucially tied to its use in the erection of tower-blocks. The construction of blocks like these had of course started before Crossman came into government. Both of Crossman's ministerial predecessors, the Conservatives Duncan Sandys and Sir Keith Joseph had encouraged their construction by, for example, a funding subsidy that was scaled to increase proportionally with the height of a building. But Crossman's programme, with its emphasis on system-building, contributed significantly to the poverty of the built environment and the blight on the lives who had to live there.

Another area in which Crossman closely involved himself was the creation of a Land Commission. Strictly speaking this was not part of his area of responsibility at all. The aim for this Land Commission, which had been promised in the manifesto, was that it should become a major player in the acquisition and release of land for building. The Commission would have powers and funds to acquire land (using compulsory purchase powers where necessary) at a lower price than the competitive market would have commanded. An additional innovation was to create a new form of tenure, 'Crown Freehold', whereby the Government would lease or sell land the Commission had acquired at reduced prices and then allow building on that land subject to the restriction that the lower price builders paid to the Government for the use of the Crown Freehold land would be reflected in lower prices at the completed stage of sale or rent. An additional responsibility for the Land Commission would be to levy a 'land betterment' tax on property values that had increased as a result of permission for a change of use.

Originally the creation of a Land Commission was intended by Wilson to be part of the work of a newly-created Ministry of Land and Planning, which was to be overseen by Fred Willey. But the proposed inclusion of planning within the remit of this new department immediately met with implacable opposition from Crossman's Permanent Secretary, Dame Evelyn, who argued that planning must not be separated from the responsibilities of the Ministry of Housing and Local Government. Crossman was persuaded that she was right and Wilson subsequently agreed.

The proposed new Ministry of Land and Planning was promptly rebranded as the Ministry of Land and Natural Resources, planning was removed from its remit and Fred Willey was left with the responsibility for creating the Land Commission, alongside a variety bag of other areas of policy, including forestry, tree preservation, commons and allotments, National Parks, the Countryside Commission and the Ordnance Survey.

Crossman was, from the start, suspicious of the plans for a Land Commission. He immediately recognised that its creation would be inordinately complex and might have unintended consequences which could impact negatively on his department. His strategy for dealing with this was to set about subtly undermining the proposal. He was assisted in this by the fact that Fred Willey's advisors, mostly drafted in from the Ministry of Housing and Local Government, believed that the Commission as originally conceived was an unworkable nonsense.[21]

Crossman set about undermining the Land Commission before it could get off the ground. His tactics included raising carefully-calculated objections, arguing for a narrowing of the Commission's scope and recommending delay in its implementation. His masterstroke was to get Wilson's agreement to the Ministry of Land and Natural Resources being absorbed into Crossman's own department. Crossman was not able completely to avert legislation but when it reached the statute book it was a very different measure from what had been promised in the manifesto. Instead of becoming the major player in the acquisition and allocation of building land, the Commission eventually emerged as little more than an advisory body. It had reserve powers to be something more, but a delay in the implementation of these powers was built into the act until a later day. This later day never arrived. Even its powers to levy a betterment tax were never used to raise more than a fraction of the revenue originally projected.

Crossman had if not strangled the Land Commission at birth, at least sabotaged it to prevent it operating as originally conceived. In a candid interview for a Granada television programme in 1972, Dame Evelyn Sharp admitted as much: "Dick Crossman and I never had the slightest interest in the Land Commission."[22]

The emasculation of the Land Commission was a rare example of Crossman and Dame Evelyn working in close harmony. For most of the time their relationship was characterised by disagreements and, frequently, blazing rows. Many years later, in an interview in 1975, Dame Evelyn commented: "He was a bull in a china shop and he felt like a bull in a china shop. I think he wanted to be a bull in a china shop, he wanted to hear the china smashing."[23]

Even those sympathetic to Crossman's side in his arguments with his Permanent Secretary had to admit some of his responsibility for the friction. Alan Watkins, in the article that had first leaked Dick's row with the Dame about taking external advice, recorded this description of Crossman: "He gesticulates a good deal. He tends to shout. In moments of excitement—and they are frequent—his straight grey hair flops over his forehead and behind the spectacles the eyes glint ferociously. Though personally the kindest of men, there is about Crossman an undertone of violence. This tendency emerges in verbal conflict and here - there is no getting away from it - Crossman is a bit of a bully."[24]

In March 1966, Dame Evelyn, the lightning rod for so much of Crossman's feuding with his own department, finally retired to be replaced by Sir Matthew Stevenson, who moved to work for Crossman from his post at the Ministry of Power. Typically, Crossman used his first meeting with Sir Matthew for a re-run of the manner of his first brutal encounter with Dame Evelyn. "I behaved as difficultly as I could," Crossman recorded in his diary, "because I wanted him to know the kind of Minister he had to tackle and I am sure the net result was to strengthen his tremendous inner complacency."[25]

Whether the two men would ever have been able to establish easy and co-operative relations is unknown, because, only a few days after Sir Matthew's appointment, a General Election was held, when Labour won a 97-seat majority. Less than six months later, Wilson reshuffled his Cabinet and Crossman left the Ministry of Housing to become Lord President of the Council and Leader of the House.

The Lord President's job is to run the Privy Council Office. The office has great seniority but is a rather empty role; its chief function is to organise the occasional ceremonies where the monarch meets with Privy Councillors to give assent to legislation passed in Parliament. Crossman, perhaps surprisingly, turned out to manage these meetings with considerable tact and discretion. The nearest occasion when matters came to something approaching friction was when Crossman pointed out to the Queen that these meetings often required ministers to travel long-distance to wherever the Queen happened to be residence, often requiring overnight travel or stays, for a ceremony that was over in just a few minutes. Crossman's implied suggestion that things could be organised more efficiently was passed over by the Queen without comment and Crossman had sufficient discretion to let the matter drop.

It was the second aspect of Crossman's new role, as Leader of the House, that was to provide him with by far the greater burden and scope. The job of the Leader is essentially to smooth the passage of the Government's

84

legislation through Parliament. Crossman took up this role with a clear self-awareness of his lack of preparation: "For days now I've been sitting down at my desk, reading the documents and mugging up the organisation and history of Parliament. It's difficult because I know as little about it as I did about housing twenty months ago. Although I've been a back-bencher for nearly twenty years I've really done very little in Parliament. I've taken no interest in procedure and not very much part in debates because I thought Parliament was a profoundly unimportant and boring place."[26]

Given that the job of Leader of the House had traditionally required not just a close knowledge of parliamentary rules and procedure, but also well-developed skills of diplomacy and negotiation, Crossman's appointment to his new role struck many MPs as curiously inappropriate. But Crossman saw his role in a new light – not just to expedite parliamentary business, but as an opportunity to effect the reform of Parliament. Crossman had been given a new stage on which to practise his talent for disruption.

The political wind was already blowing in the direction of parliamentary reform when Crossman became Leader of the House, and it was an agenda that he embraced with enthusiasm. He had for years been a passionate advocate of the need to admit light into the workings of Westminster and the diary he was keeping of his time in government, which included detailed accounts of confidential cabinet meetings, was part of his long-term plan to open-up the machinery of government for public scrutiny.

The reform of Parliament had been a topic of increasing debate ever since Labour had come to power after the war, and during the fifties and sixties the case for change had become a regular subject for discussion and a series of books and reports appeared arguing the case for reform.

In 1964, a group of academics came together to create the 'Study of Parliament' group, whose purpose was to stimulate reform. In the same year a Penguin Special, written pseudonymously by two House of Common Clerks, posed the question *What's Wrong with Parliament?* and Bernard Crick, at that time a lecturer in politics at the LSE, wrote a book on *The Reform of Parliament*. Despite the increasingly public head of steam for reform, Crick believed that it faced an uphill struggle for implementation: "Seldom has there been so much public agreement that something should be done" he wrote, "but seldom so much private agreement that nothing is likely to be done."[27]

Richard Crossman, as the new Leader of the House, seized this opportunity to prove that Crick's pessimism was unjustified. He was sure he could use both his new office and his powers of intellectual persuasion to achieve a bold series of reforms. The first that he attempted was the televising of Parliament.

The idea of parliamentary debates being shown on television was not new – it had been advocated by some Labour members as far back as 1959, but in 1963 the well-known television journalist Robin Day had written a pamphlet arguing *The Case for Televising Parliament*, an innovation which would he believed (naively as it would turn out) "develop into the most influential forum of public affairs on television".

Crossman expected that getting agreement to let cameras into the House of Commons would be an easy win. But, to his frustration, when he took the idea to Cabinet for approval it met with virtually no support. Crossman wanted the experiment to start within months, but found that amongst his colleagues in Cabinet "nobody wanted the television experiment. They didn't want a change of this sort in the Palace of Westminster."[28] Crossman had to settle for a year's delay in the introduction of television and this setback to his plan was particularly embarrassing for him, because the Conservative opposition had already signalled its agreement to going ahead almost immediately, and so he had to go back to them and explain that it would have to be delayed.

The discussion at the Cabinet meeting had seemed to be going Crossman's way, until a sudden interjection by Wilson had made clear his absolute opposition to the proposal on the grounds that extracts from speeches in the House might be used in other programmes. This, he said, could not possibly be allowed. If Crossman was surprised by Wilson's flat objection to the televising of Parliament, he should not have been. Wilson was at heart not a moderniser, but a traditionalist.

For all of his repeatedly public embracing of the 'new', Wilson was, by instinct, a politician rooted not in the now, but in the past of twenty years before. His touchstone was the Attlee government of 1945-51 and time and time again he would reach back into his recollection of his first years as a government minister, in search of strategies and ideas that he could borrow and re-present under the guise of imaginative innovation.

Crossman was to experience again the potential of Wilson's discomfort with change when, in September 1967, he asked the Cabinet to agree to a proposal that the clerks in the House of Commons, who sit at the table in front of the Speaker, should no longer be required to wear wigs. Crossman did get Cabinet agreement, but only grudgingly from Wilson who argued for a compromise whereby the clerks would still have had to wear their wigs during Question Time – the periods of Commons business when he would most likely be on the front bench himself. Crossman had at least won, but when the Conservative opposition refused to agree, the proposal had to be dropped.

In the meantime, Crossman had achieved some success by persuading first the Cabinet and then the House to agree in December 1966 to an amendment to its standing orders to allow morning sittings on two days in the week. Dick's intention behind this reform was that by introducing morning sessions on only Mondays and Wednesdays he would be able to prepare the ground for, at a later date, an extension of the reform to cover each weekday. Things did not go to plan for him. The morning sessions were unpopular and just a year later had to be abandoned. A pattern was beginning to emerge of

Crossman failures.

Another reform that Crossman took up was the use of specialist committees of the House that would have the powers to scrutinise particular aspects of the government's work and potentially strengthen the accountability of the Executive to the Commons. This was a reform that had been widely argued for over a number of years, but Crossman was to find that his Cabinet colleagues were very reluctant to agree to a change that could expose their own departments to closer scrutiny. Roy Jenkins, then Home Secretary, flatly refused to let the Home Office be subject to answering to a specialist committee and so did Tony Crosland. In the end, Crossman could only get agreement for two committees, one on science and another on agricultural policy.

These committees did not turn out to enable the scrutiny that their advocates had hoped for. The Prime Minister and the Chief Whips controlled the selection of members and although Crossman sympathised with backbenchers who thought that the membership of these committees should be independently determined, in practice he willingly went along with the whips' control of the process – in fact he was conscious that the Minister for Agriculture, Fred Peart, had only been persuaded to agree to the specialist committee on agriculture after being assured by Crossman that "the committee would be hand-picked and would eat out of his hand".[29] Crossman knew that the overwhelming majority of his colleagues were deeply suspicious of specialist committees and that the assurances he'd had from Wilson about his own support for the idea were unreliable: "When he (Wilson) is alone with me he's always in favour of specialist committees but in Cabinet he's always accepting Ministerial objections."[30]

Given that Crossman's work on parliamentary reform had not been an unqualified success, it says a great deal for his self-confidence that his final move as Leader of the House should have been his boldest yet – an attempt at reform of the House of Lords. What made his plan even more controversial was his idea that the reform should address not simply the powers of the House of Lords, but its actual composition. What Crossman proposed was to give the Lords two-tiers of membership – all members would have the right to speak, but not all of them would have the right to vote. All existing hereditary peers would, for the remainder of their lives, retain the right to sit in the Lords, but without the right to vote. When they died their membership rights would die with them and so their successors to the title would never sit in the upper chamber. Other elements to the plan included ensuring that the composition of the Lords would in each Parliament broadly reflect the composition of the Commons and, additionally, there would be limits to the ability of the Lords to delay or refuse consent to a measure that had been sent up from the lower house.

What is astonishing is not that Crossman should have succeeded – because he did not – but that he was able to get his proposal close to the finishing line. To Crossman's great credit he was able to persuade two key members of the House of Lords – Lord Carrington, the leader of the Conservatives in the upper chamber and Lord Jellicoe, his deputy – to give their support to his plan. So effective was their co-operation that when the reform was put to the vote in the Lords it passed by 251 votes to 56. The measure had already passed through its initial stages in the Commons, so it only had to return there for a final vote before it would have received the Royal Assent. But, to Crossman's bitter disappointment, before it could pass into law, the entire reform was scuppered when the government was forced to humiliatingly abandon the Bill following the withdrawal of co-operation by the Conservatives, a quarrel provoked not by House of Lords reform but by the government's decision to impose sanctions on Rhodesia, after that country's unilateral declaration of independence.

By the time of the reform's collapse, in April 1969, it was no longer Crossman's responsibility, because a year earlier, in a reshuffle, Wilson had moved Dick to another, and what would turn out to be his final, cabinet post, as Secretary of State for Health and Social Security. But the abandonment of House of Lords reform meant that within a few months of starting his new post at the DHSS, Crossman knew that his attempts at a radical reshaping of Parliament had come to nothing. Had he been able to look into the future he would have seen that the major part of the reforms he had championed would eventually be implemented. However, the length of time between Dick's advocacy of these changes and the actual realisation of each of these reforms is so great that it would be stretching the imagination to give him credit for those changes when they actually came – for example, reform of the House of Lords on lines similar to those championed by Crossman would not actually be implemented until the time of Tony Blair's government.

Crossman was originally appointed to his new Cabinet post in order to co-ordinate the work of the separate ministries of health and of social security and then to manage their merger into a new and single ministry, the Department of Health and Social Security. This new 'super-ministry' made a curious hybrid; two separate ministries spliced together for no particularly good reason and certainly to no practical advantage. The awkward nature of their union was emphasised by the two halves being located in entirely separate buildings, a considerable distance apart. Crossman found himself obliged to trek backwards and forwards in his ministerial car, a journey across the river that could sometimes take the better part of half an hour. To make matters worse, the Health building was an unappealing modern block on what Crossman described as a "ghastly site" on top of underground railway lines.

It was in the area of pensions that Crossman would plan to make his greatest reforms, but he was also determined to stir up the health side which he judged to be a "deeply inactive" ministry.[31] He deserves particular credit for the attention he gave to the standard of mental health care. He expressed serious concerns about conditions in the mental hospitals that he visited and he flatly refused to collude with a cover-up or at least a partial concealment of serious wrongdoings at a hospital in Cardiff which was supposed to provide long-stay care for patients with learning difficulties. A highly critical report of what had happened there had been written by Geoffrey Howe QC. Crossman's officials wanted to release only an edited version of that report, but Dick insisted on it being published in full. Crossman then went further and, again in the face of counter-arguments from his officials, insisted that there must be put in place a system of hospital inspections. The complete report on Ely Hospital was duly released (with the exception of names of individual patients and members of staff) and in 1969 a Hospital Advisory Service was created with the responsibility to report to the Secretary of State on hospital performance.

It was, however, on the other side of his giant department that Crossman threw his greatest weight with a highly radical attempt to completely restructure the provision of retirement pensions. Crossman's plan amounted to a complete overturn of the pension arrangements instituted following the Beveridge Report and their replacement by a completely new system. Unlike his previous roles, Crossman in this case had previous experience and a considerable amount of background knowledge. His interest in the subject had begun as long ago as 1956 when he had read a pamphlet on pension reform written by Professor Richard Titmuss, of the London School of Economics. Crossman had then gone on, in consultation with Titmuss and other academic experts, to develop a plan for a national superannuation scheme that eventually made its way into the Labour Party's manifesto in 1959. The party's promise at that election had been to introduce a national superannuation scheme that would replace flat-rate contributions with earnings-related contributions and benefits and would, when fully developed, guarantee "half pay on retirement for the average wage-earner and up to two-thirds for the lower paid workers, both men and women".

The plan which Crossman proposed to implement when he became Secretary of State was broadly similar to his 1959 proposal, but entailed compromises to the providers of private pension plans, whose stake in providing pensions had grown considerably since the late 1950s. Crossman's amended plan was that private pension plan providers should be allowed some degree of contracting-out from the national scheme, even if the benefits they offered were not as good. The economic burden of this would fall directly on the government, because Crossman proposed that 'contracted-out' pensioners would have their benefits topped-up by the State if they otherwise fell short of what they would have received in the national scheme. Since the national scheme was to be inflation-proofed this meant the government would additionally be liable for the cost of enhancing payments to contracted-out pensioners who would otherwise have received only a fixed pension for life. A further cost to the taxpayer would be widows' pensions, for which private schemes would not have to be liable. The final price that Crossman had to pay to get the industry's acceptance of his scheme was that those schemes that were opted-out would only have to pay into the national scheme at a reduced rate.

The extent of these concessions is a reflection of the bitter argument and lengthy horse-trading that was needed before Crossman could reach agreement with the insurance companies and pension fundholders. But on 19 January 1970 Crossman was at last able to stand up in the House of Commons and formally initiate debate on his National Superannuation and Social Insurance Bill. Crossman recorded in his diary his satisfaction at his performance: "I think in electioneering terms and in its intelligibility it was an able speech. I was right back at the top of my form, fully recovered, capable, rallying the Party not only to me but to the scheme."[32]

After a series of failures and uncompleted projects Crossman felt that at last he was on the verge of a major triumph. He was encouraged in this by the Bill's relatively trouble-free progress through the Committee stage. But in the spring Crossman began to be troubled by talk of a possible general election. By May the polls were beginning to move in Labour's direction and Crossman knew that this would inevitably mean the abandonment of his bill. He clung to the hope that it could be reintroduced if Labour were to win the next election, but he knew that he would not be the one to steer its next passage because he had already decided that in the longer term his intention was to leave Parliament and return to journalism as the editor of the *New Statesman*. He stood again as Labour candidate in Coventry East and on election day, Thursday June 18th, was re-elected with a majority of 12000. But nationally it was a Conservative victory and Edward Heath entered Number 10 as the new Prime Minister.

On the following Monday, Crossman wrote his last entry in his diary of his life as a cabinet minister. It was an end to a discipline of diary writing that had begun in October 1951, still in his backbench years. He had made no secret of the fact that he was keeping a diary while he was in the cabinet, a fact that was of concern to many of his colleagues and, especially, to Wilson himself. What's more he had been completely open about the fact that he was not keeping his diary as a purely private record – he had already, while in Cabinet, signed a contract for book publication and newspaper serialisation. His colleagues might have been even more concerned had they known that he was recording not just their contributions in cabinet, but also what they said in private face-to-face meetings with him.

While Crossman's diary entries include occasional passages of self-criticism, in the main they concentrate on what he judged to be his effectiveness. There are many entries in which he depicts himself as the only one who turns up for cabinet discussion with a firm grasp of the issues, the only one who has really analysed the relevant papers and the only one who can ask the penetrating questions that expose the weaknesses of a proposition or the falsity of some argument. All this is not necessarily self-inflation. He really did have an outstandingly analytic mind and he was able to absorb lengthy papers and grasp complex issues with great rapidity.

But, even allowing for an undoubted tendency to self-flattery, Crossman's intention in publishing his diary was really not autobiographical at all. His purpose was constitutional. As with the broadcasting of parliament he wanted to open-up aspects of government to the public gaze and in the case of his diary reveal not just something of the machinery of government, but particularly shine a light into its most hidden part – what went on behind the doors of the cabinet room.

When publication of the diaries seemed imminent, opposition to their appearance was particularly strong amongst senior civil servants. Sir John Hunt, the Cabinet Secretary, wrote: "There will inevitably be problems since the diary contains a blow by blow account of many Cabinet discussions, and it could therefore mark something of a watershed." Sir William Armstrong, head of the civil service, declared: "Mr Crossman breaks a tradition of mutual trust and for that matter of good manners. In my view, nothing would be the same again."[33]

Book rights had been acquired by the publisher Jonathan Cape and the newspaper serialisation rights had been sold to the *Sunday Times*. The Cabinet Office set out to suppress publication, initially by declaring that Crossman's diaries could not be published until thirty years had passed – applying the same rule as for official government papers. When the *Sunday Times* declined to accept this, the Government agreed to allow publication, but only of those parts of the text that had been officially vetted and approved. Harold Evans, the paper's editor, was initially prepared to agree to this, but changed his mind when it became obvious that the Cabinet Office would agree only to the appearance of the most trivial and mundane entries. When the government sensed that the *Sunday Times* was going to defy a ban on publication, the Cabinet Secretary wrote to Evans demanding an undertaking not to publish any unapproved extracts.

The letter was received on a Thursday and required that the undertaking be made by the following Monday. Evans immediately saw that the intervening weekend provided him with a window in which he could publish before the deadline. So, on 26th January 1975, the *Sunday Times* duly appeared with its first extract from the diaries.

With the dam now breached, the Cabinet Secretary adopted a more conciliatory approach. He asked the *Sunday Times* to submit beforehand each week's intended extracts, so that he could indicate which parts he would allow. The paper agreed to this and each week it duly received from Sir John Hunt a list of the required expurgations. Each week the *Sunday Times* complied with some of these and ignored others. The game of cat and mouse continued in this way until at last the extract was published that covered the 1966 Cabinet discussion leading to the decision to devalue. The *Sunday Times* printed this part of the diary with no cuts at all and, judging this to be a watershed in the matter, Crossman's publishers decided they could safely go ahead and bring out the first volume of the diaries in book form.

The Government decided, however, to take a further stand and the publishers and literary executors (Crossman had died two years previously) were taken to court with an action seeking an injunction to suppress publication, an injunction that relied on an archaic law of confidentiality. The defendants had hoped that the judge would deny the applicability of this law, but to their disappointment he accepted that the case could proceed on that basis. To their final relief, however, he found that there were no grounds for denying publication and ruled that the publishers could proceed to publish in full.

The genie was now completely out of the bottle and the publication of the first volume was followed by the appearance of the remaining two. The public, for the first time, read in full, without censorship, exactly what Crossman had recorded of his time as a member of the cabinet. The result was at least to diminish public confidence – if it ever existed – in a cabinet as a group of reasonable men and women intelligently weighing up public issues and coming to agreement. In the words of the Sunday Times's editor what was exposed to public view was a picture of "Cabinet ignorance and impotence".[34]

Perhaps more significantly the diaries shone a disturbing light on the then prevailing academic model of cabinet government. That model, developed by John Mackintosh, a Labour MP and a political historian, argued that essentially the country had moved into a form of prime ministerial government, in which the cabinet was not much more than an agent of the PM's bidding. But this fitted uneasily with the picture of the cabinet in Crossman's diary. The theory of a Prime Minister who gets his own way implies that the PM has at least a way in mind. But the very thing which seemed to be lacking in

Crossman's account was any sense of strategic direction from above.

Wilson's lack of strategic leadership is a persistent theme in Crossman's diaries. As early as December 1964 he wrote: "I don't think Harold has really established himself as the leader we need...I get the impression this Government isn't running itself in but just running along".[35] Five years later Crossman's evaluation of the Prime Minister had not improved: "He is just a figure posturing there in the middle without any drive except to stay Prime Minister as long as he can."[36]

The picture that emerged from the publication of Crossman's diary was a government in which the Prime Minister's sense of direction seemed to be largely a matter of hand-to-mouth expediency. If this was what prime ministerial government amounted to, it looked a lot like flying blind.

But are his diaries really an accurate record of the events he describes? Over his career there were many who had come to distrust Crossman and doubted his ability to play fair in his diary account. After Wilson had read the diaries he dismissed them, claiming "He didn't get a single fact right".[37] But a more dispassionate witness to the overall reliability of Crossman's record is his Cabinet colleague Roy Jenkins, who, although noting that Crossman often fell asleep in Cabinet, recorded his judgment that the diary was "remarkably accurate".[38] Interestingly the diary accounts provided by others, particularly Barbara Castle and Tony Benn, differ in terms of some incidents and in respect of 'who said what' around the Cabinet table – but they are in accord with Crossman's overall picture. If Wilson's government was an example of any kind of model of cabinet government, it was a model of short-termism and drift.

In retrospect it is the diaries that are Crossman's monument. Their publication not only provided vivid source materials for students of political history, they also opened the way for others to publish their record of their time in Wilson's and in other governments. Once the court case had found in favour of Crossman's literary executors and his publishers, it was impossible for any government to believe in the realistic possibility of suppressing other and future diarists.

His political achievements, as a cabinet minister, are, by contrast, relatively insignificant. His most notable success was the 1965 Rent Act which, although it had the unforeseen consequence of contributing to a reduction in the number of properties to rent, did have the notable virtue of tackling the vicious tactics of 'Rachmanism'. His other attempts at significant reform – broadcasting of Parliament, reform of the House of Lords, a revolution in pension provision – all came to grief.

Some have attempted to lessen these failures by pointing out that Crossman was in these respects clearly on the right side of reform and that although not successful at the time, many of his ideas have been advanced and even implemented since. In this respect he is hailed by some as a pioneer. This is well-intentioned but hard to accept. The intervals between Crossman's proposals and the actual implementation – or the implementation of something like them – are so great that it is hard to trace any direct connection between his work and what happened subsequently. There is a case to be made for Crossman as some kind of visionary – glimpsing what might be possible – but that is not the same as the role of political pioneer, someone who spearheads an innovation or at least puts the first steps in place.

Another defence of Crossman is that he should not be held responsible for the collapse of his main achievements, which was mostly due to events beyond his control – for example, Wilson's decision to hold a general election before the pension reform could come to a final vote. This is a fair defence, but it also has to be noted that Crossman's proposals might have been able to move forward at a faster pace – and so potentially have come to fruit – if he had not had such an abrasive relationship with his own officials.

His effectiveness as a minister – and as a member of the cabinet – was handicapped because his natural pugnacity and belligerence was made worse by the fact that by the time he became a minister he was a man in too much of a hurry. In nearly twenty years spent on the backbenches he had always been a figure confined to the sidelines – and a widely distrusted figure at that. When he became Secretary of State for Housing and Local Government, he finally had a stage on which he could make a mark – and he arrived at the Ministry already convinced that his officials would, as a matter of course, obstruct him if they could.

Crossman was, undeniably, vastly intellectually superior to the average minister, but he was determined to demonstrate this at every turn. A further negative factor was the fact that he relished a clash of minds, regarding it very much as a game. The consequence was that he would sometimes fiercely defend a particular point of view and then, after reviewing the arguments that had been put forward against him, change sides. Dick of course regarded this sort of about-turn as a good example of openness to counter-argument – and it probably was – but to his officials who found their minister shamelessly advocating a position that they had endured a vicious tongue-lashing for putting forward only the day before, it felt rather closer to perversity or hypocrisy. Tom Dalyell, an admirer of Crossman and for many years his Parliamentary Private Secretary, has left a candid description of the way Crossman "always made it difficult for someone who had to present a coherent argument to get through to the end with it. He would interrupt in the rudest way…his interruptions, implying incompetence, made it wellnigh impossible for civil servants to defend themselves".[39] It's clear that Crossman had a complete lack of self-awareness about the impact of his tempestuous style and his diary frequently records descriptions of discussion which must have seemed to those involved like an exhibition of out-and-out bullying. Yet so often Crossman concludes his description with the self-delusional judgment that everyone there had enjoyed the vigorous debate.

Crossman kept his parliamentary seat in the 1970 General Election, but even if Labour had not lost he had already decided to leave government. He had agreed to become the editor of the *New Statesman*, a job he had always coveted. Sadly, he was not a success there. His relationships with his staff were quickly marked by tension and bad feelings. Circulation began to fall and after Crossman had been hospitalised with a serious illness, the magazine's management board seized the opportunity to ask for his resignation on the grounds of ill health. Typically, Crossman used his last days at the paper to publish in it an attack on the board for its decision.

Crossman, by now in declining health, had at least the comfort of his family into which he could retreat. In 1954 Crossman had entered into his third marriage, a relationship which brought him great happiness, including two children. On his marriage to Anne McDougall, his father-in-law had given them as a wedding present the ownership of a run-down farm, Prescote Manor, dating from the sixteenth century. With the help of an efficient farm manager the estate grew in size and productivity and eventually extended to 2000 acres. Crossman loved his life at Prescote and the most tender and lyrical passages of his diary are those in which he describes events on the farm and his family life there.

Crossman died, of liver cancer, on April 5th 1974. He had stood down from his parliamentary seat at the 1974 election when he was already in the last stages of his disease. He never lived to see his diaries achieve publication, but some of the money that his books would go on to earn was spent by his wife on improvements at Prescote. Crossman would have approved.

4

James Callaghan:
Point-to-Point Navigation

James Callaghan's very first day in Wilson's government plunged him into a series of economic crises that, over months and years, was to become an ongoing, personal nightmare. As he later recorded, "I have never experienced anything more frustrating than sitting at the Chancellor's desk watching our currency reserves gurgle down the plug-hole day by day and knowing that the drain could not be stopped."[1] The state of sterling was reported to him up to four times a day, so he often had no time to react to one set of bad figures before having to absorb even worse news from the next update. As the Chancellor lurched from one critical situation to another, he had simultaneously to grapple with his cabinet colleagues, whose ministerial demands for more and more money for their departmental priorities plainly flew in the face of his daily reality.

In that kind of political weather there is little chance of being able to set a clear course ahead. Callaghan's responses to the almost continuous drain in the currency reserves were inevitably hand-to-mouth. In any event, strategic economic planning was supposed to rest not with the Treasury but with the Department of Economic Affairs, drastically limiting Callaghan's ability to establish a long-term plan for ending the economic crisis. The guidance available from his Treasury experts seemed to offer only an apparently endless series of course-corrections. Callaghan had little choice but to steer from one crisis measure to another – without compass or map, his only option became point-to-point navigation.

James Callaghan was born on 27th March 1912 in Plymouth, where his family rented a small terraced house. His father was in the Royal Navy and Callaghan had no memories of him until after his service discharge in 1912. His father then got a job in the Coastguard Service and for the next two years they lived in Brixham, Devon. In his autobiography, Callaghan's descriptions of his life during those two years are notably lyrical and, when his father died just two years later, Callaghan admitted that his father's death marked the end of the "happiest period of my childhood".

His widowed mother was left initially without a widow's pension and with no other income. They lived on the edge of poverty, dependent for the most part on the charity of members of his mother's chapel. They moved frequently and eventually returned to Plymouth where his mother was eventually able to persuade the Admiralty both to grant her a small pension and to pay the school fees that enabled Callaghan to continue as a pupil after he had reached the official school leaving age. At the age of seventeen, Callaghan took and passed the Oxford High School Certificate and was then eligible to sit for the Civil Service entrance examination in which he did well enough to be appointed to a junior clerical post in the Maidstone Tax Office.

Callaghan's life with his widowed mother had been heavily chapel-based. His mother was a severe fundamentalist and the domestic routine always included prayers, grace before meals and regular attendance at chapel. So, inevitably, when Callaghan found himself living independently in Maidstone, a long way from home, he turned to his local chapel and enrolled as a Sunday School teacher. This had the unexpected bonus of bringing him into contact with Audrey Moulton, the daughter of the leader of the chapel. Her family made him welcome and, for the first time, gave him experience of a happy family life. His friendship with Audrey led to romance and they eventually married in July 1938.

Working at the tax office also led to another and very significant branching-out. It was at this time that he started to take a much closer interest in politics, through reading and attending classes organised by the Workers' Educational Association and this study eventually led to him joining the local Labour Party. He also joined the Association of Officers of Taxes and became very active in the union's affairs, until eventually in 1933, aged just twenty-one, he was elected to its National Executive.

In 1934, he was able to get a transfer to one of the London tax offices where he continued to be active in both the local Labour Party (Lewisham) and in his union.

The work he did for the AOT was sufficiently well-regarded for the union to offer him, in 1936, a post as the association's Assistant Secretary. This was a full-time job so Callaghan resigned as a tax officer – without any regrets because his new job was at a significantly higher rate of pay. His new role enabled Callaghan to make useful contacts with a number of senior labour figures, including Hugh Dalton and Harold Laski. Equally useful, (though it was a contact established through his wife not the union) was an introduction to Hugh Gaitskell, who was teaching a University economics course being taken by Audrey Callaghan.

Soon after the outbreak of war Callaghan applied to join-up, but a regulation which excluded union officials from being taken into the services, delayed his entry into the navy until May 1940, when the AOT agreed to waive its right to exclude him from active service.

Callaghan was enlisted at the rank of Ordinary Seaman, though before long he was identified as a prospect for promotion to Second Lieutenant. But before he could take the qualifying course he had to undergo a medical, during which he was diagnosed as suffering from tuberculosis. He was admitted to hospital but eventually discharged as fit for shore duties and Callaghan found himself posted to the Admiralty where he was improbably tasked with writing a manual on Japan, to be used to educate British servicemen posted for duties in south-east Asia. Callaghan of course was completely ignorant on the subject and had to be granted access to the library of the Royal Institute of International Affairs, where he was able to research the material for his manual. It was given the title *The Enemy: Japan* and essentially consisted of notes for a series of lectures to be delivered to the troops.

Once this task was complete, Callaghan was judged fit for active duties and resumed his service at sea. But, with the end of the war now in sight, Callaghan's thoughts had turned to making a career in politics. His friend, Professor Laski, had already urged him to stand for Parliament and another useful contact, an Executive member of the Inland Revenue Association, suggested he get in touch with the local Labour Party branch in Cardiff South, who were looking for a candidate. Callaghan took advantage of some home leave to meet with the constituency committee and they were sufficiently impressed to encourage him to make a formal application to be chosen. He went on to be formally adopted and in the Labour landslide took the seat, held by the Conservative party since 1931, with a majority of nearly six thousand votes. In determining on a political career, Callaghan had decided that this new direction should be accompanied by a variation in his name. He had been born Leonard James Callaghan and up to this point he had always been known as Leonard. But in his candidature at Cardiff South he ran as James Callaghan.

Compared with some of his contemporaries, Callaghan's early time in Parliament might seem low-key. Unlike Crossman (who had quickly captured attention by becoming a thorn-in-the-flesh) or Brown (who achieved early significance by becoming an unofficial junior minister), Callaghan's beginnings in Parliament were extremely modest. He secured only an appointment as Parliamentary Private Secretary to the Parliamentary Under-Secretary at the Dominions Office. As first steps on the ladder go, this was a rung scarcely off the ground, unpaid and unnoticed. But in other ways Callaghan was able to gain a reputation as an independent voice within the party. He voted against his government over its acceptance of a loan from the USA (on terms which Callaghan judged to be punitive) and he rebelled again when the government proposed to introduce conscription. Callaghan's objection was not to the principle of conscription, but the proposed length of time during which men would be compulsorily enlisted. The government wanted a period of eighteen months; Callaghan campaigned for this to be reduced to just one year.

Despite these signs of rebelliousness (or perhaps because of them) Callaghan was in October 1947 offered his first junior ministerial post – as a Parliamentary Secretary in the Ministry of Transport. This was a busy department; its major piece of legislation, the Transport Act, which brought the railways and road transport into public ownership, came into force the month after Callaghan joined the Ministry, Callaghan was given responsibility for docks and ports and worked hard but unsuccessfully in an attempt to ensure that work was distributed to these places in a way that reflected regional fairness and balance. He was of course particularly keen to try to ensure as much work as possible for the port of Cardiff. Callaghan acknowledged in his memoirs that his

Minister, John Barnes, never involved him in important decisions, but it seems that he did at least inspire the name of 'zebra crossing' to describe the black and white stripes that were introduced to mark the roadway between the flashing beacons and is also entitled to some credit for stepping-up the incorporation of the reflective road markers known as "cats' eyes" in the road-building programme.

After the General Election in 1951, Attlee moved Callaghan to the post of Parliamentary and Financial Secretary to the Admiralty, a position clearly reflecting Callaghan's naval experience. On the face of it, this was still a very junior post, but it provided a significant opportunity for Callaghan, because the First Lord of the Admiralty sat in the House of Lords, so it fell to Callaghan to handle any business in the Commons. This gave him a good opportunity to polish his skills at the despatch box and helped to develop a parliamentary reputation as calm and confident. It was this reputation that helped to get him elected to the Shadow Cabinet in November 1951, after Labour had lost the election the previous month.

The years in opposition were a time of slow and steady progress – at first Callaghan was sent back to a previous role, shadowing the Ministry of Transport. Then, after Attlee's resignation, Gaitskell moved him to become shadow spokesman on fuel and power. A year later he was moved again, this time to shadow spokesman for education and for science. By 1959 he was shadow spokesman on the colonies (a post in which he replaced Bevan). None of these responsibilities had been of the front rank but what they did for Callaghan was to consolidate his reputation as a solid and reliable performer, never too far to the left or the right, always calm, steady and dependable.

It was his establishment as a leading figure in the shadow cabinet and a key player in the campaign at election times that gave him the confidence to stand for deputy leadership of the party in October 1960. He was a 'middle-of-the-road' candidate running against George Brown on his right and Fred Lee on his left. He was eliminated in the first round, but secured about one in five of the votes, which was a respectable loss. A little over a year later he was rewarded with a key post – Shadow Chancellor of the Exchequer, replacing Wilson, whom Gaitskell had moved to shadow the Foreign Office. With this appointment, Callaghan had clearly secured a place at the top table and, significantly, paved the way for him to succeed to the Chancellorship in October 1964.

On the face of things, it is curious that Gaitskell, a trained economist himself and a former Chancellor of the Exchequer, should choose as his Shadow Chancellor a man whom he knew had no background in economics whatsoever. The most plausible explanation is that Gaitskell presumed that as an expert himself in the field he could safely install a complete amateur who would necessarily take directions from his leader.

So far as Callaghan was concerned, it was almost a case of déjà vu; a throw-back to his wartime assignment to write a manual on Japan. He had known nothing about Japan at all, but he had been able to 'mug it up'. His natural instinct as the new Shadow Chancellor was to do the same with economics. He made contact with Ruskin College, Oxford and asked for seminars to be arranged so that he could receive instruction in the fundamentals. The forthcoming tutorials were well-intentioned and Callaghan has been entitled to credit for being willing to admit his need of an economic education. There is no evidence, however, that these seminars turned out to be of much practical use when the time came for Callaghan to enter Number 11. A few months after Callaghan had become Chancellor, Robert Neild, then the Treasury's Economic Adviser, reported to colleagues that everything had to be explained to Callaghan "like to a first-year student."[2] But then it is hard to see how any basic tuition could reasonably have equipped a complete novice to cope knowledgeably and competently with the violent economic storms which lay ahead.

After Gaitskell's death, Wilson – who had comfortably seen off Callaghan in the contest for the leadership – retained him as his Shadow Chancellor, despite having little confidence in his economic understanding.[3] Callaghan's economic naivety was on full display when the Tory Chancellor, Reginald Maudling, launched his disastrous 'dash for growth' in the budget of 1963. It was the expansion signalled in that budget that would eventually create the balance of payments crisis inherited by Labour in the following year. But in his response to that budget, Callaghan, instead of warning of any negative consequences, actually criticised Maudling for not being expansionist enough: "In my view, the Chancellor has been too cautious. I believe that there is a need for greater incentives if we are to get industry running full out. I do not believe that we can maintain it, but I think that there would be a case for arguing economically that we should have a relatively sudden spurt for a period of twelve months before we settle down to a steady rate of growth".[4]

When, shortly before the General Election the following year, the danger signs became clear - in the form of a ballooning negative balance of payments – Callaghan conveniently forgot that he had argued for even greater expansion and blamed Maudling for the poisoned fruit that his boom was starting to produce. That's politics, of course, and it is hardly surprising that Labour almost welcomed the warning signs about the balance of payments problem as a useful campaigning issue for them and one they particularly needed to exploit since for the Conservatives the effect of Maudling's expansion was to encourage a public perception that, on the back of the boom, people were becoming better off.

While the balance of payments problem was seen as politically advantageous to Labour's campaign, Callaghan was sufficiently sensitive to its implications to attempt before the election to reach a deal with Reginald Maudling. Callaghan's proposal was that if a currency slide started to develop in the run-up to the election, he and Maudling should release a joint statement insisting that there would be no devaluation. Maudling inevitably refused, but the fact that the approach was made not only indicates a surprising innocence about the reality of party politics, but more significantly is also an early indication of Callaghan's lack of understanding of what calms the market and what alarms it. A joint statement on the lines he suggested would have been most likely not to reassure the market, but to rattle it. Just as when a Prime Minister's announcement that he or she has complete confidence in a particular Minister is often a signal that that individual will shortly be gone, so a reassurance that devaluation is not to be considered is very likely to increase suspicion that it is certainly on the cards. Time and time again, after he became Chancellor, Callaghan would fall clumsily into the trap of issuing statements or taking steps that had an effect precisely opposite to his intention to calm and reassure.

On the morning of Saturday 16th October, Callaghan, only appointed as Chancellor the day before, met with Wilson and Brown to discuss the implications of the economic briefing they had all received from their officials. The headline in that briefing was that the balance of payments was expected to be around £800 million in deficit. This would be the highest imbalance since the end of the Second World War and the figure represented a twin-headed problem – firstly, paying for the imbalance and secondly maintaining the confidence in the pound against the background of such a huge deficit.

The possibility of devaluation as at least a part-solution was dismissed by the three men with effectively no debate whatsoever. In his autobiography Callaghan records that his primary objection to devaluation was that it would inevitably impact negatively on living standards and that this would be damaging for the government's prospects when, as its tiny majority made inevitable, it called an early General Election. This remarkably candid admission is in the same territory as Wilson's insistence that no incoming Labour government could have survived being branded as the inevitable party of devaluation. The reality is that Callaghan, Brown and Wilson arrived at that Saturday morning meeting with their minds already closed to the possibility of devaluation and no discussion necessary. For the next few years the question would be regarded not just as settled but as a topic that should remain firmly closed to any review.

But something clearly had to be done about the alarming trade figures and Callaghan's response was to implement off-the-shelf proposals that had already been prepared at the Treasury on the instructions of Reginald Maudling. These measures were to impose a surcharge on imports and at the same time to grant tax rebates on exports. The announcement of these measures came on October 26th, just ten days after the election and were contained in a White Paper titled *The Economic Situation*.

The rush to publish this paper may have been an attempt to live-up to Wilson's promise that his government would be energetically dynamic or it may have simply been an attempt to, as quickly as possible, pin economic blame on the Conservatives. Whatever the motive, the White Paper was an early example of the government's blindness to the danger of acting in ways that alarmed the markets. It should have been obvious that to rush out within days a paper with such a portentous title as *The Economic Situation* risked creating the impression, even before a word of it was read, that what had been issued was an emergency bulletin. To make matters worse, the White Paper clumsily revealed the figure of £800 million as the predicted balance of payments deficit. This was alarming news enough, but, to cap it all, the crowning blunder was to include a declaration that the government would not use the traditional 'stop-go' approach in order to deal with the deficit.

Just two weeks later, Callaghan delivered his first Budget. It proved to be another case of blindness to the perceptions of the market. Having started with the announcement of the negotiation of a massive stand-by loan from the International Monetary Fund, Callaghan then proceeded to declare his intention to make increases in pensions and benefits – for example, the individual state pension was increased by 12/6d a week – and the abolition of a charge for NHS prescriptions. Callaghan had anticipated that – in the light of his acknowledged need to borrow from the IMF to cover the balance of payments deficit - the market might judge these increases negatively and he believed that he could defuse concern by balancing their cost with a rise in income tax and an increase in petrol tax. His calculations were correct – the rise in these taxes would raise more than the cost of the welfare increases and so these measures were, taken together, fiscally neutral, or even slightly positive. But Callaghan had failed to anticipate that when dealing with currency trading, fine arithmetic is less important than market perception. Inevitably there were criticisms that the government was prioritising additional expenditure rather than the balance of payments.

When Callaghan proceeded, later in his speech, to announce his intention to introduce in the following year a new Corporation Tax, this inevitably invited even more criticism. The information he provided was vague – and could not be otherwise because the details had not been worked out and, indeed, the Chairman of the Inland Revenue Board had strongly warned him that the necessary detail would be so complex that to prematurely announce the intention to introduce it in his next budget defied any reasonable timetable.

The overseas holders of sterling may have been unfair in overlooking the way in which the increased benefits were being paid for, they may have been unnecessarily anxious about the proposed introduction of Corporation Tax, but the reality was that their suspicions and doubts were being fuelled by the Treasury/DEA position. The standard approach to a bad balance of payments figure was to apply at least a limited touch on the brake – a deflationary package that would cool the economy and reduce the demand for imports. Here was the new Labour Government resolutely insisting that deflation was off the table. The two measures of an import surcharge and an export tax rebate did not seem remotely adequate to the large imbalance being announced – and in any case the surcharge was suspected (correctly) of being in contravention of Britain's trade treaties.

The immediate result of the Budget was a perception

amongst overseas holders of sterling that the government was not taking its economic problems sufficiently seriously and that devaluation would eventually become necessary and might in fact be imminent. Heavy selling of pounds ensued. Wilson's response was to make a speech insisting that his government would take any measures necessary to defend the pound. This was taken to be a signal that more robust action was imminent – in the form of an increase in the Bank Rate (the equivalent of today's Minimum Lending Rate). When a number of days passed after Wilson's speech without any rate rise, the market worsened.

After nearly two more weeks of heavy selling, the Governor of the Bank of England recommended a one per cent increase in Bank Rate. Callaghan pushed for this, but George Brown resisted and, by the time he gave in, the situation had sufficiently worsened for it to be decided that the increase needed to be higher, at two per cent. But instead of calming the market, its reaction was that this rate increase had been the government's final throw of the dice and that devaluation must now be the inevitable next step. With the Bank of England's last reserves in danger the Bank's Governor, Lord Cromer, confronted Wilson and demanded immediate action in terms of massive cuts in government expenditure.

Wilson faced Cromer down, by threatening to call an immediate General Election on the issue of an attempt by bankers to blackmail the government. When the Governor tried to dismiss this possibility on the grounds that the reserves would not last long enough to hold another election, Wilson bluntly responded that in this case he would defy the requirement to maintain the value of the pound and let it float. Devaluation was one thing, flotation was another. This would have defied the Bretton Woods Agreement which bound Britain and others to peg their currency to the value of the dollar and to intervene in the market to maintain parity. The threat of dismantling the international monetary system that had held for more than twenty years was so devastating that the Governor backed down and was sent away to secure emergency loans that could restore the Bank's reserves.

Sufficiently chastened, Cromer acted with considerable speed and within days had secured loans amounting to $300 billion. So, Wilson had faced down an ultimatum from the Bank of England, but at the cost of incurring massive additional international debt. Just three weeks had passed since Callaghan had darkly reminded the House of Commons that "borrowed money must be repaid in due course". But, as was to be expected, the massive injection of funds (and the international confidence that the loans could be taken to represent) resulted in an easing of the pressure on the pound. But, below the surface, the signs of worsening trouble remained. As the Bank of England reported there was in December (just a few weeks after the Budget) "a very strong demand for forward exchange" and in the same month a deterioration in the FT-Actuaries Industrial Share Index which before the election had been on an upward trend but was now falling steeply.[5] The government was by this stage having to use new loans to make capital repayments on previous borrowings and also in December was reduced to using an accounting trick to conceal the size of the month's losses from the reserves.[*]

By this stage, Callaghan, the man who over the years had won the confidence of fellow-MPs with his reputation for cool, level-headedness, was in a state close to nervous collapse - sometimes tearful, commonly depressed and heavily reliant on Wilson for support and comfort. Any attempts to recover emotional stability were made more difficult by the roller-coaster ride of the next months. Periodic pauses in the outflow of reserves would build his hopes, only for them to be dashed again when the position once again worsened. For example, in February there were encouraging signs of a trend to convert foreign currency holdings into sterling, but by late March this trend reverted to heavy sterling sales. From April to May the picture was once again one of improvement but in late May the situation worsened once more as, in the delicate words of the Bank of England, "sentiment again faltered".[6]

Callaghan spent the uncertain early months of the year putting the finishing touches to his budget and when he presented it, on April 6th, he was apparently in one of his interludes of self-confidence. The key features of his speech were to give an elaborated description of the proposed Corporation Tax and to announce an increase in personal taxation, through higher road tax and duty on

---

[*] A loan was treated as a reduction in the loss, rather than as a means of paying for it.

tobacco and alcohol. The Chancellor also announced an expected saving of about £350 million by means of the cancellation of the programme to build the TSR2 aircraft. "The strategy of this Budget is to achieve a state of balance on our combined current and long-term capital account," he informed the House. "We have already made considerable progress. I aim to get most of the way towards closing the gap this year and to complete the process in the course of 1966."

Despite these brave words the market was not reassured and sterling continued to be weak. At the end of April, the Bank of England put a squeeze on lending by requiring banks to place 1% of their gross deposits with the Bank of England as "special deposits". Three months later, Callaghan was forced to announce additional measures, including cuts to public expenditure, a reduction in defence spending and a tightening of credit controls.

By this stage Callaghan had just about used every tool in the box – with the exception of the major lever of devaluation. The other arm of economic management – the Department for Economic Affairs – also seemed to be running into the sand. As for the National Plan's projection of 25% growth, by January 1966 the Treasury's own experts were predicting that actual growth would be no more than 16% and Brown's other project, the control of prices and incomes, had so far met with little substantial success. Prices and incomes had continued to rise in 1965 at about the same rate as in 1964. More worryingly, wages had risen faster than productivity.

In February, Wilson decided it was a propitious moment to call another General Election and, despite any negative omens, Callaghan felt able to campaign on the basis of sound economic management. The Labour Party manifesto declared: "During the past 18 months, Britain has faced, fought and overcome its toughest crisis since the War...we are winning the battle for solvency." In the House of Commons, just days before the election, Callaghan presented a confidently optimistic assurance about the balance of payments: "Our aim is to achieve external balance over a two-year period—that is, by the end of 1966. That still remains our target, and we are well on the way to achieving it." As for any worries about future deflation, the Chancellor felt sufficiently confident to be able to give the House an assurance: "I do not foresee the need for severe increases in taxation."[7]

The election campaign went well for Labour, and Wilson returned to No 10 with a stable working majority of 97. Having campaigned on a platform of economic reassurance, Callaghan then went back to the Treasury but, in his autobiography, he records that, on his return, his officials informed him that his pre-election re-assurance about the economy was unjustified by current forecasts. Callaghan's autobiography records his reaction: "I was naturally put out for I knew I would be accused of having mis-led Parliament".[8]

This is curious. Callaghan gives no details of the bad news he allegedly received from his officials[*] and

* Writing of this time in his memoirs Wilson referred vaguely to "new assessments by the Treasury experts".

significantly his budget speech on May 3, specifically included a denial of any significant alteration in the economic picture since before the election: "There have been no striking changes in the economic situation since I gave the House a review two months ago." In saying this, Callaghan may have been attempting to assure the House that the economic situation had not changed for the worse, but the reality was that he needed increased revenue from tax. His solution was to introduce a Selective Employment Tax, an idea dreamed up by one of his advisers, Nicholas Kaldor. It was, basically, a payroll tax, the ostensible aim of which was to rebalance the economy, by increasing productivity in service industries and encouraging a shake-out of employment from services into manufacturing. Its real purpose was to raise an additional £250 million in taxation, without too blatantly breaking his pre-election assurance that taxation would not be greatly increased.

Shortly after the Budget, the National Union of Seamen called a strike in support of their claim for reduced hours of work and an increase in pay. The strike lasted for six weeks and was eventually settled on what were effectively the employers' terms. The strike inevitably impacted on the pound, though the direct economic damage of the strike was actually limited. Two days later, Callaghan met with the Prime Minister and Wilson recorded a description of the meeting which is worth quoting at length: "On Friday 1st July, George Brown, Jim Callaghan and I met to discuss the economic situation. 1965 had taught us what July could mean and how suddenly crisis

could hit us. The Chancellor, with all his Treasury and Bank of England briefs before him, drew a picture of blue skies in every direction…There was no sign of any foreign exchange market problem. He was advised that we should not need to take any special action, either on the foreign exchange or on the domestic front. The seamen's strike had caused great speculative raids on the pound, but the agreement between the central banks had stabilised the situation and markets had eased after the ending of the strike."[9]

As for this picture of blue skies, the record shows that Richard Crossman was a better judge of the weather than the Chancellor. As he recorded for his diary just two days later: "I'm sure now that we are drifting on to the rocks. I was nearly sure in March before the election; but now gold reserves are pouring out of the country again and the Callaghan budget has obviously failed to inspire confidence. Very soon we shall be faced with the choice between devaluation or intensive deflation."[10]

Crossman was right about the impending choice. In facts the odds against devaluation had slightly shortened at the time because George Brown had come to accept it as not just inevitable but beneficial. Callaghan was briefly in favour of devaluation, but was rapidly talked out of it by Wilson, who persuaded his Chancellor that a package of cuts would be sufficient to get the economy back on track and, as a sweetener, offered to be the one who presented the cuts to Parliament. Less than two weeks after Crossman recorded his prediction, the Cabinet were presented with a paper that announced the need for cuts of at least £500m. Even Crossman was unprepared for this, but when he objected, Callaghan's response clearly indicated his state of mind. The Chancellor admitted that "he didn't know how we were going to get out of the mess. We have totally failed to reach our objectives, we were drifting into devaluation in the worst possible conditions...".[11]

On 20th July, Wilson, in a long speech to the House of Commons, outlined a massive package of cuts, described by one analyst as containing "every known variety of restrictive measure".[12] In explaining the need for the package, Wilson identified the impact of the seamen's strike, action taken by the US which had led to a shortage of dollars, a shortage of labour, the burden of overseas expenditure, evasion of capital movement controls, wage increases not matched by productivity.... And so on. Wilson cast blame in every direction. At least some of his colleagues recognised that all this was a smokescreen. Barbara Castle wrote: "We just are not solving the economic problem...The economic indicators are worse than they have ever been. Jim's orthodox policy just has not worked."[13]

By this stage Callaghan was looking to escape from the Treasury. Incautiously, he gave an interview in which he not only acknowledged that he wanted to move on from the Chancellorship but even revealed that the job he now wanted was Foreign Secretary. Once Wilson saw the interview it was inevitable that Callaghan would not be offered any move at all, least of all one to the Foreign Office. A new Foreign Secretary there would be, but

Wilson's choice was Callaghan's economic rival, George Brown. Brown's unsuitability for this role could not have been more evident, but the prize of thwarting Callaghan's ambition in such an overtly humiliating way made the risk of George's appointment too tempting for Wilson to resist.

So, Callaghan had no choice but to soldier-on at the Treasury. But it had come to this: the Government that had entered office in 1964 with a pledge not to return to 'stop-go', had just imposed what was arguably the most massive economic stop in the country's history. Inevitably this out-sized deflation had some positive impact. There was a lull, but the respite could never be longer than temporary. Trade figures did not worsen, but there was no sign of the balance moving into surplus, let alone sufficient surplus to repay the massive debts of over £500 million that had been incurred to maintain parity – debts which fell due for repayment in 1967.

Despite this, Callaghan felt able in his 1967 Budget to radiate optimism. "Britain is paying her way again," he declared. " We are now emerging from the valley of gloom and can begin to see the outline of the landscape we shall be travelling through in the next three years. It will be new country, especially as time wears on…Taking everything together, the overall balance of payments should improve again substantially between 1966 and 1967. We should move from last year's deficit of £189 million to a surplus in 1967 as a whole, with an even bigger one in 1968."

Just days would pass before the trade figures for the very month of the budget speech would trigger the start of a renewed slide into crisis. Over the next months the trade figures massively worsened and pressure on sterling drained hundreds of millions from the reserves. By mid-November, Callaghan, acting on unequivocal advice from within the Treasury, accepted that devaluation was now essential. He went to Wilson and faced him with the news that there was now no way the 'unspeakable' option could be avoided. Wilson had no choice but to give-in and on Saturday November 18th Callaghan announced a devaluation of just over 14%.

It was just seven months since Callaghan had announced emergence from the 'valley of gloom' and promised a balance of trade surplus by the end of the year. In July, he had declared in the Commons that "Devaluation is not the way out of Britain's difficulties". As late as 24th October he was assuring the House that he had nothing to add to his statement in July. Of course there is always a risk for a Chancellor in difficult economic circumstances. To talk too frankly about the problems can increase uncertainty; any suggestion that the Chancellor is at all gloomy or pessimistic about the situation is likely to add to instability. Callaghan was never guilty of that. But there is an opposite risk: by seeming to downplay a situation, the impression can be given to the market that the Chancellor simply does not understand the problems to be faced. That was an error into which Callaghan repeatedly fell.

Over the years Callaghan had – both inside Parliament and beyond it - built a reputation for breezy confidence. He had, in public, deliberately cultivated a manner of genial detachment which, with amused tolerance, airily brushed aside any concerns or criticisms. This may have played well with the general public, but to expert analysts his insouciance in the face of economic crisis looked suspiciously like that of a man living in a fool's paradise.

In the earlier part of his time at the Treasury, Callaghan's radiation of confidence was strictly for public consumption. In private his anxiety levels were high. But, under the strain of events, the false front maintained by the public Callaghan, started to colour the outlook of the man in private. This is the key to explain his depiction of blue skies for the Prime Minister in July. No wonder that when Callaghan met in secret with a group of ministers to reveal the impending devaluation, Denis Healey, with characteristic bluntness, asked the Chancellor "why anyone should trust him or believe his forecasts after all he has dragged the party through?"[14]

At the Treasury Callaghan had two overriding objectives – to reduce the imbalance of payments and to protect the parity of sterling. In the absence of a Treasury strategy to achieve these aims, Callaghan relied on a bewildering succession of fragmentary measures none of which promised a long-term solution and which often increased short-term liabilities Alterations in bank rate, exchange restrictions, trade controls, fiscal measures, emergency loans – at one time or another every tool in the box was tried. It was point-to-point navigation with a vengeance. It was hardly surprising that the market interpreted all this as evidence of economic mismanagement.

It was a failure and, particularly wounding for Callaghan,

it was a personal failure; all the more damaging because it was witnessed by the countless occasions on which he had pledged success. He offered his resignation and Wilson offered him as a consolation the post of Home Secretary. This opened the door to a straight swap in which Callaghan and Roy Jenkins exchanged departmental responsibilities.

His new post suited Callaghan. The law and order aspect played well to his carefully-cultivated 'stage' personality – with avuncular PC Jim on the beat everyone could sleep well at night. The broad and disparate portfolio and its piecemeal nature meant that there was no pressure on him to develop a sense of strategic intelligence; the responsibilities of the Home Secretary chiefly concerned dealing with matters as they arose. So far as Callaghan's workload was concerned, the burden of office was, with the exception of preparing a budget, broadly the same as he had been used to at the Treasury: it was a matter of reacting to day-to-day circumstances. More point-to-point navigation.

What the Home Secretary's job lacked in terms of emotional demands, it made up for in the variety of situations with which he had to deal. During his time at the Home Office, Callaghan was called on to handle an inevitably wide range of events, including the collapse of the block of flats at Ronan Point, a massive anti-Vietnam War protest outside the American Embassy, a prison riot at Durham Gaol and a confrontation with the Police Federation over police pay. Some of these were time-consuming but none of them could compare with the mental and physical exhaustion of those years at the Treasury.

Exhaustion was a remote possibility at the Home Office, particularly since Callaghan had a cursory attitude to his workload. His normal routine was not to turn up at the Home Office until lunchtime and in a note to Barbara Castle he admitted that he now had more free time than he had had in years. This saving in time spent at work inevitably came at the cost of attention to the job. Dick Taverne, who was a Minister of State at the Home Office, acknowledged that Callaghan's strength did not lie in dealing with issues. The casualness of Callaghan's grasp was fully apparent when in the House of Commons he announced "I am glad to say that less than three hours ago one of those responsible for the murder at Fulham was arrested at Bolton in Lancashire". Making it unmistakable that this was not just an unfortunate slip of the tongue, he added "the man who committed the murder this morning in Acton has also been arrested."* A hurried note had to be passed to him before he was able to attempt a correction that actually served to make matters worse: "Mr. Speaker, it has been pointed out to me that I should have said 'the alleged murder'".[15] It was left to Ronald Bell, the Conservative Member for South Buckinghamshire, to educate the Home Secretary on a fundamental principle of British justice: the arrest of the men in question was not equivalent to their conviction.

Under his predecessor, Roy Jenkins, the Home Office had handled a massive burden of legislation focused on social reform. Callaghan was determined not to follow suit. ""I haven't got a liberal image to maintain like my predecessor," he told Crossman, "I'm going to be a simple Home Secretary."[16]

Within weeks of arriving at the Home Office, Callaghan took an opportunity to emphasise his distance from any suspicion of a liberal image. On February 9th 1968, Enoch Powell, speaking in Walsall, declared that he had been startled to learn that because of their citizenship rights "200,000 Indians in Kenya alone have become literally indistinguishable from the people of the United Kingdom, so that they have an absolute right of entry to this country".[17] The speech was highly-publicised and within days it inspired Callaghan to introduce legislation to restrict entry to the UK by Asians who although currently living in Uganda and Kenya possessed British passports. The Attorney General, Sir Elwyn Jones, pointed out to the Cabinet that Callaghan's proposal would be in breach of one of the protocols of the European Convention of Human Rights but conveniently drew attention to a loophole: although the UK had signed this protocol it had not yet ratified it.[18] Despite its highly controversial nature, legislation was rushed through in just two days to impose a voucher system to control entry of these British Asians into Britain.*

His next piece of legislation, the Race Relations Act, was undeniably liberal - an outlawing of racial and national

---

* *The Times* described Callaghan's bill as "Probably the most shameful measure that Labour members have been asked by their whips to support".

discrimination in the areas of housing, employment and national services. But although in marked contrast to his immigration policy, this important and welcome reform to the law was not evidence of Callaghan's personal liberalism; he inherited the legislation from his predecessor and Callaghan's private stance can be inferred from a comment he made in the hearing of Tony Benn: "We don't want any more blacks in Britain".[19]

Settled into a quiet life at the Home Office gave Callaghan the time he needed to reflect. He was determined that the ultimate failure of his Chancellorship should not put an end to his ambitions and he knew that he needed to rebuild his reputation in Cabinet (after all the years of having been the dogsbody who opposed his colleagues' spending plans) and in the Party – and, particularly, to strengthen his place as a potential successor to Wilson. His chosen strategy was to establish his credentials with the trade-unions and while addressing the conference of the Fire Brigades' Union, he had, in a flagrant flouting of Cabinet responsibility, artfully distanced himself from the penalty clauses of the Prices and Incomes Bill, put into law as part of the May 1966 deflationary package. This infuriated Wilson and he attempted to challenge Callaghan over it in a full Cabinet meeting. But Callaghan felt able to brazen it out and Wilson's attack evaporated in the face of his Home Secretary's impenitence. It had been a trial show of strength and Callaghan's ability to survive it with impunity ensured that it would only be a matter of time before he took another and even bolder opportunity to assert his readiness to challenge Wilson. That opportunity came in 1969, when the government sought to bring trade union action into a legislative framework – *In Place of Strife*. It was Callaghan's subversion (described in the following chapter) that helped to destroy the proposal, forcing Castle and Wilson into a humiliating climbdown. From then on, it was clear that Callaghan had established himself in the role of Wilson's most cut-throat rival.

It was late in 1968 that Callaghan had to face his first real trial as Home Secretary. In October of that year there began a series of protests on the streets of Northern Ireland that turned out to be the preliminary to what would develop into years of bitter sectarian violence. The running of the province of Ulster had been for generations effectively delegated to the Northern Irish Government based at Stormont Castle. So far as the Westminster government was concerned, Ulster was best left to Ulstermen to manage and London had for years turned a blind eye to the sectarian discrimination and general system-rigging that was the stock-in-trade of the ruling Protestant class.

The street-demonstrations that started late in 1968 were the open expression of the deep resentment instilled into the Catholic community as a result of the way in which they were marginalised, disadvantaged and victimised by their Protestant masters. Since the creation of Northern Ireland in 1920 the same party – the Democratic Unionist Party – had been in continuous power. The same domination was represented at local council level. After just two years of its existence the Northern Ireland

Government had passed a law that gave additional powers to the Royal Ulster Constabulary and the Special Constabulary – powers that were used for sectarian purposes.

In 1964 a Campaign for Social Justice had been formed to work for an end to the blatant discrimination against Catholics in areas such as jobs and housing. This campaign was designed to lobby in the conventional political manner, but from the summer of 1968 onwards, protest took a more active form and marches and street demonstrations increasingly became the standard expression of protest. These demonstrations of a sense of injustice were, at this stage, not linked to the IRA and the protest movement could fairly be described as a legitimate civil-rights campaign.

At face value, Callaghan might have seemed well-placed to handle the disruption and social tension that was erupting on the streets of Belfast, Londonderry and elsewhere in the province. His carefully-cultivated manner of genial detachment might seem precisely what would be needed to cool tempers and build harmony. The fact that his father had been a Catholic and his mother a Protestant might also have seemed good credentials for someone attempting to broker peace across the divide. But, as it turned out, none of these assets would prove significant, because Callaghan completely failed to comprehend the Ulstermen's entrenched resistance to treating the Catholics as equal citizens and their willingness to back-up this determination to discriminate with the use of police violence and brutality.

It was in October 1968 that the situation escalated into high violence. A march was brutally broken-up by 'B Specials', a separate section of the police whose recruits were essentially hard-line Protestant thugs. The first reaction of Wilson and Callaghan was to rely on the leader of the Stormont government, Terence O'Neill, to calm the situation, by making some necessary concessions, including sacking his Minister of Home Affairs. In fact, O'Neill's options were constrained by the implacable bigotry of his party and the limited reforms he introduced did not extend even to something so basic as the principle of 'one man one vote' in local elections.

In 1969 the social tensions erupted into a full-blown crisis. Early in January a civil rights protest march was violently attacked at Burntollet Bridge by a Protestant gang. Police were in attendance but failed to take action to protect the marchers and it later emerged that the attackers contained many off-duty police officers. In response, O'Neill set up a commission to inquire into the causes of the civil disturbance, but this was too much for his party and when he called an election, to re-assert his authority, he very nearly lost his seat to the extremist Protestant clergyman Ian Paisley. The outcome was the loss of the DUP's overall majority at Stormont. O'Neill resigned and was replaced in May 1969 by James Chichester-Clark, whose opposition to 'one man one vote' had earlier provoked his resignation from O'Neill's cabinet.

1969 marked a slide into a pattern of appalling violence, including street riots, bombings and deaths arising from police brutality, particularly on the streets of Belfast and Londonderry. Callaghan's response was to call-in the British army to take over responsibility for law and order on the streets. This was initially well-received by the Catholics, who welcomed what they saw as army protection from sectarian violence. On 19th August Wilson, Callaghan, Healey and the Foreign Secretary Michael Stewart met with the (uniformly Protestant) leaders of Northern Ireland and agreed a joint statement, known as the Downing Street Declaration. The statement announced that responsibility for all security matters would now rest with the British Army's General Officer Commanding, leaving the province's police force to deal only with regular police duties. The B Specials were to be "progressively and rapidly relieved" of their duties. In addition, Chichester-Clark agreed to set up an independent inquiry into the recent street disturbances. The statement also laid down the vital principle that "every citizen of Northern Ireland is entitled to the same equality of treatment and freedom from discrimination as obtains in the rest of the United Kingdom irrespective of political views or religion". These were all important concessions, but in return the Stormont government had won a significant assurance that the UK government recognised that "responsibility for affairs in Northern Ireland is entirely a matter of domestic jurisdiction".[20] This assurance gambled on trusting at face value the Stormont government's commitment to ending sectarian discrimination and religious inequality. Not until 1972 would this hostage to fortune be revoked when, in the face of violence now spearheaded by the IRA, the Heath government would impose direct rule of Northern Ireland from Westminster.

In his account of his first government, Wilson describes the advice he had given to Callaghan in relation to Northern Ireland: "I had suggested that his position should be, and above all should be seen to be, 'firm, cool and fair'. He needed no such admonition." Callaghan seems to have interpreted being 'fair' to mean even-handed – which is probably exactly what Wilson meant. But it is difficult to recognise how this interpretation of fairness can be justified between, on one hand, a minority deliberately deprived of its social and economic rights and, on the other hand, a bitterly sectarian and repressive regime. The contortions that a 'balanced' approach induced were marked by such signs as an insistence on the introductions of reforms in Northern Ireland, but a willingness to accept that these would be on a scale and at a pace of Stormont's choosing. Callaghan's ultimate failure was to have trust in the good faith of Ulster's rulers.

This misplaced confidence was to have consequences that impacted on the use of troops in the province. On their arrival they had been largely welcomed by the Catholic population, who interpreted their presence as genuine protection. But when it became clear that substantial reform of their grievances was not even remotely on Stormont's agenda, community protests intensified. In this increasingly tense and hostile environment, the Army, acting in the light of the Wilson Government's explicit backing for Stormont, handled it in the way their training and experience had taught them - it was dealt with as an expression of popular insurgency against a legitimate government. Unsurprisingly, tactics developed for colonial use did not play-out well on the streets of Northern Ireland. When the army used excessive force or handled situations insensitively, it fostered a growing belief that the soldiers were just another arm of the hated Protestant majority. Inevitably, this encouraged the community to turn to an alternative source of protection. The Provisional IRA, which had emerged at the end of 1969 following a split between the old-guard IRA and more militant dissidents, became the self-appointed defenders of the Catholic communities - a role which would in time evolve into a campaign of murderous terrorism completely side-lining and eclipsing what had begun as something as patently virtuous as a civil rights movement.

It is possible that this descent into murder and mayhem could have been avoided, but for Callaghan's reliance on the Ulster's government's willingness to reform itself. His optimism was entirely unjustified and completely misplaced. The fall from power of Terence O'Neill and the rise of Ian Paisley's Protestant Unionist Party should have been evidence enough that, far from being in retreat, sectarian loyalism was increasingly entrenched and resistant to reform.

Callaghan's inability to analyse any problem below its surface details and his instinct to be content with short-term responses combined with disastrous effect in the province. It is arguable that his actions should have been not "firm, cool and fair" but bold. An Order in Council for the introduction of direct rule of Northern Ireland from Westminster had been drafted by early in 1969 and if Callaghan and Wilson had been prepared to grasp this nettle, it is possible that the course of subsequent events could have been very different. Political, economic and social rights for all, as an immediate step, could have been imposed from Westminster.

The result would, of course, have been to provoke considerable civil unrest from the Protestant majority, but although there were terrorist cells active within the Protestant community, their ability to cause havoc would have been more constrained than was the case with the Provisional IRA. There would have been no easy lines of support across the southern border for example and support from the mainland would also have been limited, because the majority of Protestants in Britain did not remotely identify or sympathise with what appeared to them as the crazed-sectarianism of their fellow churchmen in Ulster.

But, as it was, Callaghan and Wilson kept the option of direct-rule firmly out of court. Meanwhile the situation deteriorated around them, with the Westminster government increasingly distrusted by both sides. Perhaps one should sympathise with Callaghan for falling, completely unprepared as he was, into what developed into a snake pit of bitter violence, but it is clear that his failure to comprehend the depth of the sectarian corruption at Stormont led him into successive errors of judgment. He significantly over-estimated his ability to charm his way to success and, as a consequence, fell back on his now familiar approach to any problem – random tinkering with its various parts. There is a strong case for arguing that Callaghan's failure to directly challenge the bigotry and corruption of the Protestant regime contributed - indirectly if not directly – to creating the space for the IRA to move into the territory created by the civil-rights protests and enabled a legitimate protest movement to be high-jacked by terrorists.

The longer-term consequences of Callaghan's handling of the Northern Ireland situation would only become clear in the years to come; at the time he won praise for acting with what Wilson would later describe as "manifest firmness and authority". Wilson also credited Callaghan's dealings with Ulster as having played a significant part in the "strengthening of the Labour's Government's political position and standing during the second half of 1969".[21] But at the time of the Downing Street Declaration, the real service that Callaghan was performing for his party was not his Northern Ireland policy but his engineering of a piece of electoral skulduggery.

The Boundary Commission was the independent body responsible for regularly reviewing the distribution of parliamentary constituencies and devising any changes that were needed to take account of demographic shifts. Its remit was to present its report to the Home Office and the normal protocol was for its recommendations to be implemented without exception. When its latest report was received, Wilson and his cabinet immediately recognised that it presented an acute political dilemma.

Some of the changes proposed were likely to increase Labour's representation, but other alterations looked likely to benefit the Conservative Party. The challenge was to find a reason for accepting the recommendations that would favour the Labour Party while rejecting the changes that were in the Conservative interest. This would be naked gerrymandering but to maintain an appearance of respectability it needed to be presented with a manner of upright incorruptibility. It was Labour's good fortune that the handling of constituency revisions fell to the Home Office and in James Callaghan the Cabinet had the perfect frontman to justify its electoral jiggery-pokery. As Richard Crossman explained in his diary, ""Even if we are looking out for party advantage, we want to combine this with moral rectitude and, as you might expect, Jim has done this very nicely."[22]

Callaghan had of course made a career out of his talent for a carefully calculated simulation of 'moral rectitude' and it was prominently on display when he stood up in the House of Commons on 19th June to respond to a Conservative Member's call for the Commission's recommendations to be implemented forthwith. "I am sorry" Callaghan smoothly replied, "that in this matter the hon. Member's eye is constantly on party advantage. It should not be."

The political 'fix' that Callaghan cooked-up, in collusion with close cabinet colleagues, was to argue that most of the recommended changes to electoral boundaries should be delayed pending the outcome of an ongoing Royal Commission inquiring into the structure of local government outside London. This piece of sophistry came with a particular bonus – Callaghan could argue that the Boundary Commission's recommendations regarding London could be immediately implemented, because local government in the capital was specifically excluded from any recommendations that the Royal Commission would eventually make. At one stroke, Callaghan set out to circumvent changes that would benefit the Conservatives while moving ahead with changes that would benefit Labour. Callaghan was additionally prepared to implement a handful of changes to boundaries outside London, on the grounds that these were in constituencies where population growth had made them unreasonably large. The re-drawing of parliamentary boundaries in these exceptional cases was also expected to have electoral benefits for Labour. Wilson, conscious that what was being considered was highly duplicitous, kept the full Cabinet away from detailed discussions of what was going on. [23]

All this chicanery – even Callaghan's largely-sympathetic official biographer calls the episode a "cynical partisan manoeuvre" - was enthusiastically carried by the Labour majority in the House of Commons, but ran into trouble in the House of Lords, where the Conservative majority ensured it was cleverly blocked. So, when the General Election was called, for June 1970, it was fought on the same boundary lines as before.

It turned out that even the aborted gerrymandering would not have been sufficient to keep Labour in office. Despite the opinion polls seeming favourable to Labour it was the Conservatives, under Edward Heath, who came into power with a comfortable majority of 34. This was a setback for Labour politically and for Callaghan personally. But, in fact, his best days were still to come. Unfortunately for him, so were his worst days.

An immediate advantage for Callaghan emerged when Wilson, following the election, went into virtual seclusion, ostensibly to write his account of his time as Prime Minister (in reality virtually all of the book was actually written by Wilson's former Press-Secretary, now turned personal aide, Joe Haines). This meant that although in opposition, the chances increased for Callaghan to bask in what little limelight was available. A further boost resulted from his appointment as Shadow Foreign Secretary, giving Callaghan the opportunity to extend his ministerial experience in a major new field.

Callaghan's subsequent career would justify a complete essay in itself and can only be briefly summarised here. Labour's return to power, after Heath called his *Who governs Britain?* election in 1974, confirmed Callaghan as Foreign Secretary, meaning he had now held all three major offices of state. Callaghan's record as Foreign Secretary was however to be inglorious and included a humiliating appearance before the Select Committee on Foreign Affairs where he embarrassingly claimed to know virtually nothing – or to remember nothing – from his handling of affairs in Cyprus, which had led to a Turkish invasion of the island.

But Callaghan had now positioned himself closely at Wilson's shoulder as his potential successor and Roy

Jenkins' resignation from the Cabinet over his disagreement with Wilson's policy on Europe significantly increased chances of Callaghan's succession. It was surely only a matter of time. Wilson's surprise resignation in March 1976 meant that the time came sooner than almost anyone expected and, on 5 April, having in a series of ballots seen-off Roy Jenkins, Denis Healey, Tony Crossland, Tony Benn and, in the final stage, Michael Foot, Callaghan was installed at Number Ten.

His premiership was, with brief interludes of respite, a three-year downward slide into economic and social chaos. His minority government (eventually dependent for its survival on Liberal support) was marked by a fall in productivity, a rise in unemployment, depreciation of sterling, a massive emergency loan from the International Monetary Fund, strikes (including a hitherto unthinkable withdrawal of labour by the Fire Brigade) and one-day stoppages culminating in the notorious 'Winter of Discontent', in which industrial action led to headline-compelling consequences that notoriously included hospital patients being left unattended, uncollected rubbish piling-up in the streets and corpses left unburied. Faced with this crisis Callaghan seemed distant and disconnected from the reality surrounding him. He has been criticised for his lack of firm action in response to the crisis, but the reality was that any possibility of his demonstrating leadership was fatally undermined not only by his own long-standing inability to come to decisive grips with any crisis whatsoever, but also by the fact that Callaghan had, for years past, gone out of his way to offer the unions his personal backing and encouragement and was in no position to take a tough line with them.

Callaghan had decided against an election in 1978, confident that by the following year his government would be able to defeat the Conservatives, by then led by Margaret Thatcher. It was, once again, a striking case of misjudgement. In March 1979, his minority government lost a vote of no confidence and he had no alternative but to call an election. His final election broadcast was classic Callaghan – a masterclass in putting on a front of avuncular reassurance and benign righteousness. But, a few days later, he was out of office, replaced by a Conservative government with a majority of 43.

Despite this defeat, Callaghan was determined to serve as Leader of the Opposition and firmly resisted any suggestion he should step down. "There is no vacancy for my job", he modestly told his fellow Labour MPs. He clung-on as Leader until close to the end of the following year when he was succeeded by Michael Foot – not the successor that Callaghan would have chosen (he preferred Denis Healey) but, as it turned out, Foot's inadequacies and misfortunes as leader helped to absorb attention that might otherwise have retrospectively scrutinised and analysed Callaghan's own failings of leadership.

Callaghan's biographer notes that in his final days as Leader of the Opposition he had seemed to many of his colleagues "unable to point to any new direction for the future".[24] If his fellow MPs had only just noticed this failing, they had been slow to catch-on. Callaghan had never shown any sense of direction; politics for him was a series of zig-zags from one crisis to another. In his final years as Prime Minister he had become tagged as the man who, when the world was collapsing around him, blithely said "Crisis? What crisis?" In fact, Callaghan never actually said those words, but as a man who had spent so much of his career in denial of grim realities, the misattribution did represent an essential truth.

After stepping down as Leader, Callaghan acquired a few business interests and, in the process, provided further evidence of his lack of judgment. He went to work, while still a sitting MP, as an adviser to the Bank of Credit and Commerce International (the directors of which Callaghan described as "people of the highest integrity and probity"). The Bank was in fact fraudulent from top to bottom – a front for massive money-laundering and other crimes. Despite his apparent endorsement of the Bank's bona fides, Callaghan had been careful to conceal from the public record the payments he had received from it – a breach of the rules concerning MPs' outside interests.

He stood down from Parliament at the 1987 General Election and went to the House of Lords as Baron Callaghan of Cardiff. In March 2005, Audrey, his wife for 66 years, died. Callaghan's own death followed just eleven days later.

5

Barbara Castle:
Driving on the Left

When Wilson formed his first Cabinet he took care to show balance between the wings of his party. Aneurin Bevan and Hugh Gaitskell might both be dead, but Bevanism and Gaitskellism still persisted as rival hemispheres and Wilson skilfully balanced his appointments accordingly. But not all the Bevanites were or had been authentic socialists – Wilson after all had adopted Bevan's colours as a convenient, though false, flag. So, Wilson also had to ensure that within his Cabinet there was evidence of a pure socialist conscience. Barbara Castle was perfectly cast for this role. As socialists go, she was the genuine article. No one could accuse her of having been on Labour's left out of convenience or for advantage – she despised the right wing of her party and regarded her role in Wilson's cabinet as the bearer of the socialist torch, a position that was made more comfortable for her because of her self-fulfilling certainty that if she believed in something then it must be truly socialist.

She was born Barbara Anne Betts in Chesterfield on 6th October 1910. Her family were fiercely and actively socialist and this was a central feature of family life. Her father was a senior tax inspector and they were comfortably off though not affluent. They moved home quite frequently, but always in the area of southern Yorkshire. Barbara completed her schooling at Bradford Grammar School where she won a place at Oxford. She began by studying French, but then switched to Philosophy, Politics and Economics, a more natural choice for someone whose childhood had been steeped in political thinking.

It was equally natural that once at Oxford Barbara would devote more time to politics than to studying. She became an active member of the Labour Club and this commitment eventually came at an academic price; she gained only a Third in her finals and for years to come she felt acutely disappointed, even embarrassed, by her results

Back home after leaving Oxford, Barbara was unsure of what she really wanted to do next. Her only certainty was socialist politics and the local Labour Club became the centre of her life. She became its Propaganda Secretary and gained a lot of experience of public speaking. Then, less than a year after coming down from Oxford, she went with her mother to a meeting in Manchester that was being addressed by a well-known socialist writer, William Mellor.

Mellor was a fiery left-wing journalist – a former member of the Communist Party and one-time editor of the *Daily Herald*. His socialism was not at all cloth-cap. Impeccably well-dressed and with a taste for good living, he went out of his way, when addressing his working-class audiences, to parade his lifestyle. "I've just spent more on my lunch than you earn in a week," he would tell them. "How much longer are you going to put up with it?" Although he had left the Communist Party some years earlier, his viewpoint remained essentially Marxist. "The world system that is destroying hope in the world is capitalism", he wrote in an editorial for the left-wing weekly *Tribune*, "The defeat of capitalism depends on the unity of the working class… It must work to bring into power a working-class government pledged to put into operation a workers' programme swiftly, decisively, drastically. This means immediate nationalisation of the banks. It means immediate nationalisation of coal and power, land and the means of transport."[1]

After hearing him speak at the meeting, Barbara's mother invited Mellor to their home for tea. Mellor could be prickly – "volcanic" in his moods according to Michael Foot – but he was compellingly charismatic and for Barbara the attraction that day proved irresistible. Mellor, more than twenty years older than Barbara, was a married man with a family, but before long he and Barbara had become lovers and their relationship would continue, in some secrecy, for nearly ten years until he died in 1943.

His influence on Barbara would be immense. He introduced her to an extended network of socialist movers and shakers and, through him, she began to write regularly for left-wing papers and to speak on platforms for the Socialist League (which, with Mellor and Stafford Cripps she had helped to found) as well as at meetings of her local Labour Party.

By 1935 Barbara had left home and moved to London. When a sales promotion job there proved to be a dead-end, Mellor provided a lifeline by appointing her as secretary in a publishing venture he had launched to produce a magazine aimed at local councillors. When Mellor became absorbed in his work as editor of the newly-launched *Tribune*, Barbara essentially took over his role as editor of the *Town and Country Councillor*. It was local government politics that provided her next stepping-stone when, in 1937, she was elected as a member of the St Pancras Borough Council. But the opportunity that really made her name came when– at the Labour Party Conference in 1943 – she was able as a delegate for her local party to make a swashbuckling speech about the importance of early implementation of the Beveridge Report.

This speech was sufficiently attention-catching to catapult her onto the front page of the *Daily Mirror*, with a photograph and a vivid sound-bite from her speech ("Jam yesterday, jam tomorrow, but never jam today"). A year later, when the Blackburn Labour Party in search of a candidate were looking for a woman to add to their selection list, one of the party's regional organisers remembered the speech at Conference, and suggested Barbara. As it happened, the front-page coverage in the Daily Mirror had meanwhile triggered another major change in her life. Ted Castle, who had been the night editor who had made the decision to put Barbara on the front page, had been sufficiently intrigued to want to get to know her. A little more than a year later they married.

Barbara was one of six short-listed for the Blackburn nomination, the other five were men. But the panel was impressed and, despite having only just recovered from an appendectomy, she convinced them to the point of selection. She had submitted herself for selection under the name of Barbara Betts, but it was made clear to her that as the party's candidate she would need to run under her married name. So, it was as Barbara Castle that she won the seat in the 1945 General Election (becoming the youngest woman member of the House) and continued to represent Blackburn for the next thirty-four years.

Her years of socialist activity, and the contacts it had given her, made it almost inevitable that she would get the opportunity to be something more than just a novice backbencher. It was Stafford Cripps, an ally of Barbara's from the days of the Socialist League, who gave her that opportunity. She accepted his offer of a post as his Parliamentary Private Secretary at the Board of Trade and when he moved on to the Ministry of Economic Affairs, she remained at the Board as PPS to Cripps' replacement, Harold Wilson.

None of this stopped her from signalling her sense of her own independence or from demonstrating that her socialist conscience was uneasy about at least some of the Labour Government's policies. She disliked and distrusted the Foreign Secretary, Ernest Bevin, and gladly added her name to Richard Crossman's amendment of the King's Speech which set out an alternative foreign policy distanced from the government's plainly pro-US position. She became a member of the Bevanite *Keep Left* group and developed a close if unlikely friendship with Crossman.

After the 1950 Election, which drastically reduced Labour's majority, Barbara, who continued to work as Wilson's PPS at the Board of Trade, maintained her involvement with *Keep Left*, speaking at events the group organised around the country, contributing to its publications and producing some pamphlets of her own. In 1950 she succeeded in gaining a place on the party's National Executive, initially through elections for the women's section but later winning election through the constituency ballot. It was clear that her position in the party was gaining significant strength.

Despite her intense political ambition, Barbara sturdily avoided any compromise which might have eased her path to promotion. She was openly rebellious towards the party leadership and frequently spoke against her government's official line. The friendships and alliances she made clearly displayed her flag nailed to the party's left-wing. Some of these associations went back to her pre-parliamentary days – her friendship with Michael Foot for example – but others emerged through her contacts with like-minded rebels on the backbenches, such as Richard Crossman. These relationships, the tone of her political journalism and her frequent critical speeches in the House all worked to ensure that she stayed on Attlee's list of the untrustworthy.

Two of the friendships formed in her early years in the House were with the two men whose later role would be to form metaphorical bookends in her shelf-life as a front-rank politician. One was Harold Wilson, with whom she conducted a close and even flirtatious relationship when she was his PPS at the Board of Trade, and who would unhesitatingly pick her for his Cabinet in 1964 and the other was James Callaghan, who would knife her in the back in 1968 and then dismiss her from the Cabinet when he took over as Prime Minister in 1976.

The circles in which Barbara moved – particularly her membership of the *Keep Left* group - ensured that Hugh Gaitskell was not part of her friendship group. "I disliked Gaitskell intensely," she later recalled. In particular she blamed him for the split which led to Aneurin Bevan, Harold Wilson and John Freeman resigning their government posts after Gaitskell had introduced some prescription charges in his first budget speech as Attlee's Chancellor of the Exchequer.

Given her loyalty to the Bevanites, it was inevitable that her dislike for Gaitskell was entirely reciprocated. Barbara's stock among the party faithful continued to rise – she came first in the constituency party section's election for the National Executive in 1956 and was elected as Vice-Chairman of the party in 1957- but with Gaitskell now in Attlee's place as leader, there was, unsurprisingly, no call from the leader's office offering Barbara a place in the shadow cabinet. And only Gaitskell's personal invitation could have created that opportunity because, tellingly, in the parliamentary elections to the shadow cabinet, Barbara's support from her colleagues on the Labour benches had not generated enough votes to secure her a shadow cabinet place.

Gaitskell's death transformed Barbara's fortunes. As the new leader, Wilson invited Barbara to provide a shadow lead on overseas development – a role that fitted well with the knowledge and experience she had gained on a large number of overseas trips she had made, including visits to China, the Middle East, Kenya, Africa, Turkey, Greece and Cyprus. In the space of just a few weeks, either side of Christmas 1963, she went to Kenya, Uganda, Ethiopia, Tunisia, Algeria and Morocco. On the back of this extensive fact-finding travel she had built a reputation as someone with a particular interest in foreign affairs and most notably as someone with a developing expertise in overseas aid. Her very public support of the anti-apartheid campaign and related movements made it clear that her passion and belief were on the side of those struggling for nationalism and independence.

Wilson also had a long-standing interest in foreign aid and as long ago as 1953 had written a book on *The War on World Poverty*, but although he had given Barbara a role as opposition spokesperson on overseas development, this was not quite the same thing as having a shadow lead – principally because her portfolio of overseas development was not the responsibility of any single government ministry or department but was an area of work divided across a large number of separate parts of the government – the Treasury, the Foreign Office, the Board of Trade, the Colonial Office, the Commonwealth Relations Office, the Department of Education and Science, the Ministry of Agriculture, Fisheries and Food and the Department of Technical Co-operation. Wilson had already promised to end this 'divided-house' approach in his 'White Heat' conference speech of October 1963 when he had declared, "Labour means business about world development. We are going to establish a full-scale Ministry of Overseas Development with a Minister of cabinet rank." Barbara echoed this pledge in a speech in the House in February 1964: "The trouble in this country is that we have no Minister for overseas aid as a whole," she complained, adding that a Labour government would establish a Ministry of Overseas Development "with Cabinet rank". This reference to 'Cabinet rank' precisely echoed what Wilson had said in Scarborough, but behind the scenes Barbara was working to ensure that this formula was interpreted to mean more than just equivalence in rank and actually ensured a place at the Cabinet table.

Sure enough, when, on the Saturday after the election, Barbara went to see Wilson in Number 10, he not only offered her the Ministry of Overseas Development but added "In the Cabinet, of course". It is likely that had Wilson been offering the job to anyone else it would not have come with a Cabinet place. It was not the Ministry of Overseas Development that was being given that status, but Barbara herself.

Because the Ministry was new it had to be given a temporary home and a new Permanent Secretary, Sir Andrew Cohen, who was moved from the Department of Technical Innovation, where he had been Director-General. This had been the government department that handled the provision of technical guidance, support and specialised equipment as part of the wider programme of aid. He had wide experience in the field and a distinguished background that included the governorship of Uganda. He was of extremely large-build and inevitably his teaming with Barbara led some wit to characterise them as 'Elephant and Castle'.

As a new Ministry, absorbing functions that had been exercised across a wide range of other government departments, there was of course enormous scope for turf-wars with those parts of the government unwilling to relinquish their share of the reins. But Barbara had the skills and energy to make a success of a role that provoked both existing sensitivities and fresh challenges. She was, like Crossman, a minister in a hurry to make a mark, after so many frustrating years confined to the backbenches. But unlike Crossman she had the ability to be firm and insistent in argument without creating bad feelings.

But all her enthusiasm and hard work could not overcome a major difficulty – the desperate hole in the public finances meant that she was unable to secure the resources she needed to fund the kind of programme she had expected to implement. The Labour Party had, in a pre-election Penguin Special (*Why Labour*), written by a member of its Research Department, scornfully criticised the size of the Conservative aid budget (then around £153 million pounds a year): "This is less than what we spent on sending each other greetings cards, and less than a quarter of what we spend on beer…But surely we can do a great deal more than we have been doing?" But the cold post-election light of economic reality meant that, even with Barbara's fierce championship, the overseas aid budget was never going to be scaled-up to meet her expectations.

The writing was on the wall for her as early as Callaghan's budget speech just a few months after the election. Callaghan and Brown persistently resisted her attempts to secure a larger aid budget and on one occasion, when Barbara was making the case to the Chancellor for financial aid to Ceylon, he gloomily responded that in reality it was Britain that was in the need of aid.[2]

Despite all the economic restraints, Barbara was able to achieve some significant innovations. In the past, huge sums of money had been distributed in aid without any prior analysis whatsoever from economic specialists. Barbara established an Economic Planning Unit within the Ministry staffed by professional economists and would not consider any proposal that had not received approval from her economic advisers Another of her reforms was to improve the terms on which developing countries could obtain loans (in some cases interest-free) from the UK* and she was instrumental in the setting-up (by Dudley Seers, the head of her economic planning unit) of an Institute of Development Studies, based at Sussex University.

She produced a White Paper setting out the Ministry's plans. Its title - *Overseas Development: the work of the new*

---

* These more generous loan conditions had actually originated in a proposal worked-up at the Treasury under the Conservative government.

Ministry – clearly hinted at a focus that was more internal than international. The White Paper was strong on good intentions but was noticeably silent on the size of any future programme and included heavy caveats about economic constraints on overseas aid. In introducing the White Paper to the House of Commons, Barbara made no bones about the financial straitjacket within which she had to work: "This is not a moment at which it would be right to announce plans for a significant increase in the aid programme. At a time when we are taking steps to restrain public expenditure and when we must have particular regard to our balance of payments there are limits to the amount of aid we can provide." The reality behind this statement was that, for all Barbara's ambition for the Ministry and despite her fierce advocacy of its importance, she was not able to secure the budget she believed she needed and had to accept a 10% cut in the figure for which she had asked.[*]

To make it absolutely clear that this was more than just a temporary halt to the expansion of aid, it was only a few weeks after the White Paper that the National Plan – despite its wildly exaggerated expectations of growth – clearly signalled that the overseas aid budget was now of low priority. In the words of Brown's National Plan, "the amount of aid we give must be subject to restraint while our balance of payments difficulties persist, and we have to plan our aid so that the foreign exchange cost of the programme is kept to a minimum."[3]

---

[*] Castle had asked for £250 million, had been offered £216 million and had to settle at a compromise figure of £225 million.

A Cabinet Minister who cannot secure the budget they have asked for is inevitably weakened; the scope of ambitions inevitably thwarted by the lack of financial resources. But in Barbara's case the weakness extended beyond her Ministry and reached into the Cabinet room. Her status as a minister was diminished by the perception among her Cabinet colleagues that her work was judged to be of low priority. Her White Paper was full of a far-reaching ambition, but, to throw back at Barbara the words that had first launched her to national attention, it was "jam tomorrow, but never jam today".

It could not last and in December 1965, just four months after the publication of her White Paper, Wilson saw Barbara and asked her to leave the Ministry of Overseas Development and become his Minister of Transport. According to Barbara's account the offer was made to her because Wilson thought his current Transport Minister was ineffective and he needed "a tiger in my transport policy". Wilson's own recollection sympathetically notes his recognition of her frustration at Overseas Development: "Barbara was never able, against the background of financial stringency, to get the funds that she really wanted to have at her disposal".[4]

At the Ministry of Transport she found herself faced by two immediate problems – one familiar, the other less so. The familiar problem was that within the Ministry, transport was never considered or dealt with as a whole – roads and railways were handled separately, without co-ordination or strategic overview – rather as overseas aid had been parcelled out across so many different ministries and departments.

The less familiar problem was the Ministry's Permanent Secretary, Sir Thomas Passmore – a highly-regarded civil servant whose distinguished background and glittering career had prepared him for every circumstance except the possibility of not getting his own way. From the start he and Barbara were at loggerheads over matters both of policy and practice. To Barbara, whose personal determination was formidable, his obstructiveness was intolerable – and to make matters even worse his habit of loudly playing his violin during his lunch-hours cannot have endeared him to his workaholic minister.

The Labour Party manifesto had committed the government to creating "a national plan for transport covering the national networks of road, rail and canal communications, properly co-ordinated with air, coastal shipping and port services". This was a major challenge, but perfectly suited Barbara's belief in socialist planning, and her appetite for imposing order on complex and multi-headed problems. This alone might have been enough to have provoked conflict with her Permanent Secretary, but additionally the manifesto promised to impose at least a temporary halt to the pattern of rail closures that had followed the Beeching Report and led to a colossal reduction in railway services. Barbara fully subscribed to the idea that the railways had a key part to play in any attempt to create an integrated transport policy and this was to be a massive point of difference between her and her Permanent Secretary.

Sir Thomas had served under and greatly admired

Ernest Marples, the last transport minister of the Conservative government. Marples operated in ways that were at least curious – in his work he chose to run the Ministry from his home in Belgravia and in his private life he enjoyed being caned while wearing ladies underwear. So far as the direction of transport policy was concerned, he was from top to bottom a minister who believed in running down the railway network and instead building roads. This policy had a number of attractions for him – not least the opportunity it created to place multiple and highly lucrative road-building contracts with his own firm of Marples Ridgway (as Minister of Transport he had been required to sell his shares in the company, but he secretly retained control of them and used his powers as minister to line his own pockets).[*] His legacy in the ministry was a team of officials and in particular a Permanent Secretary who believed that road was king and that, in terms of any national policy, rail was part of the problem not part of the solution.

Within days an opportunity to reinforce the officials' negative view of the railways arose when the National Union of Railwaymen announced their intention to call a national strike. The threat of industrial action arose from a pay claim made by the NUR the previous year which had been referred by George Brown to his newly established Prices and Incomes Board, because the claim exceeded the government's norm. The Prices and

---

[*] In his last years, after he had left Parliament, Marples fled to Monaco to avoid arrest for tax fraud but died before any charges could be brought.

Incomes Board concluded that the railwaymen should receive no more than British Railways had already offered (which in itself also exceeded the norm) and outlined a future direction in which any subsequent pay increases were to be linked to productivity and not, as common before, based on rates of inflation or ideas of comparability with other occupations.

The intention to strike plunged Barbara Castle and George Brown into a round of tense negotiations with the leaders of the National Union of Railwaymen – discussions made more difficult by Brown's alternation of periods of brilliant persuasiveness in the negotiations with spells of drunken belligerence. In the end the union leaders had to be invited to a meeting at Number 10, where Wilson believed he could persuade them to call off their strike over whiskies and sandwiches. When the union leaders judged the sandwiches to be too few and too dainty, the refreshments were changed to much thicker sandwiches, beer and sausages. Wilson's approach was to combine fraternal sweet-talk ("We're not two sides, you know"), with a blunt insistence that the economic situation did not allow an improved offer (softened by some vague talk about revisiting the wages issue in the future once the strike had been called off).

When this did not seem to have been sufficiently persuasive, Wilson gave Barbara a chance to speak. Wilson had concentrated on the economics of the situation; what Barbara now focused on was her vision for the place of rail in a new national transport policy. She stressed her commitment to the railways, talked in terms of investment and expansion and promised to involve the union in discussions about future policy.

It did the trick. After some more haggling the NUR men voted to call off the strike. *The Times* on the following day declared: "All credit to Mr Wilson for getting the railway strike called off without the payment of any further ransom money." Wilson clearly deserved some credit – particularly for sticking firm on the refusal to increase the offer on the table – but credit was also due to Barbara for providing the union with a face-saver, a 'take-away' that provided cover for their climb-down.

It was a good news story for the government and cleared the way for, within days, an announcement that there would be a General Election on March 31st. In Blackburn, Barbara's overall vote slightly decreased but her share of the vote was up and she returned to the Ministry of Transport to continue working on her national transport policy and the refinement of a Road Safety Bill, the groundwork for which had been laid under her immediate predecessor.

The most eye-catching element of this Road Safety Bill was the introduction of roadside breath-testing and, for the first time, a statutory definition of the blood-alcohol concentration level which was to define the threshold of drunk driving.[*] While these measures met with broad support there was some opposition, including some from unexpected quarters. "Minister, this is a rotten idea. You're spoiling my fun as a motorist," objected one BBC

---

[*] The limit was set at 80mg per 100 millilitres of blood; at the time of writing this remains the maximum permitted concentration.

interviewer.[5] Even Richard Crossman, who agreed with the reform, worried that it was being seen as a "really unpleasant attack on working class drinkers. We are in danger of becoming known as the government which stops what the working classes really want."[6]

Undeterred by any opposition – which included poison pen letters sent directly to her - Barbara continued to work on the provisions of the Bill as originally conceived and significantly tightened its provisions – for example police could require a breath test on suspicion of drunk driving instead of, as first planned, the breathalyser being used only in random checks. A further and particularly significant tightening of the law in Barbara's Bill was to introduce a one-year disqualification penalty for drunk driving; until then the offence had generally incurred only a fine. Within months the change in the law was proving its value – for example, the deaths from road accidents at Christmas fell from 158 in 1966 to 98 in 1967. In the first year after the passing of the new law, deaths on the road dropped by 1200.

The greater part of Barbara's time in the Ministry during this year was spent not on the road safety measures but on developing her vision of an integrated transport policy. Her White Paper on this was published on 27th July 1966. It contained not a detailed policy but a framework of ideas that would outline the shape of policy to come. Its keynote was that "transport must be planned as part of the national effort as a whole" and that the need was to "plan different forms of transport in relation to each other".

It signalled an important change with regard to the railways. Her Conservative predecessor, Ernest Marples, had, in his 1962 Transport Act, laid down that British Railways must operate so as to make a profit or at least break even. This was impossible without cutting services to the bone and even beyond – hence the Beeching cuts. Barbara's White Paper rejected the goal of 'breaking even' and set out instead the government's intention to provide a subsidy to ensure the continuation of unprofitable routes that were seen to be "socially necessary". In addition, Barbara promised capital investment – government funding to modernise the infrastructure, including rolling-stock and track. On top of this public investment, British Railways was to be given a chance to increase its income by a policy of steering more goods traffic back onto rail. This re-balancing of goods traffic from road to rail was to be overseen by a new body, a National Freight Corporation, which would be required always to direct goods traffic to the railways whenever this would be efficient and economic. Urban transport in large towns and city areas was to be updated and improved through the work of newly-formed Passenger Transport Executives which would plan and manage the integration of local train and bus services, which in turn would benefit from increased government investment and subsidies.

What was outlined in the White Paper was nothing less than a major structural overhaul of national transport policy and it was clear that the legislative implications were massive. The Transport Bill that was to follow was unsurprisingly monumental, running to 2377 pages and needing 45 committee sittings before it made its way onto the statute book. At the time it was the largest piece of non-financial legislation since the Second World War.

But although the vision behind it was undoubtedly Barbara's, she was not to be the one who would finally oversee the final passage of her Bill. By the end of March, the government seemed to be losing support, having just lost four by-elections. Wilson was looking to a cabinet reshuffle to restore the government's image and as part of that offered Barbara a move. When Wilson had first raised with her this possibility, the job they both had in mind was at the Department of Economic Affairs, but after Roy Jenkins put his foot down, Wilson cooled on that idea. After some more thought, Wilson offered her instead the Ministry of Labour, replacing its current occupant, the trade unionist Ray Gunter.

Barbara was not impressed by the offer. To her it represented no improvement in status and status was a keen preoccupation within the cabinet – as shown by this pompous example from the diary of Richard Crossman, shortly after she had become Minister of Transport: "I started with a meeting with Barbara at her own Ministry. I had decided to show courtesy to a junior in the Cabinet by going to see her rather than making her come across the river to see me."[7] Barbara's response to Wilson was that she would only consider the post if the job-offer was restyled as the Secretary of State for Employment and Productivity. When it was additionally agreed, after discussion between Wilson and Crossman, that Barbara should also be named as 'First Secretary of State' (essentially the most senior member of the Cabinet) she accepted the new post. In terms of increased status this was very demonstrably signalled when, at the first subsequent Cabinet meeting, Barbara found herself seated not at the far end of the cabinet table but right in the centre, directly opposite Wilson himself.

When Barbara started in her new role, in April 1968, she was under no illusions about the challenge that she now faced, working, as she described it, at "the very focal point of unpopularity". She was moving into a zone where maximum danger – which had so far been averted – could not be far in the future. The potential flashpoint was in the government's relationship with the trade unions and particularly the policy restricting wage growth. An incomes policy had been openly advanced by Labour even before it came to power in 1964 but it had managed to sell to the TUC the idea of an incomes policy not as a form of wage restraint but as a way of planning income growth. That was what was promised in Labour's 1964 manifesto: "To curb inflation we must have a planned growth of incomes so that they are broadly related to the annual growth of production."

But once elected, the decision not to devalue forced the government to use wage restraint not as a mean to ensure planned growth, but as a tool to provoke deflation. Taking the Unions along with this approach – and its accompanying apparatus, the National Board of Prices and Incomes – had called for monumental efforts of persuasion by George Brown, including a marathon twelve-hours of talks with the TUC on the eve of their annual conference in 1965. In the first years of its income policy the government managed to just about retain the grudging support of the Unions and, despite industrial resentment over restraint, the number of working days lost due to industrial action remained relatively stable between 1965 and 1967.

But the relationship with the unions was undeniably deteriorating. It was clear that the state of friction – at first something like a fragile truce but then degenerating into more of a hostile stand-off – would eventually blow up into major conflict. The inevitability was obvious to many trade union leaders – some of whom could not understand why it had not already happened. In 1967, Clive Jenkins, General Secretary of ASSET (Association of Supervisory Staffs, Executives and Technicians), declared: "The British unions look tired. They *must* be suffering from exhaustion or they would not be acquiescent to measures of a Labour government which will turn them into departments of the State."[8] To the eye of the general public, however, the unions did not seem quite the submissively docile creatures that Clive Jenkins depicted. A National Opinion Poll taken in August 1966, just after the economic crisis measures of July, revealed that people were three times more likely to blame the problems on the unions than on the employers.

At the same time as Barbara moved into her new role, a Royal Commission was in the process of completing a bulky report on trade unions and employers' associations. The idea for setting up the Commission had originally come from the previous Conservative government, but the idea had been dropped in the face of the refusal of the TUC to co-operate with any such enquiry. At the time of the original suggestion Wilson had opposed it, dismissing it with the quip that any such commission would "take minutes and spend years". But, soon after the election, Wilson had come to see some advantages in going ahead with the idea – perhaps not least because his dismissive joke highlighted something which he could turn to advantage. Royal Commissions did indeed have a reputation for consuming time with very little outcome and in this case a long-drawn-out enquiry could have the advantage of creating a hiatus – when questions of trade union reform could be safely put on the back-burner pending the Commission's report. So, after a rapid piece of legislation that dealt with the TUC's original objection, a Royal Commission started its work in April 1965.

As the Commission toiled on, Wilson became increasingly concerned about the ability of the government to keep the lid on its pay policy and increasingly doubtful about the ability of the trade union movement to continue even a cosmetic display of co-operation. Wilson had been extremely shaken by a six-week strike by the National Union of Seamen, in June and July 1966, and during its course Wilson had told the House of Commons that the strike was being influenced in its course by a "tightly knit group of politically motivated men". The Prime Minister was roundly criticised for giving voice to what was judged to be an inflammatory invention, but years later it was revealed that MI5 had supplied him with intercepts which showed that strike leaders were taking instruction from the headquarters of the British Communist Party. The progress of the hard left was unmistakable and, for Wilson, deeply troubling. The election in 1967 of Hugh Scanlon, a militant left-winger, as President of the Amalgamated Engineering Union and, the following year, of Lawrence Daly, another hardliner, as General Secretary of the National Union of Mineworkers did not bode well and Wilson was very aware that George Woodcock, the generally conciliatory and co-operative Chairman of the TUC was due to retire, almost certainly to be replaced by someone much more confrontationally minded.

The traditional special relationship between the trade unions and the Labour Party was, for Wilson, a double-edged sword. It could be represented as a strength, reflecting the co-operation that a Labour Government could expect from union leaders – at the last TUC conference before the 1964 election Wilson had promised that the unions and a Labour Government would be "partners in a great adventure". Or the relationship could be seen as a weakness with a Labour Prime Minister effectively in hock to the movement which provided such a large share of the party's finances, held, by right, nearly half of the seats on the party's National Executive and wielded the power of their large block votes at party conferences.

By 1968, Wilson was worried about the impact that industrial disputes were having on the image of his government. Strikes and unofficial stoppages were becoming increasingly common (1968 would record nearly two million more days lost to strikes than in the previous year). Whilst some of the disputes were very short-lived and were of limited impact, others were not – one highly-volatile and therefore headline-catching strike lasted from December 1966 to January 1968. After a punishing series of by-election defeats, nearly six hundred council seats lost in the local elections in May and with the national opinion polls running against Labour, Wilson recognised the danger that the Conservatives would attempt to take the high ground and represent themselves as the only party able to take an assertive stand against the unions.

While in government the Conservatives had avoided addressing the issue of trade union reform, preferring to leave matters well alone, in the hope that the unions would put their own house in order. But in opposition that mood began to change. In February 1966, the Shadow Cabinet considered a paper which argued for reforms including the creation of an Industrial Relations Court that would have wide-ranging powers that could include the outlawing of some forms of industrial action. On the back of this paper, the party set up an Industrial Relations Group, which set out to develop the ideas of the paper into a concrete policy.

That policy was launched two years later on 8 April 1968 (coincidentally, or not, on Barbara's first day as Secretary of State for Employment and Productivity), set out within the luridly-purple covers of a pamphlet titled *Fair Deal at Work*. In its foreword, the Conservative leader, Edward Heath, declared that his party's policy was "to provide

Britain's industrial life with a new framework of rights and obligations". The key message of the pamphlet was that industrial relations needed a reform of the law and that Conservative policy was to ensure that this legal overhaul would tackle a wide number of issues, including collective bargaining, restrictive practices, industrial pressure-tactics and industrial action intended to promote "sectional objectives".

Wilson was rattled by this policy initiative - but his natural response lines were blocked. It would have suited him to be able to take a statesman-like position and declare that it would be wrong to pre-empt the findings of the Royal Commission and that any plans must wait until there had been time to consider any recommendations the Commission was going to make. This line was however not of much service in terms of putting the issue on the back-burner, because the Commission was about to complete its work. Its final report was expected to be published by November of that year and so any breathing space would be purely temporary.

An alternative fall-back position could have been provided if the imminently-published report were about to recommend tougher laws to inhibit strikes and stoppages. Wilson could then have used the Commission's recommendations to provide respectable cover for adopting its tough line (or a slightly watered-down version of it). But this potential avenue was also closed off, because Wilson already knew – from his outgoing Minister of Labour, Ray Gunter – that the report was not going to recommend any significant tightening of the law whatsoever.

Without any cover available from these alternatives, Wilson turned to his new Secretary of State for Employment and Productivity for a way forward. He wanted a lead from her on how to respond to the Conservative proposals and suggested that a committee of ministers should be established to collaborate on the work. The group, when it was eventually formed consisted of only five, comprising Castle, Gerald Gardiner, Sir Elwyn Jones, Fred Peart and Fred Lee. The inclusion of Gardiner and Jones was highly significant because they were respectively Lord Chancellor and Attorney General, essential members from the start because it was taken for granted that the purpose of the committee was to frame future legislation. The other significant point about the committee is the name that was noticeably missing – James Callaghan. His exclusion – almost certainly on the grounds that he was considered 'unsound' on the matter of trade union reform – was to play a major part in the crisis that would eventually develop.

Barbara's strategy was to wait until the Royal Commission's report was published (it was always referred to as the Donovan Report, after the name of the commission's chairman, Lord Donovan) and then allow a decent interval for consultations with the employers' organisations and the unions about the Report's recommendations. Meanwhile the new committee would work in secret on its own proposals that would then be put out as a White Paper.

The Donovan Report was published on 13th June 1968. Its conclusions were broadly that while management and unions needed to improve their ways of dealing with one another, a significantly tighter legal framework around their roles and responsibilities would be unhelpful or impractical. The Commission's basic article of faith was that problems in industrial relations were simply down to ignorance about ways of doing things better. It followed that reform should, on the whole, be a voluntary matter between and within the employers and the unions.

At the start the membership of the Commission was broadly balanced between those who favoured a much more closely-regulated system and those who were opposed to it. During the Commission's work there were rumours of manoeuvrings by the rival camps, but ultimately those who favoured minimal legal intervention and an avoidance of legal penalties carried the day. In any case the inclusion on the Commission (at his own insistence) of George Woodcock – General Secretary of the TUC– effectively gave the union voice a veto over its conclusions, because any notes of dissension from him would automatically undercut the commission's findings. Barbara Castle described the report as having "Woodcock's fingerprints all over it".[9]

Evidence of the contortions necessary to accommodate the divisions within the commission could be seen in the way in which any firm conclusion it reached was often hedged around with some form of escape clause. For example, one of Donovan's recommendations was the establishment of a register of trade unions and employers' associations. But, the report stressed, while registration of itself by any trade union would be 'essential', it would not be compulsory. Another recommendation was the creation of an Industrial Relations Commission that would review cases and problems arising from disputes relating to procedures or collective agreements. But, once again twisting in the wind, the Donovan Report also laid down that this Commission should not set out to arbitrate in these disagreements or, by and large, be able to impose any penalties for not complying with its recommendations.

All this back-bending to the side of the unions had nothing to offer that suited Wilson. He had already decided to take action in the opposite direction, explaining to Denis Healey that he had given up on the possibility of the unions reforming themselves. "I had a go at incomes policy," Healey recalled Wilson saying, "but there was no chance of getting enough support for that. So I am going to switch to curbing the power of the unions."[10]

If Castle had been at all disposed to disagree with Wilson's cynicism, her experience in her first months as Secretary of State for Industry and Productivity would have changed her mind. Her new department had taken on responsibility for the Prices and Incomes policy that had previously rested within the Department of Economic Affairs. Almost from the moment she started her new job Barbara was plunged into a series of industrial actions that sometimes turned-on national wage disputes that challenged the Prices and Incomes policy, but just as often were factory-level walkouts organised not by top-level union officials but by local shop-stewards. Not a week passed without her having to deal with some or other strike or the threat of one.

Amongst the disputes that she had to handle within the space of just a few weeks were a claim on behalf of 70,000 busmen, a dispute with the engineering union, a threatened seamen's strike, an inter-union row in the steel industry, a railway strike and a walk-out by sewing machinists at Ford's Dagenham plant (years later used as the basis of the feature film *Made in Dagenham*). Many of these disputes were official – that is they were threatened or called by the national union's leadership or one of its authorising committees. But strikes of this kind were in a minority of industrial disputes. Between 1964 and 1967 out of the total of around 2.5 million working days lost due to union action, nearly 2 million were as a result of unofficial action. These were walk-outs or strikes called by local shop-stewards and were often staged on the basis of grievances that to the outside world seemed minor or trivial. But the pettiness of these disputes could be in inverse proportion to their wider impact, as the shut-down of one plant led to shortages that halted production elsewhere.

A notorious example had been the dispute that broke out in November 1966 in the Roberts-Arundel works in Stockport. The trouble began when the company installed vending machines to replace the existing arrangement whereby men brewed their own tea with water boiled in their electric kettles. From that acorn developed a strike of 145 workers that lasted nearly eighteen months and eventually threatened to bring out a million workers across the north-west of England. That strike only ended when the American owner of the plant pulled the plug on the business and put the factory building up for sale.

The Roberts-Arundel strike had ended by the time Barbara arrived at the Department of Employment and Productivity but it would not be long before she was faced with a fresh example of a strike that was not so much a dispute as an episode of industrial madness, almost tailor-made to make a mockery of the wishful thinking and light-touchery of the Donovan Report. On November 11 1968, a machine-setter working at the Girling brake factory in Cheshire was asked to turn-on an oil valve. He refused on the ground that the instruction was coming from a supervisor who was a member of a different trade union. When the man who had given the instruction then turned-on the valve himself, it prompted a walkout by 27 men who claimed that only members of their union had the right to operate that valve. As a result of their action 500 other Girling workers had to be laid-off. The company was a vital link in the supply chain of components to the car-making industry and within days the shortage of its disc brakes meant that 5000 workers had to be laid off in Ford factories that had no involvement in the original dispute whatsoever - a stoppage that cost Ford half a million pounds a day. The action was unofficial, but the strikers' union (Amalgamated Union of Engineering and Foundry Workers) was ambiguous in its approach –

asking the strikers to return to work while at the same time declaring that their action was fully justified. The strike dragged on for 23 days.

The frustration and public indignation resulting from the strike inevitably intensified demands for tighter legal controls on the way in which industrial disputes played-out. Inevitably too it highlighted the general toothlessness of the Donovan Report's recommendations when applied to real-world situations like Girling. When the Commission's report had been published, Barbara had been careful to keep her public responses neutral – neither praising the report nor criticising it, merely announcing time for further consultation before a White Paper would be produced. But behind the scenes she had continued to consider alternatives to Donovan and, to help her formulate a new policy, she arranged for a residential conference in Sunningdale where there could be detailed discussion of what reforms were needed. It happened that the weekend booked for this conference was just four days after the start of the Girling strike, so as participants turned up for her conference that dispute was a significant part of the news background to their discussions.

On the first day of the conference the *Times* had run with a story headlined STRIKE CRESCENDO ATTACKED BY TORY MP. It reported a speech by Robert Carr, Conservative Shadow Spokesman on Employment and Productivity, in which he branded unofficial strikes as "the scourge of British industry". He accused the government of a "failure to give Britain an up-to-date system of industrial relations and trade union law" and warned "it is committing national suicide to allow things to go on this way".[11] With the Conservatives now in full attack on the industrial relations front and the trade unions apparently quite content to provide them with ample ammunition, Barbara was only too well aware that inaction or only luke-warm reform was not a political option.

The conference was to run from Friday evening until the Sunday. For the first part – from the Friday evening until late afternoon on Saturday – Barbara, her two junior ministers and a small group of her officials were joined by a group of external experts and by Peter Shore, Secretary of State at the Department of Economic Affairs (by now drastically reduced in its authority and scope from its heyday under George Brown). The advisers and Shore would stay until before dinner on the Saturday. Once they had gone, Barbara would be left to work alone with her officials until the conclusion on Sunday.

The group of experts was on-the-whole more or less balanced between the interventionist and the non-interventionist camps. They comprised Professor Hugh Clegg (who had been a member of the Donovan Commission and was the author of a key chapter of its report), Campbell Adamson (the incoming Director General of the CBI), George Turnbull (the Deputy Managing Director of the Leyland car company), Jim Mortimer (an official of the Draughtsman and Allied Technicians Union), Len Neal (Director of Industrial Relations at British Rail), Aubrey Jones (the head of the National Board of Prices and Incomes) and Donald

Robertson, a Professor of Applied Economics and occasional Department of Employment and Productivity trouble-shooter (who would shortly be asked to investigate the Girling dispute).

In the first part of the conference Barbara remained in listening-mode, giving nothing away about the direction of her own thinking. But on the Sunday morning, with only her officials present, she opened-up and disclosed exactly what she had decided should be in her White Paper. Her plan amounted to a taking-forward of Donovan's chief recommendations but with crucial additions – additions that were a clear rejection of Donovan's view that legal sanctions were an inappropriate way of handling industrial disputes.

Barbara had decided that there needed to be three new legal powers. One was to give the Secretary of State the right to require a strike ballot whenever that was judged to be in the national interest. Another was to create, as recommended by Donovan, an Industrial Relations Commission but, contrary to the recommendation made by the Royal Commission, to grant it the power to enforce any decision it came to in cases of an inter-union dispute. The third additional power was to require a cooling-off period where workers were proposing to walk-out in breach of agreed procedures – and since the overwhelming majority of strikes were unofficial, and therefore not in line with agreed procedures, this last power would be something approaching a catch-all intervention.

With the Secretary of State's intentions made clear, her

officials started work on turning them into a White Paper. When, a few weeks later, Wilson saw a first draft he was delighted, judging that this policy initiative would completely take the wind from the sails of the Conservative's current line of attack; Barbara had, he said, "not so much out-heathed Heath as outflanked him".[12] Wilson, who had all along insisted that preparations for the White Paper should be kept leakproof, decided that, to keep things under wraps, the next stage should be to limit any wider discussion of the proposals to just a small group of handpicked ministers. His plan was to sew up agreement amongst a chosen few, with a view to then taking the White Paper to full cabinet and presenting it almost as a *fait accompli*.

It would not be long before Wilson's plan to ensure early-stage secrecy was blown apart. On the 12th December the *Guardian* had a front-page scoop headlined 90 DAYS 'COOLING' PROPOSED FOR UNOFFICIAL STRIKES. The piece below disclosed that "Mrs Castle and her departmental officials and Junior Ministers" had decided on including in her White Paper a cooling-off period in any dispute where it was believed that "an opportunity for second thoughts would help in securing a peaceful settlement".

The news item, well-informed and clearly based on a leak, seemed a breach of Wilson's insistence that the White Paper's plans should for the time being remain a secret. But it may be that Wilson did not find the leak entirely displeasing. The opinion polls were running strongly against the Government; in that month a Gallup poll recorded a Conservative lead of 20 percent (up 4.5 per cent from the previous month) and the National Opinion Poll was even worse – a Conservative increase of nearly 9% from November. The *Guardian's* splash – which clearly revealed that Barbara was proposing to steal the Conservatives' clothes – may have provided Wilson with some welcome relief.

There was one sentence in the report which, perhaps seemingly insignificant at the time, actually touched-on what would become a major source of trouble for Wilson and Castle. In the second paragraph of the story, its writer (the paper's Deputy Political Correspondent, Ian Aitken) pointed out that the cooling-off mechanism "has yet to go before other departmental Ministers and eventually will have to be endorsed by the Cabinet before the White Paper is published at the end of January". This almost throw-away line probably did not perturb the ministers who were finding out about the cooling-off proposal for the first time from that morning's newspaper. They were all used to leaks and would have been confident that the contents of the White Paper would in due course be put through all the usual preliminaries – scrutiny by other ministries and thorough examination at sub-committee level before going for final approval to the full cabinet. They would have had no idea that Wilson's intention was to by-pass all the usual formalities and go straight to Cabinet for something like a rubber-stamping.

But if no ministerial hackles were raised by the leak in the *Guardian*, things would shortly change catastrophically as a result of a serious blunder by Barbara. On December

19 she had a meeting with George Woodcock, of the TUC, to talk about a current dispute in the steel industry. During the conversation she abruptly decided – "on an impulse" was how she recalled it – to tell Woodcock the details of her proposed White Paper. There are differing accounts of his reaction, but it is not in dispute that he recommended that she meet with his Finance and General Purposes Committee and tell them what she had just shared with him.

Barbara agreed to Woodcock's suggestion and a meeting with Woodcock's senior colleagues was arranged for December 30th - what had begun as impetuous indiscretion now escalated to blind recklessness. In the meeting Barbara disclosed her entire hand, outlining not just a few points from her White Paper but essentially summarising her entire plan. She was sharing with the TUC's top-table information that was, up to that time, still being held back from the great majority of her cabinet colleagues. Inevitably, the next day's *Guardian* had got hold of the story: "The government", the paper informed its readers, "has finally lost patience with the unions' attempts to put their own house in order voluntarily and is preparing for a period of massive intervention in industrial relations. This uncompromising message was given by Mrs Barbara Castle, Secretary of State for Employment and Productivity, when she met leaders of the Trades Union Congress yesterday to discuss her plans for the reform of union law."[13]

The *Guardian's* story was under the by-line of John Torode, the paper's Labour Correspondent, which inevitably pointed to the leak having come from within the TUC. Torode included all the details that Barbara had disclosed of her plan and so his two-column report essentially provided a precis of the forthcoming White Paper. His report referred to the fact that "her proposals have not yet been finally approved by the Cabinet" – a point which must have been read by astonishment by her cabinet colleagues, who had at that stage not even been given a first chance to talk about her plans let alone not having yet "finally approved" them. The difficulties that Barbara was about to have with her Cabinet colleagues were going to be much worse because of the offence she had given by putting them at the back of the consultation queue while she prioritised instead discussions with the TUC.

Of course trouble was inevitably expected from James Callaghan. When, on January 1st, Barbara was confronted by Crossman, furious at the way in which her White Paper was being bulldozed through, she explained that "we had to do this because of Jim Callaghan".[14] It had been obvious for some time that Callaghan had been manoeuvring to become the 'trade union man'. His ambition was still firmly set on replacing Wilson at Number 10 and the trade union constituency was for him the obvious source of potential support.

Back in May 1968, Callaghan, while speaking at the annual conference of the Fire Brigades' Union, had promised that the present compulsory powers over wages would be replaced by a voluntary policy. The *Times* reported the following day that he had given the union "the strongest possible assurance so far that the Government know they have driven the trade unions as far as they could be expected to go in tolerating legislative control of wages".[15] His confident assurance that wage control would be voluntary by the autumn turned out to be as wildly inventive as his economic forecasts when Chancellor of the Exchequer – by the autumn the Government was in fact tightening its attempt at the control of wage inflation - but Callaghan was not at the conference to show-off his forecasting skills, he was there to advertise his solidarity with trade unionists.

There was nothing subtle about Callaghan's pitch; he was a "friend and fervent believer in the trades union movement" he told the conference and the report of his speech in the *Guardian* acutely noted that Callaghan "has now openly aligned himself with the trade union members in Parliament".[16] This 'alignment' was a naked pitch to a considerable source of votes in any future leadership contest - at the time 132 Labour MPs were trade-union sponsored.

But when the Cabinet met to discuss the draft of Barbara's White Paper on January 3rd, it was Crossman who led the attack. According to Barbara's own account his approach was venomous, but Crossman's diary shows his usual blissful unawareness of the effect he was having on the feelings of a colleague. Callaghan also weighed-in describing the penal clauses of the White Paper as an unprincipled overturning of everything for which the trade union movement had stood and fought. The timetable for launching the White Paper was tight –

publication had originally been scheduled for January 9th, a date set when Wilson had reckoned on everything being agreed on the basis of just one Cabinet meeting. But once debate began in the Cabinet room it became obvious that this timetable had no chance of success - even when the meeting had been extended into an afternoon session it was clear that it would not get through the Cabinet that day. In the end it would take three further days of work in Cabinet committee and another three meetings of the full Cabinet before Barbara was able to rally sufficient support amongst her colleagues to finally overcome the resistance, by an advantage of around two to one.[*]

The White Paper, *In Place of Strife*, was finally launched on Friday 17th January, more than a week later than originally planned. Press comment was generally favourable. On the day after publication the *Times* declared: "The unions would be foolish indeed if they try to work up resistance to the White Paper proposals." But working-up resistance was exactly what the unions set about doing. Their tactic was not at this early stage to show head-on resistance, but to work behind the scenes to stoke up opposition among their union-sponsored MPs. Discreet meetings were arranged where, without seeming to dictate a line for those MPs to follow, it was strongly suggested that it was in their interests to work to have the penal clauses dropped. The impact of this was revealed when Barbara had a meeting with the majority of

---

[*] No formal vote was taken but Wilson reckoned up the balance of those for and against on the basis of their views.

those sponsored MPs on January 20th. Next day's headline in the *Times* precisely captured the mood: 'Reform proposals evil, unions MPs say'.

What had started amongst the trade union sponsored MPs soon spread into the wider Parliamentary Labour Party. On January 30[th,] the *Guardian* reported that Barbara had had to defend herself before a "highly critical and occasionally hostile meeting of Labour backbenchers". Further humiliation was to follow. On 3rd March, at the end of a debate on the White Paper, fifty-seven Labour MPs voted against the government and around thirty more abstained. Then, on March 26th, Labour's National Executive voted to reject any legislation based on *In Place of Strife*. In blatant defiance of the convention of collective cabinet responsibility, Callaghan voted for the motion of rejection.

Faced with dissent on this scale the government decided to switch tactics. Instead of a full Industrial Relations Bill, implementing the White Paper as a whole, it was decided to put through only a short measure, essentially concentrating on just the four penal provisions. The thinking behind this switch was that a longer bill would drag out the embarrassment of internal opposition and, at the same time, delay its implementation until close to the election. Barbara had her doubts about the idea – in particular she was worried that resistance would be increased when the measure was seen to be all about penalties, with no chance of these being seen to be offset by those provisions in her White Paper that were judged to be union-friendly. But her objections were overcome; a short and snappy bill would, it was agreed, proceed briskly through Parliament and mean that the new law would have become well-embedded before the government had to face the next election.

When the TUC heard rumours of this plan they asked for a meeting with Wilson. He insisted that he was not going to shelve a measure simply because the TUC did not agree with it, but refused to say whether or not a short bill was being contemplated. He added that the only alternative to his legislation would be for the TUC to put forward a plan of their own that would achieve what the White Paper aimed to achieve. This suggestion was almost certainly a throwaway line, made only for effect – the whole point of introducing legislation was that he had no expectation that the TUC would be able to reform the movement from within. But, as things were to turn out, his gesture would later provide him with a lifeline out of very deep trouble.

When it was finally confirmed that there would be only a short bill it was, curiously, announced not by Barbara but by Roy Jenkins, as part of his budget speech on April 15th. "We need", he said, "to facilitate the smooth working of the process of collective bargaining in industry and to help to prevent the occurrence of unnecessary and damaging disputes, of which we have seen all too much recently, and which are totally incompatible with our economic objectives. The Government have, therefore, decided to implement without delay, during the present Session, some of the more important provisions incorporated in the White Paper 'In Place of Strife'."

The next day Barbara announced to the House exactly

what "the more important provisions" were. She started with what may have been interpreted as sweeteners – describing those elements that were concessions to the unions. In fact, Barbara would not have considered these parts of the bill as being in any way sugar-coating for the pill. She believed that the whole thrust of her White Paper had been pro-union – strengthening some protections and proscribing some activities which to her mind were 'unsocialist' and therefore not legitimate trade union behaviours.

The first measures she announced were to give employees the absolute right to belong to a trade union and to require employers to recognise and negotiate with unions represented in their workplaces. This led her on to more controversial ground – the bill would include clauses to deal with inter-union disputes. Under the new law she proposed that the TUC should first be given an opportunity to resolve any one of those disputes – but in the event of their failure the Secretary of State would have the power to decide (after taking guidance from the new Commission for Industrial Relations) which union or unions the employer should negotiate with. The element of the bill to which she then turned was the most controversial of all – in the case of an unofficial strike the new law would give the right for the Secretary of State to impose a 28-day return to work for 'conciliation'. Refusal to comply could be subject to a fine that, if imposed, would be collected not through the courts but by attachment of earnings – Barbara softened this point by referring vaguely to the possibility of any monies collected being used for purposes that contributed to well-being amongst workers.

Barbara finished by stressing that "in the weeks that lie ahead, before the Bill is presented, and while it is being discussed in Parliament, the Government will still be prepared to consider any alternative proposals from the T.U.C. for achieving its purposes equally effectively and equally urgently." This gave encouragement to the TUC to search for ideas of their own that could persuade the government to drop the legislation. Its response was what it called a *Programme for Action*, which went through a series of drafts in the hands of Vic Feather, then head of the TUC's Economic Section. The final version made a concession on inter-union disputes whereby the TUC would arbitrate on the quarrel and its decision would be binding on the unions involved. But on unofficial strikes there was only the promise to tighten up an obscure TUC rule that theoretically could result in unofficial strikers being "reported to Congress". This was a tepid concession which hardly seemed likely to get any grip on the rash of unofficial strikes that, almost on a weekly basis, resulted in hundreds – sometimes thousands – of other workers being laid off in collateral damage. And even this limp package came with a price-tag – it was conditional on the government dropping any penal powers from its proposed Bill.

So far the TUC's response seemed to Wilson to be playing into his hands. The lack of a clear commitment by the unions that would make the proposed penal powers obsolete served to reinforce a public perception that the

TUC was at best impotent in the face of wildcat strikes and at worst happy to collude with them. Then, on June 1st, Wilson and Castle had a secret meeting at Chequers with Vic Feather, Jack Jones and Hugh Scanlon. At this meeting the union leaders made plain a complete lack of interest in co-operating with the government to reduce industrial stoppages and their total determination that the law should not and would not be allowed to intrude into the area of union action. The penal clauses seemed to hold no threat for them – in fact they boasted of the ways in which they would circumvent the proposed new law and make it useless. In a very real sense it was not the penal clauses that for them were the issue – their central argument was that the government had no right to interfere with the workings of trade unions and that they would oppose on principle any legislation that seemed to hinder their work. This was plainly a constitutional defiance. In that secret meeting the question at issue was the one with which Edward Heath would face the country five years later – *Who Governs Britain?*

It was, Barbara confided to her diary, a crisis that was "irreconcilable". Wilson was sufficiently alarmed by what he had heard from the union side that he took the precaution of writing up an account of what had occurred. But at this stage Wilson was convinced he still had the upper hand and that the Parliamentary Labour Party would, despite all its negative noises, ultimately swallow any doubts and, through self-interest if nothing else, vote through measures that any potential rebels could see were strongly supported in the opinion polls.

But for once Wilson had miscalculated. In fact, while the trade-union sponsored MPs had as expected remained strong in their opposition to the measures, some of Wilson's original support had been ebbing away as doubtful or nervous Labour MPs began to switch sides. On 17th June, the Cabinet received a stark warning from Bob Mellish, recently appointed by Wilson as Chief Whip, in the belief that he would impose any necessary discipline. Mellish told the Cabinet bluntly that he could not deliver the votes they would need for their Industrial Relations Bill. The Chief Whip was telling the Cabinet no more than what they could read in their morning papers. That day the *Guardian* carried a front-page report of a letter sent the previous day to Wilson from the Chairman and Vice-Chairman of the Parliamentary Party and the Chief Whip that made clear the Bill was dead in the water. "The letter," the Guardian told its readers, "is said to make it quite plain to the Prime Minister that not even if the Commons were kept sitting well into August would there be any chance of the Bill getting through the Commons".

Wilson and Barbara now found themselves precariously poised on a stool, two legs of which (the TUC and the PLP) were offering no support at all and the third of which (the Cabinet) was on the verge of giving way because the Callaghan faction was drawing to its side Cabinet members who had originally supported the Bill but now worried that perseverance with it was threatening the very survival of the Government. Even Roy Jenkins, who had promised support to Barbara from the very start, now fell away. Tony Benn, another former supporter who now jumped ship, recorded in his diary an account of the way in which Wilson responded to the evidence that the Cabinet would no longer support the legislation: "Harold and Barbara then became extremely bitter...In the end he said he would meet with the TUC tomorrow and he would tell them what he thought, do what he thought necessary, and the Cabinet would either have to uphold him or repudiate him."

The next day the morning papers implied that Wilson and Castle were still hoping the TUC would give ground. But, in reality, Wilson and Castle sat down with the TUC leaders in a negotiation that was in effect a one-sided deal. An editorial in the *Guardian* that morning described the TUC as being threatened with a blunderbuss. But the TUC leaders arriving at the meeting already knew that the blunderbuss was loaded with blanks. Douglas Houghton, the Chairman of the Parliamentary Party, had tipped-off Vic Feather about the extent of the defection of Labour support and so the trade union leaders arrived knowing that *In Place of Strife* was a bust-flush. But despite their sense of victory the TUC was prepared to offer Wilson at least a fig-leaf of dignity in defeat. After a face-saving show of back-and-forth, the union leaders offered a formula - the TUC would enter into a "solemn and binding" agreement to place an obligation on a union to get back to work any of its members taking unofficial action.

The words "solemn and binding" had the stamp of high moral righteousness – and in those days there would have been some who even recognised its biblical roots. But it would not be long before it became a standing joke. Wilson and Castle, it was said, had been rescued by their friend Mr Solomon Binding. In any event the undertaking, however solemn and binding, was worthless and Wilson and Castle must have known it. The following day in the House of Common, Edward Heath pressed Wilson to say what would happen when unofficial strikers ignored their union leaders and carried on striking. Wilson replied that "the T.U.C. will place an obligation on the unions concerned to get their members back to work. It will then be the duty of the unions concerned to do this, including, where appropriate, the use of their rule books". His answer was, unsurprisingly, greeted with laughter.

The headline in the next day's *Daily Mirror* proclaimed WILSON PLEDGES: WE'RE BACKING THE TUC, a reference to a television broadcast the Prime Minister had made the evening before, complimenting himself and the TUC on completing the 'solemn and binding' agreement. A more downbeat assessment appeared on an inside page under the headline CHEER NOW, WEEP LATER. That cynical tone was to be entirely justified. Unofficial strikes continued. In July, the month after the agreement, 306,000 days were lost due to unofficial action. The following month the figure rose to 514,000. Over the summer and beyond, the unofficial strike route was taken by, to name but a few, refuse collectors, miners and car delivery drivers.

Vic Feather was inclined to be seen to be more proactive in at least appearing to implement the agreement, but behind him stood the powerful union bosses who not only had no interest in reining-in unofficial strikers, but actually welcomed them as evidence of the independent assertion of workers' rights.

After the final meeting with the TUC, Barbara's immediate reaction was to suggest to Wilson that there could still be a short Industrial Relations Bill, this time implementing some of the other, less controversial, proposals put forward in her White Paper. But Wilson refused to countenance the idea. *In Place of Strife* was officially dead and buried. Speaking to her officials she compared the events of the last two days to an execution.

The outcome had been a massive personal blow for Barbara. At the Ministry of Overseas Development her grand plan for aid had been strangled at birth, deprived of the funding it needed. At the Ministry of Transport she had masterminded a major piece of reform but had moved to another job before her plans reached the statute book (and her successor, Richard Marsh, had actually trimmed back the legislation on some points she regarded as critical). And now, at the Department of Employment and Productivity, she had once again been denied a crowning achievement.

In Place of Strife may have been discarded, but Barbara had another cause immediately in hand – an Equal Pay Bill. This had its origin the previous year when Barbara had been piloting her Prices and Incomes legislation through the House. This was needed because the powers established through the 1966 Prices and Incomes Act were due to lapse and the government had determined to extend them into the next years. But during the progress of the renewal powers, Barbara came under some pressure to allow exemption to scrutiny of pay increases where they were the result of moves towards equal pay. After a hurried consultation with the Chancellor of the Exchequer, Roy Jenkins, Barbara stood up in the House and announced her commitment "to enter personally into discussions with both sides of industry directly with a view to agreeing a timetable for phasing in the implementation of equal pay over an appropriate period. No doubt the House will ask, 'What period'? Clearly—and I am sure that the House will accept this—any final answer on that ought to await the outcome of the discussions I have. But I myself say that, if equal pay for women in the public service could be phased in over seven years, our industrial women deserve no less generous treatment."[17]

Those discussions had produced mixed results. The CBI was, as to be expected, hostile to the idea of equal pay and even the TUC found itself in an ambiguous position. Union leaders had always been theoretically committed to equal pay – but the commitment was less one of principle and more one of tactics. That is to say that trade unionists were in favour of equal pay when any resulting pay award would also increase the pay of men. They were less keen on equal pay when it merely closed the differential between men and women or risked a potentially lower pay rise for men because whatever money was available for a pay increase might go in greater share to women. The formula of 'equal pay for equal work' had originally appealed to the TUC, but it had then moved sharply away from the idea when it became evident that the principle would involve processes of job analysis and classification that could result in structural distinctions in pay between groups of men who had until now been paid at the same rate.

Within months of abandoning *In Place of Strife*, Barbara was pressing to move forward with an Equal Pay Bill. Support within the Cabinet was uneven but with Wilson's backing she got approval to go ahead in time to make the announcement as part of her speech to the annual party conference in Brighton. The announcement was enthusiastically received in the hall, despite her warning that full implementation of equal pay might not happen for another six years. Her Equal Pay Act received Royal Assent on 29 May 1970, although the wording of the Act set 29th December 1975 as the due date for its implementation.

The passing of her bill was, for Barbara, a cause for much-needed personal celebration, but the Conservative victory at the General Election, just a few weeks after the Equal Pay Act was passed, was to mark a watershed in her political career. In the subsequent voting, to elect Labour MPs to places in the shadow cabinet, Barbara was successful, but only just, squeezing into the last place available. Callaghan topped the poll; another straw in an ill-wind. In opposition, Barbara shadowed her old department, Employment and Productivity, and, without embarrassment, led the Labour assault on Heath's Industrial Relations Bill. That legislation, though admittedly based less on *In Place of Strife* and more on the party's ideas from its *Fair Deal at Work* pamphlet, nevertheless set out to achieve very similar ends to those for which Barbara had striven as Secretary of State. That did not in any way deter her in her fight against the Bill and she admitted taking pleasure in the disarray that followed its passage into law when the unions, taking advantage of weaknesses and loopholes in the new Act, rode a cart and horses through it. Barbara's pleasure in the way in which the unions circumvented the new law does not seem to have been tempered by a recollection that the TUC had warned her that it would be exactly the fate of her own proposed legislation.

After the passing of the Industrial Relations Act, Barbara moved to shadow social security, but failed to retain a shadow cabinet seat in the 1972 parliamentary party elections. Wilson offered her a place anyway, but she declined. Then in 1974 when Heath lost the *Who Governs Britain?* election, Barbara once again had a place at the cabinet table, this time as Secretary of State for Health and Social Services. She still had a keen appetite for reform and put through significant improvements to the state's welfare and pension systems, including the introduction of child benefit to replace the old system of family allowance.* But the writing had been on the wall ever since Callaghan had insinuated himself into the position of 'leader in waiting' and, when Wilson resigned in 1976, one of Callaghan's first acts as Prime Minister was to sack

---

* The Child Benefit Act was passed while Barbara was Secretary of State but not implemented until after she had been dismissed from the Cabinet.

Barbara from the cabinet.

She left Parliament in 1979 and was elected instead as a Member of the European Parliament. Just a year later her diary of her time in the 1964-70 cabinet was published – another volume, her diary of her years in the second Wilson government, would appear in 1984. Six years later she became Baroness Castle of Blackburn and though nearly blind in her last years, remained politically active up until her death after a fall at home in 2002 at the age of ninety-one. The next day's *Guardian* led with the news: "Barbara Castle, Labour heroine and champion of women's rights, dies at 91". On an inside page, Denis Healey described her as "the most remarkable woman in the history of the Labour party".[18]

Barbara Castle was a towering figure. With the exception of Wilson, she was, during the 1964-70 government, the cabinet member with the highest public profile. Instantly recognisable she was a hugely popular figure and even during the row around *In Place of Strife*, was always greeted warmly at trade union events. She was a compelling speaker, good at working-up a set piece and capable too of improvising a speech on the spot in a way that held and enthused an audience.

Her natural territory was the big picture. She was never minded to tinker or to tweak. Her instinct was always to work on a broad canvas, even if the scale of her ambition seemed likely to outstretch the resources available or outdistance potential support She was, like Crossman, a reformer on the grand scale.

She brought to her plans a great intelligence and an acutely sharp mind. Hers was not an academic brilliance – like Wilson's or Crossman's – but a penetrating intelligence, capable of shrewd analysis and quick to make the connection between problems and potential solutions. She was hugely energetic with an immense capacity for work and the pages of her diary often carry the reader along on a whirlwind of relentless activity.

Her greatest weakness was the lack of support on her own backbenches. This was a long-standing pattern. Her failure to get elected to the shadow cabinet through the parliamentary vote in the years of opposition had been a marker. Her low tally in the same vote in 1970 and, two years later, her failure to get any place at all revealed a persisting dislike or mistrust. Some of it was down to sexism of course. She was never afraid to use her femininity – she was always impeccably dressed and according to one account brought-in a hairdresser every day to make sure she always looked her best. She could be jolly, clubbable and even flirtatious. But the sharp edge of her intelligence was always in evidence and what might have been admirable in a man was, for many Labour men, a challenge to their masculine pride.

Given her strengths, Barbara's misjudgement of the political viability of her trade union reforms, calls for explanation. Partly this lies in her over-reliance on Wilson's assurance that he could get her White Paper approved by the Cabinet without the need for it to pass through the conventional stages of procedure. In one sense her confidence in Wilson was not misplaced. Wilson probably could have fixed the Cabinet on its own – what he could not fix was what eventually developed into a triple alliance which combined considerable opposition within the Cabinet with hostile resistance from the trade unions and a threatened revolt on his backbenches. This coalition was too strong for even Wilson to face down.

A second factor playing into Barbara's carelessness was her failure to understand just how controversial her proposals were. It will be recalled that at her Sunningdale conference she had not shared her thinking with the group of external advisers. So no direct challenge had emerged from that group. Meanwhile Barbara's own officials shared her enthusiasm for reform and, while their like-mindedness no doubt created congenial working relationships within the Department, it meant that Barbara never faced a robust critique of her plans from her own civil servants.

Barbara's sense of false security had been compounded by her conviction that her plans would gain strong public support. A National Opinion Poll survey towards the end of the year had revealed that 62% of people favoured making unofficial strikes illegal (revealingly the figure was almost as high amongst trade unionists). A *Guardian* report on December 31st had pointed out, what had been in Wilson and Castle's mind almost from the start, that "Mrs Castle's proposals are quite simply an attempt to steal the thunder from Mr Edward Heath". If Barbara had given any time at all to reckoning on how her White Paper might play with her own backbenchers she might have expected, given the low relative state of Labour in the polls, that on the whole they would judge that stealing thunder from Mr Heath was, in terms of the political weather, meteorologically wise.

Of course, it is not for civil servants to warn their ministers about political difficulties. But that is exactly what parliamentary private secretaries are supposed to do. But Roy Hattersley, her joint PPS at the time of *In Place of Strife*, has recorded her reaction when he briefed her about Douglas Houghton's work to turn Labour backbenchers against the proposals: "Her rage against both the message and the messenger was terrible to behold and so violent that I thought I would be lucky to get away with only my hand cut off."[19] If Barbara had been able to handle more calmly reports of a falling-away amongst backbenchers she might have received earlier warning of forthcoming difficulties and been better placed to meet them.

Another question – one which puzzled trade unionists at the time – was how to reconcile her proposals with her well-advertised socialist faith. She lived socialism with every bone of her body. But hers was a distinctive strand in the socialist tradition. She had grown-up steeped in the socialism of the progressive middle-class – in the Sidney and Beatrice Webb tradition – not in the down-to-earth working-class socialism born out of grinding poverty and squalid surroundings. Hers was the socialism of her long-time lover in the thirties and forties, William Mellor – with his kid-gloves and chauffeured cars. She saw herself as a stout defender of trade union rights, but that defence stopped at the point when, as she saw it, those rights were being exercised not in the interests of economic justice but in the cause of beggar-my-neighbour.

In Place of Strife ended in a humiliating failure, but it is hard to deny now that she and Wilson had been right in principle. Any doubts about the good sense of what she was trying to do could not survive the near-satanic misery that was to be inflicted by the unions under Callaghan in the 'Winter of Discontent'. Wilson to his credit stuck with Barbara until there was no other alternative but to give up. Even then he managed to square a formula that was not on the face of it an unconditional surrender. Roy Jenkins, in retrospect, neatly summed-up what is probably the fairest judgment on the White Paper's fate: "It is a sad story from which he (Wilson) and Barbara Castle emerged with more credit than the rest of us".[20]

Barbara was a favourite of Wilson's because he knew she was a highly gifted minister who repeatedly created much-needed 'good news' for his government. She held nothing back from him in terms of outspoken criticism – but, given Wilson's penchant for troublesome women, this was no doubt also part of the attraction. She in turn loved Wilson for his strengths but was infuriated by his weaknesses.

In the final judgment it is her work at the Ministry of Transport that was her greatest political legacy – the best evidence of her calibre as a minister. Her hoped-for rebalancing of rail and road transport is today a seemingly lost cause, but today's Passenger Transport Executives are an effective survival from her Transport Act. Her greatest achievements of all are bound-up with her introduction of key road safety measures that, largely unaltered since then, are now taken for granted. Her introduction of the breathalyser and, for the first time, the establishment of a defined limit to a driver's blood-alcohol level has, over the years since, saved many thousands of lives. It is not many ministers whose political legacy has such humane significance.

6

Denis Healey:

Politics as a Martial Art

Denis Healey commanded enormous intellectual firepower. Instinctively combative, he was always primed to mount a devastating attack on the arguments of those he disagreed with and fiercely argumentative in the defence of his own corner. Everyone who got into a debate with Healey walked away knowing that they had been in a fight. He was a bruiser – on at least one occasion quite literally when, in 1965, he aimed a punch at Colin Jordan, the leader of Britain's tiny but disruptive group of neo-fascists.

Denis Winston Healey was born on 30 August 1917 in Kent, but his family moved a few years later to Bradford where his father had been appointed as the Principal of Keighley Technical College. Early in life Denis acquired a taste for voracious reading. "When you asked what he wanted for a present," his mother later recalled, "he always said 'books'."[1] His wide reading would in time equip him with an extensive knowledge not just of classic fiction and poetry but also of history, philosophy, psychology, economics and politics. He became a good piano player too and acquired a deep knowledge and appreciation of music and art. Throughout his life this cultural background – his 'hinterland' as he called it – was something in which he took enormous pleasure and pride.

He won a scholarship to Bradford Grammar School, the same school that Barbara Castle would eventually attend – though he was in the sixth form by the time she was enrolled. He was hugely successful at school, standing out academically even in a school whose selective intake combined with its high teaching standards enabled it to take pride in sending around a dozen of its pupils to Oxbridge in any year. In his last year at school he won a scholarship to Balliol College, Oxford.

At the end of his first year at University he joined the Communist Party, convinced that it was only communists who were prepared to take on the fight against fascism – at that time Chamberlain's government was, of course, resolutely committed to appeasement and the Labour Party's stance was, at best, one of standing-by and wringing its hands. But because Communist Party policy was that its members should join the Labour Party – to take it over from within – Healey also joined Labour. It was as a Communist infiltrator into the Oxford City Labour Party that he was able to stage what, up to that point, was his most overt political act.

In August 1938, the Conservative MP for Oxford City

died while on a walking holiday. Quentin Hogg (later to become Lord Hailsham) was adopted as the Conservative candidate but, in the months before nominations closed, the issue of appeasement reached a newly-intense heat when, in September, Chamberlain and Hitler signed the Munich Agreement. Sensing an opportunity to overturn the long-standing Conservative majority, the local Liberal Party candidate announced his willingness to stand down in favour of an independent candidate, Dr Lindsay, (Master of Balliol College), provided the Labour candidate would do the same. But Labour's man, Patrick Gordon Walker,[*] initially declined to withdraw before being eventually forced to do so after manoeuvring by the secretary of the local Labour party, Frank Pakenham (prior to his later incarnation as the loopy Lord Longford) and by Denis Healey (who had recently been elected as the local party Chairman) and the other communists who had been able to work their way into a controlling role in the local party organisation. Healey recalled campaigning with "enormous enthusiasm" but the campaign was, to say the least, unsophisticated. The Lindsay campaign's slogan 'A Vote for Hogg is a Vote for Hitler' was met by Hogg's supporters with the riposte 'Vote for Hogg and Save Your Bacon'.

---

[*] Patrick Gordon-Walker would become a *cause-celebre* in the 1964 General Election when he lost his seat at Smethwick to a local racist, Peter Griffiths, who, as the new Conservative MP for the constituency, was immediately branded by Wilson as a "parliamentary leper".

Just before the start of Healey's final year at Oxford, war broke out. "Denis, you can put away your books," his mother said to him on hearing the news, "War's been declared."[2] Healey immediately joined up, ignoring the Communist Party rule against volunteering (this was the time of the Hitler-Stalin pact). His enlistment was however deferred for a full year and this gave him the time to go back to university to finish his degree.

It had always been inevitable that at Oxford, he would once again excel – he graduated with a Double First. He had, some time before, planned that after finishing his degree he would spend a further year studying abroad, on a Commonwealth Scholarship, but then another option opened-up when, on the back of his academic record, he was offered a Junior Fellowship at Merton College.

In the event all options had to be put aside for the duration of the war. When France fell, Healey renounced his membership of the Communist Party and by late 1940 he was square-bashing with other new recruits in Harrogate. Before long Private Healey got commissioned as a Second Lieutenant and trained in movement control - handling troop transits and other logistical tasks. He was then posted first to North Africa and then to Sicily. In the invasion of mainland Italy he served as a beachmaster at both the Salerno and Anzio landings. The job of a beach landing officer is immensely challenging and demands not just huge organisational skills but also clear and rapid thinking, self-discipline and sheer courage – especially vital when, as at Salerno, the landing is directly opposed by the enemy. Healey's work as a beachmaster earned him two mentions in despatches. By the end of the war he had been awarded the MBE and promoted to the rank of Major.

By then Healey's mind was already turning in the direction of a career in politics and in the early summer of 1945 he was, through a family connection, invited to apply for selection as the Labour candidate for the Yorkshire seat of Pudsey and Otley. He was still abroad on service when the selection meeting was held, but a friend (and member of the local party) read his presentation to the committee on his behalf. He was duly selected and, when the General Election approached, the army gave him the special leave that was afforded to all those in service who were standing for Parliament. One of the first things he did on return to Britain in May 1945 was to travel to Blackpool to attend the Labour Party conference, where he had a chance to speak, in battledress, on what was to become his specialism, foreign policy. His speech was enthusiastically received in the hall and attracted the attention of the inveterate talent-spotter Hugh Dalton.

The Pudsey constituency had a Conservative majority of over 21000 and so was clearly a safe seat for that party, but the strength of Healey's personal campaign and the national swing to Labour meant that in the end it was a close-run thing – Healey did lose but by less than 1700 votes. Meanwhile Hugh Dalton, assuming a Conservative victory in the seat was inevitable, had already ear-marked Healey as the ideal man to fill the vacant post of Head of the International Department at Transport House, the Labour Party headquarters. Healey's speech had impressed Dalton with its clear grasp of international issues and future priorities – a knowledge that had been acquired not just through his time in the army but from numerous, extended trips abroad made in Europe before the war. In addition, Healey spoke several European languages – including fluent and well-accented French, Italian and German.

The International Department had essentially two main areas of work. One was to revive the Labour and Socialist International, through establishing or renewing contacts and relationships with socialist parties and groups across Europe – connections that had of course been broken or interrupted by the war. Its other responsibility was to develop materials and publications that addressed international and foreign policy issues from Labour's perspective. When Healey arrived to take up its leadership, the department was a scarcely-functioning unit. Its previous head had made a resentful departure a year before, leaving a staff of just two to run things on their own. But the rudderless state of the department gave Healey the opportunity to give it his own steer – essentially to create the department anew in his own image. He was never going to be content with merely reflecting policy made elsewhere – he was determined to seize the initiative and have a shaping hand on policy as it was made.

Across Europe there was a great appetite for organised resurgence among socialist groups and individuals (some of whom were literally emerging from hiding). Healey with his flair for languages and his energetic enthusiasm was well-placed to be not just in the thick of this revitalisation but actually leading and directing it. He quickly perceived the danger that some socialist parties would be attracted not to democratic socialism but towards the alternative of communism. Although still in some ways to the left of his party, Healey had no doubt at all that the reconstruction of Europe depended on rejecting the pull of Soviet Russia and embracing instead a solidly democratic platform. He argued this case repeatedly in meetings, conferences and speeches and his efforts were closely observed and valued by the Foreign Secretary, Ernest Bevin. Others were watching too. In March 1948, the US Ambassador to Italy, James Clement Dunn, sent a telegram to his State Department praising Healey's robust handling of the pro-communist Italian Socialist Party.

A collaborative relationship quickly developed between Healey and Bevin. Denis provided Bevin with briefings and other intelligence based on his meetings across Europe and, in return, overseas diplomats were instructed to identify local opportunities for Healey to make useful contacts and approaches. By May 1947 this symbiotic relationship created an opportunity for Healey to act as an unofficial spokesman for Bevin by writing a pamphlet that effectively set out the case for the Foreign Secretary's policies.

Ernest Bevin was a towering figure in Attlee's government – as he had been in the war-time coalition where, as Minister of Labour, he had been one of Churchill's favourites. Bevin's policy at the Foreign Office was a determined move towards a reduction of Britain's overseas responsibilities, coupled with a drive towards persuading the United States to shoulder a larger share. He was a man of enormous abilities but unfortunately these did not extend to a command of fluent argument and this created considerable scope for his critics within the Labour Party to attack his policy for what they perceived as its pro-American and anti-communist bias. A group of these MPs – Richard Crossman, Michael Foot and Ian Mikardo – got together over an Easter weekend in 1947 to collaborate on a pamphlet attacking Bevin's policy which they published under the title *Keep Left*. It argued for a rejection of American influence in Europe in favour of a new "Third Force", a cross-European socialist alliance with Britain and France at its heart. The release of the pamphlet was timed so as to stir-up anti-Bevin sentiment before that year's party conference in Margate.

Healey, who was in complete agreement with Bevin, quickly saw an opportunity to defend the Foreign Secretary by writing a counter-pamphlet that would set out a coherent and robust argument for Bevin's policy. His pamphlet, *Cards On The Table*, was also produced in time to affect opinion at the next Party Conference. Bevin's biographer, Alan Bullock, set the pamphlet in its context: "For once Bevin had the case for his policy put for him by one of the ablest young men in the Labour Party, whose intellectual powers were fully equal to those of the Keep Left group and who wrote with a force and economy which Bevin could never achieve."

Of course it helped Bevin, and irritated his critics on the

backbenches, that the pamphlet came as an official publication of the Labour Party. But Healey had not acted entirely independently; the text had been checked before publication by Foreign Office officials and Bevin had encouraged if not instigated the pamphlet's appearance – though he was anxious for his support and involvement in it to be kept confidential. Behind-the-scenes collaboration between the Foreign Office and Healey would continue until Bevin's death in 1951, eventually becoming so open that, in 1951, the *Economist* felt able to refer to "the little Foreign Office of Transport House".

Both the 1950 and 1951 elections came and went without Healey running again for Parliament. In his autobiography he writes airily of having been at the time of those elections weighing-up other moves-on from the International Department – including the possibility of a Professorship at Aberystwyth University and the Foreign Editor's post at the *Daily Herald*. Neither of these seems likely to have been even briefly attractive to Healey and, although he does not mention it, it seems likely that he must have turned down approaches from constituency parties keen to attract him as their candidate in either 1950 or 1951. If he did reject invitations it could have been because he believed that his present position at the International Department had more to offer than starting-out as an MP. By the beginning of the decade Healey had achieved a position of such influence in the Foreign Office that some officials there even referred to him as the "little Foreign Secretary". This degree of scope and significance was vastly more than any new MP could hope to have.

But, in March 1951, Bevin resigned, seriously ill and just a few weeks away from death. The end of Bevin's term at the Foreign Office seems to have triggered in Healey a recognition that it was time to leave Transport House. A General Election followed that October, but because there had been a General Election the previous year, local constituency parties were generally inclined to put forward the same candidate again, especially in the safer seats. But after the 1951 election one of Labour's MPs, James Milner, was granted a peerage (after being disappointed in the election for Speaker) and this created a vacancy in Leeds South East. There was a Labour majority there of nearly nine thousand, making it a safe seat – and so one for which there would be plenty of competition for Labour's nomination.

When Healey was approached about the possibility of his applying for nomination it was significant that the approach came not from the local party itself but from one of its activists, whose motivation was that he wanted to dish the chances of John Rafferty, a local Councillor and the Acting Chairman of the local party, who had convinced himself that he was a definite shoe-in for the nomination. Healey agreed to throw his hat in the ring and he and Rafferty were joined by two other would-be candidates, a local councillor and the former Labour MP Aidan Crawley. The first round of voting was inconclusive and after a number of subsequent ballots it came down to a straight choice between Councillor Rafferty and Healey. During the time taken for this series of votes, support for

Healey had grown and eventually he was convincingly confirmed as the local candidate.

The by-election was held in the first week of February and, as was to be expected, Healey won by a majority of over seven thousand. Campaigning had to be halted on the day before the election when the death of George VI was announced. Within an hour of the election result being declared, Healey performed his first duty as an MP when he attended Leeds Town Hall for the proclamation of the accession of Elizabeth II.

He had caused some disquiet during the campaign by seeming at times more preoccupied with international affairs than local issues and, unsurprisingly, once in Parliament he continued to focus on what had become his recognised specialism and area of expertise. His maiden speech, made in May, was on foreign affairs, addressing the state of West Germany, the threat to unification from East Germany and the importance of West Germany contributing to its own defence. This concentration on foreign affairs was to continue – the first twenty-seven of his speeches were on international issues and it would not be until February 1954 that he spoke in the House on any other topic.

But his formidable knowledge and experience inevitably recommended him to the opposition front bench. Early in November 1954 he was invited to speak from there, again on the role of West Germany in European affairs including defence. It was part of Healey's good fortune that the next five years were to present a useful succession of international situations and other problems that gave him great scope to demonstrate his abilities as a specialist in foreign and defence policy. One of the most significant of these opportunities came with the Suez Crisis in 1956, during which Healey was a vehement critic of the government's actions – "In the whole of my political life," he later recalled, "I have never been so angry for so long as I was during the Suez affair".[3] The government's approach was for Healey anachronistic; an attempt to evoke our imperial past. In August he spoke in the Commons of the impression "that an enormous section of the Conservative Party is in favour of unilateral military action by Britain, to try to bring back the nineteenth century".[4] Healey also detected a throw-back to the Prime Minister's personal history, with Eden determined to present himself again as the man who would have no truck with appeasement. Healey argued that what should have been a straightforward issue concerning the free movement of oil had been misused by the Prime Minister as an opportunity to replay his 1930s stance against dictatorship. The geo-economic consequences of Eden's lack of judgement would, Healey believed, include aligning all the Arab countries on the side of Egypt and increasing Russian influence in the Middle East and Asia. Healey's very evident passion and anger helped to counter a perception in the House that in the past while his interventions and speeches had been deeply-informed, they had been almost too dry to be persuasive. Healey later recalled "The strength of my feelings over Suez led me at last to speak like a human being with emotions rather than like a soulless automaton".[5] Given that

Gaitskell was initially inclined to be more supportive of the Eden government's action, Healey's stand over Suez was not only impassioned, it was assertively independent.

Throughout his time as a backbencher Healey worked hard to stay deeply well-informed about world politics and issues. He travelled frequently and widely – often to international conferences or as part of a parliamentary delegation, but also on personal trips and holidays. He travelled to the United States at least once every year and his visits to Europe and beyond included stays in Norway, Sweden, Poland and Russia. During his travels Healey not only acquired first-hand knowledge but also made useful contacts, developing personal connections across the world.

Despite all these interpersonal links Denis was not what would have been judged in the House as a sociable individual. He was in some respects something of a parliamentary outsider– well-connected but socially distant. Some of this was because of his work schedule but much of it was due to the fact that people found him intellectually very intense – and not just about politics (in 1952 Crossman recorded a long evening with Healey and Hugh Dalton during which Healey occupied a lot of the time talking about existentialism). Healey's interests and enthusiasms did not make for the kind of small-talk or gossip that oiled the wheels in the House's bars and smoking rooms. For a man who was to be frequently at or close to the centre he was also, paradoxically, something of an outsider.

Given this sense of distance, his election in November

1959 to a place in the shadow cabinet was unpredicted – the *Guardian* described it as "surprising". The post Gaitskell gave Healey was relatively low-level - junior spokesman on foreign affairs (with Aneurin Bevan as the shadow lead). Even when Bevan became too ill to work, Gaitskell did not allow Healey to act as his stand-in. Instead, Gaitskell took on the foreign affairs lead himself, though he did allow Healey to handle the brief at parliamentary questions. Even after Bevan's death, in July 1960, though Healey was then formally recognised as the official opposition speaker on foreign affairs, in practice Gaitskell retained the oversight of the brief for himself.

In December 1961 Healey moved from the Foreign Office brief to shadow the Colonial and Commonwealth Office. On the face of it this was a step-down from shadowing the Foreign Office, but in this new role Healey was able, for the first time, to be really taking a lead. Typically, he threw himself into the new role. Within days of taking up his appointment he was off on a month's fact-finding tour of West Africa.

The Commonwealth and Colonial Affairs portfolio was, at this time, anything but a backwater. Current issues included the restrictions on immigration embodied in the Commonwealth Immigrants Bill, the break-up of the Central African Federation, the concerns of the Commonwealth countries about Britain's application to join the Common Market and a spate of nationalist disturbances in British Guiana, Aden, Brunei and elsewhere.

Healey's opposite number in government was Reginald

Maudling, but as a result of a curious re-assignment of responsibilities it was R A Butler, as Home Secretary, who had the oversight of Central African affairs. And in one of Healey's first outings at the despatch box as Commonwealth and Colonial Affairs spokesman he found himself up against Butler, who attempted to patronise Healey on account of his inexperience in this area. Healey was onto this in a flash and quickly skewered Butler – and others who tried to follow his example – with a series of broadsides demonstrating his grasp of the facts. Despite the change of focus it was business as usual for Healey: confident mastery of context, principle and detail.

Then, in January 1963, with virtually no warning, Gaitskell died. The election of Wilson as leader opened-up a new opportunity for Healey when he was asked to take on the shadow lead on defence, an area that he had long studied as an inseparable aspect of his work on foreign affairs. In the Labour Party's 1964 manifesto the sections on each of these areas showed clear evidence of Healey's influence.

But, for all Healey's brilliance, there was amongst his colleagues a persisting lack of popularity. In the November 1962 parliamentary elections to the Shadow Cabinet, Healey's vote dropped by almost a fifth. Many were alienated by what struck them as an arrogant display of self-confidence, his appetite for fierce argument and an interpersonal style that could be caustic even with his Labour colleagues. Those in his party might admire him, but they did not always find him likeable. The judgment of the far-left Labour backbencher Ian Mikardo reflected the feelings of many when, although recognising Denis as "an outstanding talent" who was always "penetrating and enlightening", he described him as "a political bully wielding the language of sarcasm and contempt like a caveman's cudgel".[6]

Less than a year before the election Healey delivered a Fabian Society lecture on *A Labour Britain and the World*. It was vintage Healey – a sweeping *tour d'horizon* which aimed to set out the major objectives for a Labour Government's defence and foreign policy. There was, however, no reference to the nitty-gritty question of what defence policy the country could afford or alternatively how the country could pay for what defence policy was needed. The defence bill was at that time around £2000 million a year, amounting to nearly 7% of GDP, of which a large proportion was spent in overseas currency. The bulk of this budget was made up of what could be described as 'legacy costs' – commitments 'East of Suez' that had their origin in Britain's imperial past.

The term 'East of Suez' was used elastically. Sometimes it was a strictly geographical description, applying to bases and operations in the Middle or Far East, such as Aden, Singapore, Hong Kong, Malaysia or the Persian Gulf. Sometimes the description was stretched to apply to any defence deployment outside Europe. The phrase 'East of Suez' also had a significance that went beyond the geographical. For some, Britain's presence 'East of Suez' was a demonstration of our continuing ability to project power at long-distance and thus earn a right to a place at the 'top table'. For others 'East of Suez' represented not a cause for pride but a source of national embarrassment, a pretentious and money-wasting clinging to an outworn imperial façade.

The Labour Party's election manifesto had committed the government to ensuring that defence expenditure represented value for money and, following the General Election and within days of Healey's confirmation as the incoming Minister of Defence, he gave an interview to the *Times* asserting that his general policy aim was the need to "get the best value for every pound spent on defence" and that cuts were to be expected in the current defence spending plans. The report – under the headline SOME DEFENCE PROJECTS LIKELY TO BE CANCELLED - noted that Healey was tackling his new role with "characteristic zest" and ended with an oblique reference to the expected impact of Healey's abrasive manner in Whitehall Gardens (the home of the Ministry of Defence): "The forecast for Whitehall Gardens is anything but dull. There are likely to be some fresh winds, it will be cold in places and there is a chance of scattered thunderstorms." [7]

Just over a month after the election, Wilson assembled a defence conference held over a weekend at Chequers. The main focus was to be the identification of cuts that could be made in the defence budget inherited from the outgoing administration and in particular to evaluate the viability of three highly expensive defence aviation projects. The procurement systems at the Ministry of Defence had for years been incompetently managed. Inter-service bickering about requirements and specifications had been allowed to run riot, project costs had spiralled beyond control and contractors were likely to be continually plagued with changes to design requirements (or in some cases allowed to fall short of the specification on which they had been contracted). This complete breakdown of control had been possible because the Ministry had been a revolving door for a succession of dimly-lit ministers[*] without either economic grip or political grasp.

Amongst the problems to be considered at that weekend conference were three costly aircraft projects, of which the most problematic (because the most expensive) was the development of the TSR2 – a 'state of the art' tactical strike and reconnaissance aircraft being built by the British Aircraft Corporation. The specification for this hugely expensive project had been frequently changed mid-stream and because of this, as well as because of serious technical problems, the TSR2 had fallen behind schedule and costs were continually escalating. By the time of Healey's arrival at the Ministry of Defence the basic fuselage had, after four years of work, been flight-tested only once. By the end of the weekend at Chequers the future of the TSR2 seemed highly doubtful and the other two projects – a transport aircraft and a vertical-take-off and landing fighter – also looked likely to be scrapped.

As well as reviewing these expensive projects, the

---

[*] Denis Healey believed that Duncan Sandys, Minister of Defence from 1957 to 1959, was an honourable exception to this otherwise dismal parade.

Chequers conference had also to discuss important strategic issues. One of these was whether or not to continue with the purchase of the submarine-based Polaris missile system, which had been agreed between Harold Macmillan and President Kennedy in 1962. By the time of the election, the programme was still in its earliest stages, with only one submarine completed. In the Labour Party manifesto, Wilson had allowed some incautious reservations about the continued purchase of Polaris and, inevitably, this opened the Chequers conference to the argument that this was the time for Britain to renounce its own status as a nuclear power. Two of those at Chequers that weekend – Lord Chalfont (Minister for Disarmament) and George Wigg (Paymaster General) - argued for exactly that. Their arguments were demolished by Healey with, according to one account, "lethal candour"[8] and by the second day of the conference it was clear that the government would go ahead with Polaris.

Another strategic concern was how Britain should respond to the US proposal for a multilateral defence force. The Americans hoped that this plan would thwart any expansion of nuclear capability into other European countries, by bringing all nuclear weapons in Europe into a combined mixed-nation force under the command of NATO (and thus effectively under the command of the US). In a speech in the US before the election Wilson had criticised the plan on the grounds that it would, he said, "give the appearance but not the reality of shared nuclear control". Healey, like Wilson, was against the multilateral force and the Chequers conference agreed that it should be opposed. Wilson had already arranged that he and his defence team would visit Washington in early December and it was agreed that during those talks whilst they would agree to continue with Polaris they would attempt to change the Americans' minds about the multilateral force.

One of the urgent issues that Healey had to tackle in his early days at the Ministry was the need to harmonise the inter-weaving rivalries of the services. Many of the problems, past and present, were due to inter-services friction and feuding and the consequent backroom plotting. A key player in this disruption was Lord Mountbatten, the monumentally vain and deceitful Chief of the Defence Staff, who had risen effortlessly throughout his career by the strategy of blaming others for his mistakes and taking the credit for their successes. In his autobiography, Healey records his first substantial meeting with Mountbatten after arriving at the Ministry of Defence: "His charm, self-confidence and good looks enhanced a reputation for radical independence".[9] Healey confided a more candid and accurate impression to his private diary. Mountbatten was, he noted, "most untrustworthy".[10] At the time Mountbatten's appointment was due for renewal; Healey told him he had to go.

Healey was determined to provide the leadership that this highly complex ministry had long needed but not had. He made a point of attending joint meetings between defence staff and Ministry officials – something his predecessors had not bothered to do. He insisted on taking an active part in the annual NATO crisis simulation exercise, contributing in real-time as Britain's Defence Minister. He listened carefully to advisers but would never be talked into a decision that he had not independently weighed-up. Above all, he brought to the Ministry a relentless insistence that defence and strategic issues were fundamentally economic questions. This did not mean that Healey was a hatchet man, taking an axe to anything that would improve the balance sheet. But he understood the relationship between military power and the economic strength needed to pay for it. In a parliamentary debate, a little over a month after the election, Healey drew attention to the financial reality of the UK's defence burden. "One thing I have already learned from my first five weeks in office" he told the House, "is that Britain is spending more on her defence forces than any other country of her size and wealth."[11] He clearly indicated that a reduction in the defence budget was economically inevitable but, as Wilson had already told the House, no details could be announced until after the forthcoming talks in Washington.

The talks with the US were set for early December. In his own account of his 1964-70 government Wilson stresses that for their journey to Washington he and his defence team flew in a Comet, after he had insisted that the flagship British airline, BOAC, should fly them in a British-built plane rather than an American Boeing 707, which, he snootily points out, had been the transatlantic plane of choice for his Conservative predecessors. If Wilson's insistence on flying British was intended as a demonstration of national prestige and pride then it was misjudged. BOAC had phased-out the use of the Comet on its scheduled transatlantic flights some years before, preferring to use the more efficient and much more capacious 707; by 1964 the makers of the Comet were on the point of ceasing all production. So, when Wilson and his colleagues landed in Washington,* they did so in an obsolete plane no longer capable of meeting current demands. Hardly the best image for a Prime Minister determined to forge a 'New Britain' at the cutting edge of a technological revolution.

Once in America, the first priority for Healey and Wilson was to provide reassurance. On a previous visit to the US, while still Leader of the Opposition, Wilson had suggested to President Johnson that a Labour Government might cancel the Polaris agreement. Now Wilson hastened to undo the damage and assure Johnson that Britain would go-ahead – though Britain's plan was now to build one less submarine than originally intended. By way of further assurance, Wilson told Johnson that Britain was still committed to a worldwide involvement in defence and security and that in particular it would maintain its role 'East of Suez'. There was, nonetheless, still one awkward element in the discussions, when Johnson unsuccessfully pressed Wilson for military support in Vietnam.

Healey's role meanwhile, in separate discussions at the Pentagon, was to offer a further sweetener by suggesting

---

* Due to the Comet's limitations Wilson's flight had to be made in three hops, needing a stop-over at both Prestwick in Scotland and Gander in Canada.

that Britain might cancel Britain's own TSR2 programme and purchase instead the American F111. As for the US plan for a multilateral force, Healey's strategy was to undermine the proposal not by outright opposition but by the suggestion of an alternative to be known as the Atlantic Nuclear Force. This, like the American proposal, would bring nuclear weapons under a single umbrella of command but, unlike the US plan, would not involve mixed-nation crews on any ships or aircraft. This variation was sufficiently subtle to hold some attraction for Johnson and Robert McNamara, the US National Security Adviser, and they were willing to consider it. In the meantime this put the MLF plan on the back-burner where Healey hoped it would eventually fade away. This tactic worked and, in time, both the MLF and Healey's Atlantic Nuclear Force, were quietly abandoned.

Back in London, Healey, with his officials and service advisers, had begun serious work on a comprehensive Defence Review which had to take place in the context of a drastic reduction in the defence budget. Callaghan had at an early stage identified defence as a prime target for savings in public expenditure. This was partly because the defence shopping list included so many big-ticket items and partly because overseas defence commitments had significant implications for the balance of payments. Callaghan had accordingly persuaded the Cabinet to agree to a £2000 million ceiling on annual defence spending, to be achieved by 1970. The current spending plan (inherited from the preceding Conservative government) would breach that ceiling by about 16%, making the need for cost reductions not only essential but urgent. Almost as soon as he had returned from Washington, Healey despatched a team of service personnel and ministry officials to begin discussions about the purchase of the F111 attack fighter. Healey knew that not only was this a cheaper alternative to going ahead with Britain's own TSR2, but that the American planes would be available sooner than the TSR2 which was still at the early stage of development and already running into problems. The TSR2 programme by this stage was costing around £1m a week, with no certainty of final success.

As a first step towards creating budget savings a decision was taken to cancel two projects – the development of the P1154, vertical take-off and landing fighter plane and the HS681, a transport aircraft. The order for the P1154 – which had been intended for use by both the Navy and the RAF – was however replaced for an order for the RAF of a similar plane, from which the P1154 had evolved. This new order would in time lead to the airforce being equipped with the now famous Harrier Jump Jet. The cancelled HS681 was replaced with an order for the American-built Hercules – a transport plane that, in one version or another, continued to be the backbone of RAF logistics into the twenty-first century. So although Healey had cancelled two projects, the replacements he had commissioned were good choices that proved their worth over many years.

Cancellation of the TSR2, considered a high-prestige project, was always going to be more problematic. Because the plane was of British manufacture there were

British jobs at stake and Healey needed to square his colleague, the Minister of Aviation, Roy Jenkins. Eventually Jenkins was persuaded – in part because there seemed little hope that the TSR2, even if successfully built, would find an overseas market. But even with grudging support from Jenkins, Healey had to work hard to get, and only by a narrow margin, the Cabinet's agreement to scrap the TSR2.

All these contractual changes had helped to reduce the projected budget by about £220 million a year. This still left a shortfall of around £200 million to save annually in order to meet the agreed ceiling of £2000 million by 1970. The next project to be reviewed was a plan to equip Britain with a new fleet of aircraft carriers. The case for or against a carrier became a battleground between the RAF and the Navy. The RAF argued that an aircraft carrier was not cost-effective and that more firepower could be provided more cheaply by using the new F111 planes from land-bases. The Navy made a poor case in response, not making enough of the argument that a carrier's role was particularly to provide aircover for the fleet's other ships and not envisaging at all the scenario in which Britain would need airpower at sea at an impossibly long distance from any land base (as would happen years later in the Falklands).[*]

In carrying out the Defence Review. Healey was

---

[*] Although this possibility was not then advanced as an argument for retention of a carrier capability it is likely that the idea would have been dismissed at the time as improbably unlikely.

uncomfortably aware that the country's traditional strategic positioning and undertakings had shaved the thin red line to an unsustainable extent. In recent years the UK had, on repeated occasions, operated without any strategic reserve at all and frequently its agreed complement of forces deployed in Germany had had to be reduced in order to meet deployment needs elsewhere. One of the consequences of this overstretch (which was compounded by a decline in recruitment) was the straitjacket it imposed on the adjustment or realignment of defence policy. The lack of any meaningful operational flexibility constrained both the response to any unforeseen emergency and the ability to operate proactively in ways that could reduce the possibilities of instability in the future.

But Healey's opportunities to rescope the budget against a fresh assessment of priorities were always going to be limited. An obvious target for any recalibration of defence policy in a time of budgetary constraint was the burden of UK deployment 'East of Suez'. Cutting back on this burden could simultaneously reduce expenditure, improve the balance of payments and massively reduce pressure on military resources. Healey was never an advocate of complete withdrawal but at this stage any significant reduction in deployment in the Middle or Far East would have been rejected by Wilson who regarded Britain's status as a world power as being synonymous with an 'East of Suez' presence. "I want to make it quite clear," Wilson told the House of Commons in December 1964, "that whatever we may do in the field of cost effectiveness, value for money and a stringent review of expenditure, we cannot afford to relinquish our world role - our role which, for shorthand purposes, is sometimes called our "east of Suez" role…".

Within the Foreign Office too any idea of withdrawal was an unthinkable lowering of the flag, damaging to both national interests and prestige. A convenient ally in this resistance was the US, which strongly argued against any UK withdrawal from the Middle or Far East and, as a key contributor to the foreign loans Britain needed to stave off economic crisis, was in a position to back up its position with the implicit threat of cutting off or cutting back on any further financial support.

Given these tensions, the outcomes of Healey's defence review were more cautious than bold. There were to be reductions in the numbers of service personnel in Cyprus and Malta and a complete withdrawal from Aden (which was in any case coming to the end of its time as a British Protectorate). The most controversial outcome of the review was the cancellation of the project to build a new aircraft carrier (a project which had been initiated in the Macmillan years). This decision provoked the resignation of the First Sea Lord and of the Navy Minister, Christopher Mayhew. who objected not just to the cancellation of the aircraft carrier but also to the principle of shaping defence policy to the budget. In his view the policy should come first and the means then provided to pay for it.

The cancellation of the aircraft carrier caused enough controversy to ensure that Healey's White Paper could not be described as a damp squib, but its overall scope fell well short of anything that could be described as a strategic reset. It had, however, more or less made the savings required, though Healey acknowledged that a further £50 million would have to be cut in order to reduce the defence budget to the Treasury's ceiling of £2000 million by 1970.

Within weeks of the White Paper's publication the 1966 General Election was underway. The party manifesto boasted that the defence review was evidence of a "new realism" but described it as being "only the first step in a phased programme which should bring substantial cuts both in commitments and in expenditure by 1969-70". This ambiguous statement could be taken to mean no more than the progressive working through of the cuts already announced, but also allowed for the possibility that further defence cuts would be announced in due course.

The manifesto had boldly declared that Britain had, economically speaking, "weathered the storm" but it would be only a few months before a freshly-developing exchange crisis made it painfully plain this was no more than wishful thinking. By 20 July, Wilson was announcing the need for further deflationary measures to reduce demand, including a cut in defence spending of £100 million.

The implication was plain. The proportion of the defence budget tied up in the 'East of Suez' deployment was huge. The Far East commitment as a whole amounted to around £200 million annually, of which around £40 million was spent just on our base in Singapore. The reduction that Healey was now required to make made it inevitable that it was to the east that he had to look to find it. By October 1966 Healey was ready to brief a small group of the Cabinet about his plan to cut deployment in south-east Asia by half. Crossman was the only member of the group to suggest that Healey should go the whole hog and end all East of Suez commitment. Healey's answer was that "our allies would never allow that".[12]

By February 1967, as part of his defence estimates for the coming financial year, Healey was able to announce that 25000 men and 6000 service families currently stationed outside Europe would be returned to the UK. As a result of this and other measures he expected defence spending to come-in just under the target set (in 1964 prices) of £2000 million a year. The *Guardian* praised Healey for bringing "order, logic and a scheme of priorities for spending into the biggest and least manageable spending department in Whitehall".[13] But the Opposition and even some of his Cabinet colleagues believed that he had not done enough. Significantly, a large number of Labour MPs abstained in the Commons vote to approve the estimates. These political pressures and the worsening financial situation were causing even Wilson to back away from his commitment to a world role in defence.

The governments of Australia, New Zealand, Malaysia and Singapore knew from the February Defence White Paper that the British presence there was to be reduced.

But in a series of meetings during the spring and early summer, they were given the further news that complete withdrawal was being considered by the mid-1970s. This news was not well-received but in early July, against the advice of Herbert Bowden (the Secretary of State for Commonwealth Affairs), the Cabinet agreed a new Defence White Paper (the third in two years) which announced that withdrawal from the UK's bases in Singapore and Malaysia would be completed "in the middle 1970s".

A few days after the White Paper appeared, Callaghan, speaking in the House of Commons in response to an Opposition motion of censure on the economy, declared "the new defence policy published last week will during the coming years bring into harmony British economic policy, British foreign policy and British defence policy. The three will march together for the first time since 1945...Last week's White Paper will, in my view, be regarded as a historical landmark in the success story of the Government's policy to reconcile military and foreign obligations with economic strength."[14]

This confident reference to 'economic strength', cannot have been based on anything more than a Micawberish confidence that 'something would turn up'. The search for that 'something' would become increasingly desperate. By September, Callaghan was reduced to scratching around to raise penny-packet loans from Swiss banks, the inadequacy of which in comparison with Britain's needs only served to draw attention to Callaghan's psychological capacity to integrate breezy confidence with humiliating despair.

On November 16th, when it was revealed to the Cabinet that the Chancellor and the Prime Minister had agreed to devalue, Callaghan ran rapidly through a list of cuts in public expenditure that would need to accompany the move – one of these was a further reduction of the following year's defence budget by £100 million. Once more Healey was into the process of cutting. At this point it was evident that the withdrawal from Singapore and Malaysia could not be delayed until the mid-1970s. In the January following devaluation the Cabinet agreed that our withdrawal from Singapore and the Gulf would be completed in 1971.

By now Roy Jenkins had replaced Callaghan as Chancellor and the decision to accelerate withdrawal from the Far East conveniently opened the door for him to call for further defence cuts – in particular, on the grounds of the reduced role implied by withdrawal, the cancellation of the purchase of the American F111 aircraft. Despite Healey's dogged resistance (and fierce opposition from George Brown), the Cabinet finally agreed with Jenkins and, on January 16th, amongst the cuts in public expenditure announced by Wilson was the confirmation that the order for the American planes was to be cancelled.

Healey did not allow his case to go by default. Tony Benn, who voted for cancelling the F111 contract, recorded his admiration for the way in which the Defence Secretary argued his corner: "Healey made the most formidable case in favour of the F111, calmly and quietly, and with considerable power of argument".[15] Denis's biographer argues that Healey's longstanding position as a political loner prevented him from winning over colleagues to his side. Healey's preference to be always a lone-ranger was no doubt unhelpful in the F111 crisis, but it seems unlikely that any alliance could have given him the votes he needed – the Cabinet voted 12 to 9 for cancellation. The reality was that those in favour of cancellation were a disparate group. Some were concerned only to make the necessary cuts in spending, others were temperamentally inclined to resist defence spending in the first place and some were in favour of purchasing the F111 but believed that another of Jenkins' cuts – the postponement of the raising of the school leaving age – would be presentationally toxic if, at the same time, a large spend on military aircraft was allowed to go ahead.

By the time of this setback, Healey had been at the Ministry of Defence, in a state of almost continuous retrenchment, for three years. This was longer than any previous holder of the office[*] since Winston Churchill during the Second World War. He was ready for a change and when George Brown flounced out of the Cabinet in March 1968 it created a vacancy for the post for which Healey was especially qualified – Foreign Secretary. But by then Wilson was in one of his recurring states of suspicion about attempts by his colleagues to oust him. In

---

[*] Until 1964 all Healey's predecessors had been Ministers of Defence. But in that year the post was elevated to that of Secretary of State for Defence.

this mood he was not going to offer any advancement that might add to the credibility of a potential rival. Both Jenkins and Callaghan had now acquired the prestige of having held two of the 'great offices of state', Wilson was in no mood to add distinction to another perceived rival by making Healey his new Foreign Secretary.

Wilson was at least right to recognise Healey's potential as a rival. He was not a leading contender, like Jenkins or Callaghan, but he was clearly in contention. His public profile had been generally subdued – he was too hard-working and self-contained to have cultivated the press relationships that helped to keep his colleagues' names in the papers. But an appearance he made on David Frost's show in late December 1967 had provided him with an extended opportunity to display some of his argumentative flair before a large television audience.

The invitation from Frost had been to be interviewed about defence but Frost found Healey more than a match for the interviewer. Healey believed he had scored a particularly wounding point when he turned to the audience and asked them to agree with him that Frost had not been properly briefed by his researchers. Healey thought that this had particularly struck home because Frost liked to create the impression that he did his own research. An additional wounding edge to Healey's strategy was that it turned the table on Frost who was fond of inviting his audience to show how much they sided with him rather than his interviewee. The *Times* described Healey's performance in the interview as a "courageous stand under the fire of hostile questions" and recorded the opinion that "Mr Frost came out a bad loser."[16]

Wilson did not watch the interview live – at the time he was spending his Christmas holiday in his home on the Scilly Isles. But he was briefed the next day on what had been said and was infuriated by an exchange during the programme in which Frost had accused the "Number 10 publicity machine" of circulating to the press the story that Healey was in favour of selling arms to South Africa. Healey piously denied that anyone in the Cabinet would use publicity in that way, though he was well-aware that Wilson was a past-master at leaking and habitually used leaks to advantage himself and embarrass or discredit one or more of his colleagues.

Given the history of suspicion and antagonism it was hardly surprising that Wilson rejected the chance to move Healey to the Foreign Office in Brown's place. Healey might at that point have resigned and looked for another career outside Parliament – at one time there was even a rumour that he was about to be offered the soon-to-be-vacant post of Secretary General of NATO. But although deeply demoralised by his failure to retain the F111 - "the first time in my life I've seen him really broken," his wife recorded - he determined to stay at Defence.

There were to be more battles over defence cuts, but Healey, despite all the ground that he had had to give, was still full of fight and he managed to beat off attempts by Jenkins and others to abandon the work on a Harrier Jump-Jet. In doing this he saved the aircraft that, in an updated form, went on to play a critical part in the

Falklands War in 1982. There was another attempted squeeze on his budget when a fresh economic crisis prompted Jenkins once again to seek savings from defence. But by now Healey was dug in for a final stand – he threatened resignation if the proposed cuts were made and, partly because of his resistance and partly because the economic situation slightly eased, Jenkins backed off.

In the year before the 1970 General Election, Healey was sounded-out over his willingness to become the party's campaign manager, with direct oversight of the campaign itself and the management of Transport House, the party headquarters. But Healey, despite considerable pressure, turned the idea down. It did not appeal; Healey was a politician more interested in policy and action than in politicking itself. Although when the actual campaign began in the summer of 1970, Healey did play a leading part at the party press conferences, in the party-political broadcasts and in touring the country to stump-up votes.

Despite all the troubles of the Wilson government the polls did suggest that there was a chance of re-election. Just a few weeks before election day the polls were showing a clear lead for Labour. In one poll the party's lead reached eleven points. Wilson was sufficiently confident to map out the appointments for his next Cabinet – including the decision to move Jenkins to the Foreign Office and to install Healey as Chancellor of the Exchequer. But in the final days of campaigning – in hot June weather – the latest trade figures were released showing another deficit in the balance of payments. These bad trade figures were in fact only a temporary imbalance due to the purchase of two jumbo jets, but the inevitable impression was that Labour was still not competent at managing the economy.

Healey retained his seat, but overall it was a bad night for the Wilson government. The Tories secured a forty-three seat lead over Labour and an overall majority of thirty. For Healey the result came as a "bewildering shock". But despite all the bruising arguments that had centred around defence – or more particularly around its budget – and despite all the cuts he had eventually been compelled to implement, Healey looked back on his years as Minister of Defence as a period of relative success. He remains probably the best-informed defence minister in its departmental history and his ability to forensically analyse a case and trenchantly argue it through on its merits or against its defects meant that the service chiefs had at their head the most formidable ally they could have wished for. He moulded what had previously been separate service ministries into a unified Ministry of Defence and introduced modern management approaches to streamline its work. He managed the East of Suez fall-back with considerable skill and although many projects were scrapped on economic grounds, he was able successfully to defend developments that were to be of crucial importance in coming years.

It had been almost six years of immensely hard work – with the exception of the Chancellor of the Exchequer no minister had faced greater challenges or had to fight fiercer battles. And despite his vigorous pugnacity and his trenchant style of argument, Healey had won widespread admiration from his Cabinet colleagues. Roy Jenkins, for example, despite having had bitter arguments with Healey over defence cuts, regarded him as an "outstanding Minister".[17]

Wilson owed Healey a personal debt of gratitude. Healey had not been an unqualified admirer of the Prime Minister but despite differences and suspicions had remained essentially loyal. By the end of the 1964-70 government, Healey was clearly a potential successor to Wilson, but had never been an active plotter against him. Wilson did, however, deny him the Treasury brief he had been promised if Labour had won. Instead Healey was appointed as Shadow Foreign Secretary, a role for which he was supremely equipped after his many years of involvement in international affairs. But just two years later he was on the move again when Roy Jenkins quit the Shadow Cabinet over what he regarded as Wilson's hypocritical double-dealing regarding Edward Heath's policy of negotiating Britain's entry into the Common Market. This created a vacancy for the Shadow Chancellorship and Healey happily accepted this move which would, for the first time in his career, expose him to a political challenge which daunted and to an extent unnerved him.

Healey's performances as Shadow Chancellor were uncertain and unconvincing, an impression made worse by the fact that despite clearly not having yet mastered his brief, his speeches and interventions in the Commons continued to be marked by what the political commentator Peter Jenkins had once described as

Healey's customary air of "impatient superiority". But, despite these limitations, when the Heath government fell in the *Who Governs Britain?* election of 1974, Wilson appointed Healey as his Chancellor of the Exchequer. Given the thinness of Healey's fulfilment of the shadow role this was a risky appointment – a risk made far greater by the economic situation.

Within a few weeks Healey had to deliver his first budget. When Healey rose to present it to the House he admitted that the period of its preparation had been "the most exhausting three weeks of my life".[18] But these early days turned out to be just a foretaste of what was to come. In retrospect his turbulent years at the Ministry of Defence proved to be a walk in the park compared with the torrid battles in which Healey would have to engage over the coming years. The state of the economy was even worse than it had been in 1964. As Chancellor he had to deal with a massive balance of payments crisis, partly caused by a massive hike in oil prices following the Arab-Israeli War, overseas speculation against the pound, spiralling inflation, rising unemployment, and trade union pressure on wages. The economic crisis would eventually reach a level so critical as to require borrowing at an eyewatering level, including a five billion dollar credit line from the US and other banks and then another loan of nearly four billion dollars from the International Monetary Fund, this last a credit arrangement which came attached to humiliating conditions.

When, at last, the economy was showing positive signs of recovery and the opinion polls began to look good for

Labour, it seemed as though a General Election in 1978 (one year earlier than necessary) might keep the party in government. But James Callaghan (who at that stage had been Wilson's successor as Prime Minister for only two years) decided to hold-off until the following year. It was Sunny Jim's final miscalculation. By the spring of 1969 the country had gone through the misery of the 'winter of discontent' during which the trade union movement had, in an orgy of self-destructive strike action, queered Labour's pitch. The Tories entered government under Margaret Thatcher.

Healey returned to the backbenches after a continuous run of five years as Chancellor, from the time when Wilson returned to Downing Street to when Callaghan left. But the battle-hardened Healey had further struggles to face. He was the obvious candidate to succeed Callaghan as Party Leader and had Callaghan stood down immediately or soon after his General Election defeat it was as good as certain that Healey would have been his successor. But Callaghan having dithered about the date of that election then proceeded to hang out his tenure as Leader of the Opposition. In the meantime, the Labour Party, particularly in terms of the active members at the local constituency level, was undergoing a sea-change. Entryism – the infiltration of the membership by left-wing extremists – was changing the party landscape.

Up to this point the election of the Labour leader had always depended only on the votes of sitting Labour MPs, but the activists on the left had secured a forthcoming change in the rules to ensure that the leadership would be elected by a formula combining votes of the constituency parties with those of the trades unions. On the face of it this change could be represented as a more democratic process. In fact, the domination of the left-wing activists at local level and the unrepresentative nature of the block votes exercised by the trade unions meant that this change was using ostensibly democratic means to secure undemocratic ends. The imminence of this rule change finally prompted Callaghan to jump - in the knowledge that if he further delayed resigning then the election of his successor would, under the new rules shortly to be introduced, be won by a hard-left candidate.

So the Labour MPs had, for the last time in the party, the right to choose their leader. Healey, in the meantime, had lost some support, but the expectation was that he would still be comfortably elected by his fellow MPs as clearly not only the most qualified to succeed Callaghan but also the most able to stand up to the pressures from the extreme left of the party. But it was not to be Healey's day. A significant number of his erstwhile supporters defected because of pressure from their local parties. Others, who in their hearts were fully supportive of Healey, turned out to be paradoxically willing to withhold their vote from him precisely because they felt that the best way to defeat left-wing extremism was to provoke a split, and that the election of a left-wing leader would help to make more likely the formation of a breakaway centrist party to which they would be then able to transfer their allegiance. The final binding agent in this curious anti-Healey coalition was the number of MPs who actively disliked Healey, who resented his aggressive brand of politics and in some cases had been on the receiving end of his belittling tongue.

The result of the election was that the leftish Michael Foot was elected leader by the Parliamentary Party. Foot was a man of many gifts, unfortunately none of them applicable to the task of party leadership or management and so many Labour MPs were relieved or at least reassured when one of Foot's first acts was to appoint Healey as his deputy. Healey's role as deputy offered at least the hope of ensuring some rationality at the top. But this hope was for the left-wingers a threat. Healey's place as the new Deputy Leader immediately came under attack and it became clear that under the new rules an attempt would be made to replace him.

Meanwhile, on 26th March 1981, the Social Democratic Party was launched, an overtly breakaway movement from traditional Labour and an attempt to seize centrist ground. Just a few days later, on appropriately enough April Fools' Day, Tony Benn announced his intention to challenge Healey for the deputy's office. Benn, an MP since 1950 and a foolishly incapable minister in both Wilson's governments, had by this stage abandoned any attempt to make politics about results and instead turned to the easier business of protest. The ensuing contest between Benn and Healey became a vicious battle. At open meetings, organised by the Party for the two candidates to speak, Healey was repeatedly shouted down by mobs of angry Bennites. In the interests of his one-sided concept of free speech Benn did nothing to restrain his supporters. Even Michael Foot, himself an inflammatory rabble-rouser in his palmy days, was shocked by the tactics of Benn and his supporters. "Planned hooliganism" was Foot's opinion of the Bennite campaign, though when it came to the ballot for the post of deputy leader Foot did not vote for Healey – or for that matter for Benn either.

When it finally came to the voting for the deputy leader's post, Healey scraped a win by less than 1% of the votes cast. The win was marginal, the damage in terms of the party's image was colossal. The news pictures and footage of the contest, with its baying mobs of hard-left Bennite supporters, had added the final confirmatory touch to a widespread perception of Labour as characterised, in Healey's judgment, by "disunity, extremism, crankiness and general unfitness to govern".[19] That image was firmly cemented in place by the adoption of a manifesto for the 1983 election so stuffed with the demands of the extreme left as to make Labour unelectable even before the polls had opened. One senior Labour MP, Gerald Kaufmann, described the manifesto as the "longest suicide note in history". The result was a foregone conclusion; Labour's vote dropped by over 9% and the Party sustained a net loss of over 50 seats.

Foot resigned, but Healey decided not to run again for the leadership and stood down from the post of deputy. Foot was replaced by the left-leaning but generally right-thinking Neil Kinnock and Healey was replaced by the sensible figure of Roy Hattersley. Healey continued to serve as an MP until 1992, after which he went to the

House of Lords as Baron Healey of Riddlesden. He lived to the age of 98, by which time he had established a reputation as an older statesman, a gifted photographer and author. He was often spoken of as the "best Prime Minister we never had".

Healey was battle-hardened long before he became an MP. As a Landings Officer during the campaign in Southern Italy he had masterminded complex logistical operations under devastating fire. It turned out to be a metaphor for his life in politics. He never shrank from a fight – and he initiated many of them. He was highly intelligent, intensely well-informed and masterful in argument. In those qualities he resembled Richard Crossman, but whereas Crossman enjoyed an argument for its own sake, for Healey argument was always directed to a purpose. He was always convinced of the rightness of his own position (again unlike Crossman who would deliberately assume a particular position just for the sake of being difficult) and saw no reason to hide his sense of superiority over those who argued against him. But success in politics is not simply a matter of demolishing the arguments of others, it is about mobilising others in support of your position.

He was a superb Minister of Defence – no one else could have argued the case against military retrenchment so knowledgeably and so forcefully. His civil servants and senior officers respected his expertise and drew considerable strength from it. He was on top of his policy agenda; sufficiently so to write himself large parts of the numerous defence white papers. Even if he did not always win the case against defence cuts, he was sufficiently powerful to keep the retrenchment within limits, for example enabling Britain to retreat from East of Suez while still preserving a considerable degree of international prestige.

Healey had many political admirers, but few political friends. The political commentator Peter Jenkins described Healey as "the cat who walked alone". He worked immensely hard but was too indifferent to his own support to spend time cultivating it. And his impatience with what he saw as weaknesses in the arguments or ideas of others led him into exchanges that could be brutally wounding for those on the receiving end of his put-downs. His ultimate weakness, perhaps the essential reason why he never reached the very top, was not that he had few friends but that he had too many enemies.

7

Roy Jenkins:
Politics à la Carte

On Sunday 12 July 1964 readers of the *Observer* were able to read the first of what would be two articles provocatively titled *How Not To Run A Public Corporation*. The pieces were written by Roy Jenkins, since 1950 the MP for Stechford, a constituency on the eastern side of Birmingham. Jenkins had established a reputation for occasional journalism and had actually won an award for his innovative style of in-depth analysis. He had been writing features for the *Observer* since 1962 and the two articles which appeared in successive weeks in mid-July 1964 on the troubles of a public corporation were a dissection of the way in which the British Overseas Aircraft Corporation (which would eventually be subsumed into British Airways) had got itself into serious difficulties through dithering over whether it should equip itself with the American Boeing 707 aircraft or buy instead the British-built Vickers VC10– dithering compounded by muddled-thinking at the Ministry of Aviation which controlled BOAC. In his articles Jenkins was particularly critical of what he saw as a lack of hard-headed economic analysis at the heart of the decision-making process at both BOAC and the Ministry of Aviation. He finished by warning that this was precisely the kind of critical analysis that had yet to be applied to the plan to build an Anglo-French supersonic aircraft – the Concord (at that stage still spelled in Britain without a final 'e').

These articles caught the eye of Harold Wilson, then still Leader of the Opposition, who immediately marked Jenkins down as a possibility for the Ministry of Aviation, should Labour win that year's General Election. So it was largely on the back of those *Observer* pieces that, on the Sunday morning immediately after that election, Jenkins went to see Wilson in Downing Street to become the new Minister of Aviation.

Roy Harris Jenkins was born, on Armistice Day 1920, in Pontypool, South Wales. He was to be the only child of a highly political family. His father was a trade union activist and a prominent figure in local politics who briefly went to prison in 1926 for his part in a mass picket supporting a miners' strike (his absence was misrepresented to the young Roy as due to an extended visit to Germany). Roy's father became a County Councillor, a local magistrate, an official of the Welsh Miners' Federation and had a seat on the Labour party's National Executive. In 1935 he was returned as the Labour MP for Pontypool and just two years later Clement Attlee chose him as his Parliamentary Private Secretary. So by the age of 15 Roy Jenkins was already coming into contact with prominent Labour personalities – not only Attlee, but Herbert Morrison, Hugh Dalton, Ernest Bevin and others.

Although Roy had won a scholarship to the prestigious Monmouth Grammar School his father chose to send him instead to the local secondary school, where he encountered rather indifferent teaching. But his father was also intent on Roy getting to Oxford and so at the age of sixteen he spent nearly a year at what was the rather pretentiously named Cardiff University College – it was in fact something more like what we would today call a sixth-form college. But Roy had better teaching than he had received at school and, in particular, learned to write essays that would meet the expectations of Oxford. He became so practised at this that one of his tutors at Balliol College would eventually tell him "I am not sure how much you know but you write it in a fine style which I could not teach you and which will be of more value to you than anything I could."[1]

For Roy, writing was to become almost a parallel career to his life in politics. He would become a prolific writer of book reviews, essays, full-length biographies and studies of political history. This body of work would eventually earn Jenkins so much distinction that Harold Wilson one day observed rather ruefully that while he had only a political life, with nothing much else to fall back on, Roy always had his books.

The time spent at Cardiff paid off. Roy applied for an Oxford scholarship but although he was not successful at that, he was instead offered an unsubsidised place at Balliol College where he would read Philosophy, Politics, and Economics. By the time Jenkins arrived at Balliol the college had long since established a reputation as what

Jenkins himself would describe as "a great forcing house" of politicians.[2] His fellow-students at the College included Anthony Crosland, Denis Healey and Edward Heath. Jenkins inevitably involved himself in both the Labour Club and the Oxford Union and what with those activities and a fair degree of socialising his academic studies took very much a back seat. It was only thanks to a couple of months of intensive revision prior to his finals that he managed to gain a First, though it was made clear to him that it had been by a scrape.

For most of his time at Oxford, Jenkins had a busy social life but the closest thing to a romantic attachment was to his fellow undergraduate Anthony Crosland. The intensity of their relationship only adjusted to a level of nothing more than close friendship when, a year before his Finals, Jenkins met, at a Fabian Summer School, his future wife, a Cambridge undergraduate named Jennifer Morris. It was 1945 before they married, but their partnership endured until his death over sixty years later. The endurance of this marriage did not however exclude for Roy countless affairs. For Jenkins, love, as it would later be in his politics, was never to be confined to the set menu.

By the time Jenkins had completed his Finals in June 1941 he was immediately eligible for conscription, but the War Office deferred his joining-up for six months until, in February 1942, Jenkins reported for training preparatory to joining a Field Artillery Regiment. It is easy to misjudge the life of a soldier at this stage. Their common experience might be thought to be fighting in

North Africa or up against the Japanese in the Far East. In fact for the great mass of soldiery the daily experience was an apparently never-ending life of training on home soil. This was to be Jenkins' experience for nearly two years until the end of 1943 when he was posted for special intelligence work at Bletchley Park, the home of Britain's top-secret code-breaking operation.

On the face of it, the rationale for this transfer is not obvious. Jenkins had no special gift for mathematics and only a very limited knowledge of German. What he could bring to the work, however, was the same combination of abilities that would serve him so well throughout his life – high intelligence, sustained concentration and the ability to break a problem down into its component parts. He realised, for example, that he did not need to become at all fluent in German in order to pick out what was essential in decoded messages. All he needed was a comprehensive mental dictionary of the key vocabulary. He set to compiling giant lists of German words with their translation and his retentive memory enabled him to mentally store these words, to discern their forms when they started to emerge from their coded form and so recognise what any message concerned, even if he could not understand the message's overall sense.

In the final years of the war Jenkins started actively looking for a parliamentary seat. He made unsuccessful attempts to win selection for a series of safe seats in the West Midlands but lost each time to rival candidates who would be duly returned for Labour in the 1945 General Election. In January 1946 he was demobbed and went to work for the Industrial and Commercial Finance Corporation, an organisation founded the year before by the Bank of England to create a mechanism by which credit could be provided to medium-sized and smaller businesses. But while working there, on assessing applications for business loans, Jenkins continued to look for an opportunity to get into Parliament.

In April 1946, his father died and his parliamentary seat became vacant. It was almost inevitable that Jenkins should be included in the selection process to find a candidate for the by-election but, despite the intimacy of the family tie, he was not eventually selected. It was almost certainly for the best, because a seat that can be characterised as 'inherited', is inevitably open to suspicion that it would not have been gained on merit.

But in 1948 an opening appeared at last. The Labour MP for a run-down constituency in London, Central Southwark, resigned and although the seat was to disappear in a pending boundary reorganisation, it was an opportunity that Jenkins could not resist. Jenkins was at last selected and on April 30th 1948 he finally became an MP. His maiden speech was well-received; he had taken the trouble to write it out and memorise it beforehand which may have given an over-impressive sense of an ability to speak extemporaneously – in any event he was never to repeat this memory trick in the House again. He had at last achieved his parliamentary goal, but he knew he was living on borrowed time. The next election would be due in 1950 and with his current seat becoming redundant he needed to find a new parliamentary home.

Although he was now a sitting MP, Jenkins did not find it easy to find another constituency willing to select him. But after a number of unsuccessful attempts in London and elsewhere he was finally chosen as the Labour candidate for the constituency of Stechford, an area on the outskirts of Birmingham to the south-east of the city centre. It was an area that was then rapidly expanding, as a result of developments including a large area of newly-built council housing in the district of Shard End. His selection came just a few months before the General Election in the late February of 1950. Jenkins came home comfortably with a majority of over twelve thousand. He would continue to represent the seat for just over a quarter of a century.

Given Jenkins' later reputation as a man of the political middle ground (there was even a nod to this in the title of his autobiography *A Life at the Centre*) his standpoint at this early stage of his career was distinctly leftist. He was, for example, a great admirer of Aneurin Bevan and supported both wider nationalisation and even the assimilation of public schools into the state system. In 1951 he wrote a pamphlet, *Fair Shares for the Rich*, the title of which was a clever piece of Swiftian mockery, because its essential argument was that the rich should, through punitive taxation, have their share drastically reduced to an equitable level.

This leftish phase was not to last long and even at the time did not run that deep. His fellow-MP Woodrow Wyatt (who had beaten him for the nomination at Aston, Birmingham in 1945) characterised Jenkins at this stage as being "caught between two worlds".[3] Gradually Jenkins moved towards a position that although still socialist was distinctly pragmatic. For example, when in the spring of 1951 Bevan quit the Cabinet (together with Wilson) over the introduction of some prescription charges, Jenkins took the view that these charges were reasonable and justifiable. By 1953 Jenkins would publish a book called *Pursuit of Progress*, which was a clear counter-argument to the Bevanite cause. Increasingly Hugh Gaitskell could rely on Jenkins as part of a group providing a voice on the party's right and by the time in 1959 when Labour lost its third General Election in a row, Jenkins was amongst those who blamed the loss in part on a too-ready identification with old-style socialism including an over-heavy emphasis on nationalisation.

Just a few months before that election Jenkins clearly established himself as a standard-bearer in the move towards less control and restriction in the area of private morality, when his parliamentary support and advocacy led to the passing of the Obscene Publications Act of 1959, a major liberalisation of the law which had until then suppressed material judged to be offensive to public decency. His campaign had begun in 1954 when he had become part of a newly-formed action committee set up by the Society of Authors. This committee drafted a bill which aimed to allow against any charge of obscene publication a defence of merit – a plea that the work was of literary, artistic or other merit. A bill on these lines was introduced by Jenkins under the 10-minute rule in March 1955. It was unsuccessful, as was a second attempt when the bill, with some modifications, was presented by a Conservative MP, Hugh Fraser. Another try was made in 1957, but was not given enough parliamentary time to succeed. In 1958 another attempt was made and despite attempts by the Crown's Law Officers to subvert the bill, it was Jenkins who persuaded the Home Secretary, R A ("Rab") Butler to relax the objections and enable the Obscene Publications Act to reach the statute book.

Just two years later the Act would be triumphantly vindicated when Penguin Books was found not guilty of obscenity in publishing D H Lawrence's *Lady Chatterley's Lover*. Addressing the jury the Counsel for the Prosecution, Mervyn Griffith-Jones, condemned the book with a phrase which in turn condemned him to ridicule: "Is it a book you would wish even your wife or servants to read?" The literary merit justification, under the new Act, provided the defence with an open goal and a string of witnesses, including Jenkins, entered the witness box to testify to the book's good character. The jury agreed and Lady Chatterley left the court a free woman. It was a landmark case, but for Jenkins the passing of the Act and its subsequent vindication was also a marker. His leading role in the campaign for reform had established him as a prominent defender of social liberalism, an early demonstration of the attitudes that would enable him as Home Secretary, six years later, to support the introduction of major social reforms.

Jenkins' success in securing the passage of the Obscene Publications Bill came just a few months before the 1959 General Election. There were encouraging signs for

Labour in the election lead-up. Hugh Gaitskell's campaign seemed to be going well and then, just over a week before polling day, he carelessly announced that an incoming Labour Government would not introduce any increase in income tax. This promise was widely scorned as being either blind to economic realities or just dishonest. The Conservatives duly won the election and Harold Macmillan remained as Prime Minister.

Gaitskell would not live to fight another General Election. In 1963 his sudden death removed him from the political scene, just when Labour seemed again in the ascendant. Jenkins was badly affected by the death. In an obituary for the *Daily Mail* he wrote "It is by far the biggest unexpected loss to British politics this century. Without him a shadow falls over the whole political prospect." Forty years later, in his last-ever piece of journalism, Jenkins, only days before his own death, wrote for the *Guardian* another tribute to Gaitskell. "He was", he wrote, "the one politician over the past 50 years whom I have loved".

In his memoirs, Roy Jenkins recalled that when, soon after Gaitskell's death, the contenders for the party leadership started to emerge, he experienced a feeling of "revulsion" at the prospect of a Wilson victory. In the contest Jenkins chose to support George Brown, believing that despite his obvious problems, he was a man of great intellect and good judgment. When Wilson won, Jenkins felt a sense of deflation and, for a time, considering leaving politics following an approach to sound him out about his willingness to become the next

Editor of *The Economist*. While he was considering this, he went to see Wilson to let him know about the offer. This was not so much to put Wilson in the picture about Jenkins' possible departure from the Commons as a disguised attempt to truffle-out some hints about what plans Wilson might have for Jenkins in the event of a Labour win. Wilson gave Jenkins a clear signal that he might expect some kind of a government post, though not, at least at first, in the Cabinet. By the time the 1964 General Election came, Jenkins had rejected the idea of leaving politics and threw himself into campaigning in Stechford in the hope of not just a Labour victory but also some initial step into government.

Once it was clear that Wilson had won, Jenkins had to spend an anxious two days waiting to hear whether Wilson would come good on his hint about a place for him in government. It was not until the evening of the Saturday after the election that Jenkins was formally invited to meet with Wilson on the Sunday morning. That same evening, however, Jenkins was tipped-off by George Brown that when he went to see Wilson he was going to be offered the Ministry of Aviation. Jenkins was considerably encouraged by this news – not least because it meant that he was going to be given a department of his own, rather than being second-in-command to someone else, and that it was an area of policy in which he already had considerable knowledge.

The meeting at Downing Street on the Sunday morning was even more encouraging. Wilson indicated that the Ministry of Aviation would be Jenkins' home for only a year or two, after which he would have a new post within the Cabinet. Wilson's idea at this stage was that the Ministry of Aviation should restrict itself to the management of civil aviation and that the business of procurement of civil and military aircraft should be transferred to the Board of Trade. But Jenkins was able to use his acquired expertise in the subject to persuade Wilson to let the Ministry retain all its current responsibilities without hiving-off any of its functions.

Once installed in his Ministry, Jenkins had to undergo several days of intensive briefing to bring him up to speed on his new responsibilities. The management of civil aviation, including aircraft procurement, was as already explained an area in which he had considerable knowledge. But the procurement of military aircraft was completely outside his experience, as were the intricacies of rocketry and various space initiatives. But the most immediate priority was the matter of Concorde.

The joint decision to build a Franco-British supersonic airliner had been reached in November 1962 when bilateral projects of that kind were hoped by the Conservative government to help win over French resistance to British membership of the Common Market. But at the time when the agreement to build Concorde was signed, there was as yet no detailed design of the proposed aircraft, let alone any projected costings. All that existed was a three-view drawing that committed the design to nothing more specific than a delta wing and rear-mounted engines. Without a design or detailed specification, the best forecast of how much this would all cost was in the region of £150 million. But when Sir Richard Way, Permanent Secretary at the Ministry of Aviation, appeared before the Public Accounts Committee in the same month as the agreement was signed, he had to admit that this £150 million price tag was "not a great deal more than an inspired guess".

By October 1964 the estimated cost had risen to £280 million, but although a substantial increase there was no reason to believe that this estimate was any more realistic than the guesswork of two years earlier. Even under the Conservative Government there had been growing concern about the viability of the project. In July 1964 the then Prime Minister, Sir Alec Douglas-Home, received. from a senior official, a secret memorandum which acknowledged that "The rational course would probably be to drop the Concord".[4]

Given this background of concern about unquantified costs it was unsurprising that within days of the 1964 election George Brown and Jim Callaghan decided (against the advice of Douglas Jay, President of the Board of Trade) that Concorde should be cancelled. Jenkins, whose department was responsible for Concorde was not consulted and the first he knew of the decision was on his third day as Minister when his Permanent Secretary alerted him to the intention to include an announcement of the cancellation in the forthcoming White Paper, *The Economic Situation*. Jenkins learned that the draft of the White Paper was to be discussed at the following day's cabinet meeting and he got agreement to join the meeting to put the case for not cancelling – or at least for not cancelling at this stage and certainly not for in effect issuing the French government with an abrupt *démarche*. Jenkins was, however, unable to persuade his Cabinet colleagues to reverse Brown and Callaghan's decision and when the White Paper appeared a few days later it contained what was in effect an only-slightly-coded announcement of a unilateral decision to cancel: "The Government have already communicated to the French Government their wish to re-examine urgently the Concorde project".

It turned out that Jenkins was entirely right to anticipate serious difficulties with the French government. Brown and Callaghan had mistakenly assumed that the basis of the Concorde project was nothing more than a conventional commercial contract that could be cancelled by either party. It turned out that the plane was actually subject to three contracts: two of them were commercial contracts, one of them between manufacturers of the airframes and one between manufactures of the engines. The third agreement was not at all a simple contract but an agreement between the French and British governments to proceed on the basis of shared work and costs. This inter-governmental agreement was not a contract as such but an international treaty. Any cancellation of Concorde would therefore be a breach of the treaty with all the potential penalties of law and damages.

The abrupt announcement in the White Paper caused a major breach in relations between the two governments. Late in October, Jenkins set off to Paris to meet with his counterpart, the French Minister of Works and Transport. Shortly before his departure Jenkins received a Foreign Office briefing warning him to prepare to be received with "cold enmity".[5] In fact the atmosphere was not explicitly hostile. But the French were determined to hold the British government to its treaty obligations and this sense of their legal rights was inevitably strengthened by a generous measure of Gallic *amour-propre*.

On November 5th Jenkins had to reply to an Opposition motion criticising the proposed cancellation. It was the first time that he had spoken in the House from the front bench. His speech was a skilful defence of the British position, making the most of the loophole that, whatever the British government's de facto position, the actual wording in the White Paper said only that the project should be urgently re-examined. He pointed out that the projected costs had already increased massively and were expected to spiral even further upwards at a time when the government had just inherited a huge trading deficit. Not only was there a vanishing prospect of a financial return on the project (the treaty optimistically made provision for the British and French governments to share equally in any profits made by the sale of Concorde) but the likelihood was that BOAC would need to be paid a subsidy to operate the aircraft when it eventually went into service. His speech was an extremely well-constructed argument and was judged impressive even by his opponents. Jenkins himself regarded this speech as his 'proving' moment in his life as a minister, the occasion when he became a "high-stake parliamentary player".

Discussions with the French dragged-on. It would not be accurate to describe them as negotiations because so far as the French were concerned there was nothing to negotiate. Instead of argument they chose instead to assume a position of innocent puzzlement – they must surely be misunderstanding the British because, of course, there could be no cancellation as the commitment was enshrined in an international treaty. Gradually the British realised they had no choice but to concede. The UK law officers advised that if the Wilson government unilaterally revoked the treaty, the French would be able to take the British before the International Court of Justice in The Hague where they might expect to win as much as £200 million in damages – more than three billion pounds in today's terms. By January a form of words had to be found that would paper-over an embarrassing retreat and Jenkins duly went to the House of Commons to announce, with a straight face, that the urgent re-examination of the project had now been completed and Concorde would go ahead.

It had been a chaotic affair that had caused considerable damage to Franco-British relations, but the fact remains that the economic argument against the costs of the Concorde project was fully-justified and became even more unmistakeable in the coming years. In the end only 16 Concordes were built, of which Air France and BOAC took seven each (without payment). Only the fact that the taxpayer footed the bill for design, development and construction and that the planes were effectively gifted to the two national airlines enabled Concorde to be operated commercially at all. Seen from the exterior Concorde was breathtakingly beautiful. The present author vividly remembers the thrilling sight of Concorde passing directly over his Yateley home at low height on its way to the nearby Farnborough Air Show on 7 September 1970. But though outwardly magnificent, the interior of the plane was absurdly cramped and passengers paid premium prices to be transported in conditions little better than a modern-day low-budget airline.

In Concorde the Wilson government had inherited a project that was a money pit. The Conservative Minister of Aviation originally responsible for Concorde, Julian Amery, had failed to ensure that there was a cancellation clause in the treaty and the Treasury had been deliberately excluded from any careful evaluation of the long-term financial implications and the eventual true costs.[6] The Wilson government's attempt to cancel it may have been misjudged and mishandled, but Concorde had, from the first, been an economic disaster in the making.

But Concorde was not the only money-losing project on Jenkins' desk. Just a few weeks before the General Election the TSR2 military aircraft had undergone its maiden flight. This plane was designed as a tactical strike aircraft intended for multiple uses. It was intended to combine the capabilities of a manned bomber with those of a ground attack aircraft and to be able to be armed with either conventional or tactical nuclear missiles. The design specification required that it should only require a short take-off and be capable not only of operating at high speed but of doing so at high, medium and low altitudes. This mish-mash of requirements was the outcome of considerable inter-service squabbling and, unsurprisingly, incorporating these diverse and sometimes competing capabilities ensured that the design and manufacture of the TSR2 would pose complex problems with both cost and manufacturing implications and leading to inevitable delays in production.

To add to these inherent problems the Conservative government that had commissioned the TSR2 had taken the opportunity to force greater integration in the British aircraft manufacturing business by requiring, as a condition of winning the contract, formerly competing contractors to merge under a single umbrella, the British Aircraft Corporation. This may have been in itself a sensible step to greater coherence within the industry, but inevitably a new manufacturing organisation, (the result of a shotgun marriage between four separate companies) having to invent itself from the ground up, was not the ideal setting for the design and development of a highly complex and technically innovative aircraft.

In August 1964, just a few weeks before the TSR2's maiden flight, the service ministers met with the Minister of Aviation, Julian Amery, to discuss the aircraft's progress. The briefing note to prepare them for that meeting referred to multiple problems caused by "deplorable technical delays, ineffective management and cost escalation…and by extreme tardiness in doing anything to remedy the Ministry of Aviation's own inadequate organisation."[7]

When the TSR2 had its maiden flight at Boscombe Down on September 28th 1964, the Conservative Minister of Aviation was forced to deny claims that the plane had already cost British taxpayers £250 million. His denial was accurate; at that point the costs to date amounted to around £160 million. But there was still a long way to go, and a great deal of money to be spent, if the plane were to reach the final manufacturing stage. The maiden flight had proved the plane could at least get off the ground, but major technical problems remained to be solved and there were already serious concerns about design flaws – replacing an engine, for example, would take RAF ground crew about 24 hours, a ludicrous length of time for a plane in the course of operational deployment.

The TSR2 was not expected to be ready to enter service until late 1968 or early 1969. Jenkins calculated that by this stage the plane would have cost around £13 per head for every man, woman and child in the country. There was moreover no prospect of any financial return by selling the TSR2 to overseas buyers. The only potential buyer, the Royal Australian Air Force, had shown an initial interest but then dropped out. The case for cancellation was overwhelming – and even Denis Healey, the Defence Minister, agreed.

Healey's plan was to replace the TSR2 with the purchase of an American alternative – the F111. Jenkins was convinced of the need to cancel TSR2 but had concerns about the impact on industry (around 1600 people were employed on just the design side of the TSR2 alone) and reservations about the need for any replacement at all.

The matter was eventually resolved in favour of cancelling TSR2 and placing an option to buy the American alternative - but it took two Cabinet meetings at the start of April 1965 to reach the decision. The announcement of the TSR2's cancellation was made to the House of Commons a few days later, not by Roy Jenkins, but by James Callaghan in his budget speech on 6th April.

For Jenkins there were crucial lessons to be learned from the mare's nests exemplified by both the Concorde and the TSR2 projects. The first point was that any future projects had to be minutely scrutinised and managed in order to ensure efficient production that represented value for money. British aviation contractors, Jenkins told the House of Commons, had come to believe that the government held open a "bottomless purse". The second lesson to be drawn was that Britain should no longer be attempting independent large-scale complex aviation projects. The future had to lie in collaboration, either with the US or with partners in Western Europe. Jenkins persuaded Sir Edwin Plowden, a distinguished economist, to carry out a review into the UK aircraft industry and the subsequent report validated Jenkins' view that the future of aircraft manufacture in this country depended on collaboration with overseas partners. As Jenkins had warned the House of Commons even before the cancellation of the TSR2, it was the "end of the road for exclusive British manufacture for an exclusively British market".[8]

Meanwhile, on the civil aviation side, Jenkins had determined on a change to the way in which a number of regional airports and aerodromes were to be operated. He decided that a new authority should be created, the British Airports Authority, and the control of Britain's four international airports – Heathrow, Gatwick, Stansted and Prestwick - should be transferred to this body away from their current management by the Ministry of Aviation. This was a sensible rationalisation that recognised that the organisation and running of major airports would now be best served not by the civil service but by specialised and more efficient management. The bill was actually seen through the Commons by Jenkins' Parliamentary Secretary, John Stonehouse, who long after his time at the Ministry of Aviation would achieve considerable notoriety for his interest in flight of a different kind.[*]

In little more than a year Jenkins had distinguished himself at the Ministry and had, in the course of handling difficult and complex controversies, established himself as a leading figure in the House of Commons. His speeches were carefully-argued and coolly-logical but lightened with flashes of wit – for example he warned the House that there could be no overseas sales expected for TSR2 because it was "as firmly geared to an exclusively British market as is a week's holiday at a Butlin's holiday camp". His early establishment of evident authority in the House of Commons had been remarkable and Wilson was sufficiently impressed by the summer of 1965 to describe Jenkins as being "in a class by himself".[9] In fact as early as

---

[*] In 1974 Stonehouse faked his own death. When he was found to be still alive, he was arrested and after conviction on fraud charges he received a seven-year prison sentence.

the previous January – when Jenkins had been at Aviation for just three months – Wilson had attempted to persuade him to become Secretary of State for Education. This would have been an immediate step into the Cabinet, but Jenkins was not attracted by the portfolio and turned it down.

But it would only be a few months before another opportunity came and this time it was more than just an entry into the Cabinet, it was a step into the first rank of ministers. Jenkins had earlier in the year more than hinted to Wilson that Home Secretary was the post he would most want to have and, in the summer of 1965, Wilson made Jenkins an 'under the table' promise of that job, though in the end the offer was not formally and publicly confirmed until nearly the end of the year. But by 22nd December 1965 Jenkins had become the new Home Secretary, at the age of just 45, the youngest Home Secretary since Churchill.

The intervening Christmas period gave Jenkins time to think himself into his new responsibilities. But in effect he had, many years before, already determined on what would be his new agenda. Just before the 1959 General Election, Jenkins had written a Penguin Special titled *The Labour Case*. In one of its chapters, *Is Britain Civilised?*, Jenkins had elaborated on the libertarian outlook that had prompted his earlier work on the Obscene Publications Bill. In his 1959 book Jenkins set out a case for widespread social reform that focused on what he saw as the "need for the State to do less to restrict personal freedom". He identified specific reforms – abolition of the death penalty, decriminalising homosexuality and suicide, relaxation of the divorce laws and the legalisation of abortion. By the time, seven years later, when Jenkins became Home Secretary only one of these reforms had reached the statute book – the abolition of capital punishment.* For Jenkins the time had now come when he could implement those remaining reforms that for him were a necessary step to creating a civilised society.

But Jenkins' first challenge at the Home Office was to deal with his Permanent Secretary. Sir Charles Craik Cunningham, GCB, KBE, CVO had been the most senior civil servant at the Home Office for the previous ten years and had single-mindedly stamped his authority not only on his staff but even on the three home secretaries he had served so far. In April 1959 Sir Charles addressed the annual conference of the National Association of Probation Officers. The title he chose for his address was *The Home Office Looks Ahead*. In reality, Sir Charles' ideal of vision at the Home Office was that the Secretary of State should not see anything that ran counter to the Permanent Secretary's own ideas and views.

When a decision had to be reached at the highest level, Sir Charles would present the Home Secretary with nothing more than a bald recommendation of what should be done. No alternatives were offered and no background information or briefing was provided that might enable the Home Secretary to make his decision in some kind of an informed context. No criticism or review

---

* The abolition of capital punishment was approved initially for five years only. It was banned completely in 1969.

of alternatives was allowed that might admit any penetrating daylight into Sir Charles's decision-making process. Of the three home secretaries he had managed before Jenkins, two were supine and spineless, easily dominated by the Permanent Secretary. The third, R A Butler, certainly possessed the political nerve and character to stand up to Sir Charles, but 'Rab' was simultaneously both Conservative Party Chairman and Leader of the House and with these other jobs on hand only too glad to leave Sir Charles in charge at the Home Office.

Over the Christmas holiday, Jenkins prepared himself for his new role and quickly saw from the papers already provided that the Home Office had become institutionally rigid and unresponsive and that a major block to progress was the Permanent Secretary himself. A confrontation was inevitable and Jenkins determined that from the start he would have to assert his authority over that of his Permanent Secretary. In his memoirs Jenkins described the ensuing meeting as the most difficult he ever had with a senior civil servant. Jenkins had a long list of changes that he insisted be made. Some were changes of personnel; Jenkins particularly emphasised the importance of recruiting new talent from other departments, including bringing-over his previous Principal Private Secretary at the Ministry of Aviation. This was a red rag to a bull; Sir Charles had always been intensely insular and resistant to bringing-in from other ministries officials who might have different views or expectations about how things should be done.

All this was, from Sir Charles' point of view, insupportable enough, but Jenkins went on to insist that in future all ministerial decision-making was to be supported by a file record of fully-informed analysis, open discussion and background study. To the Permanent Secretary this must have seemed to amount to something like insubordination on Jenkins' part and the inevitable face-to-face row was continued on paper when Sir Charles submitted a memo insisting that what the Home Secretary was asking for was impossible. In Roy Jenkins, however, Sir Charles had finally met his match and despite a sneakily underhand attempt by the Permanent Secretary to recruit the junior ministers to his side, the reforms which Jenkins had demanded were largely made. But there was to be one further and decisive move by Jenkins. On account of his age Sir Charles was due to retire in six months' time, but he had gained the previous Home Secretary's informal agreement that he should stay-on. Jenkins would have none of it and at the due date Sir Charles finally left.

The first two of the personal freedom reforms that Jenkins had identified in his book of 1959 actually passed into law in the first months of his time as Home Secretary. But technically these were not Home Office reforms at all. The Abortion Act and the Sexual Offences Act (which decriminalised homosexuality above the age of twenty-one) were both private members' bills. However, they would never have passed into law had not Jenkins ensured that they received sufficient parliamentary time for them to pass through all the necessary stages. But

Jenkins did more than merely facilitate the passage of these bills – he actively supported them by speaking in their favour in the House. The Government position in regard to both of these reforms was one of neutrality, but no one was left in any doubt about the Home Secretary's position. As he explained to the House regarding the Abortion Bill,[*] "The fact that the Government's collective attitude is one of neutrality does not – and, I think, should not – preclude me from expressing my own views on this issue…I certainly shall have no hesitation in voting for the Second Reading of the Bill."[10] This explicit advocacy, from the Government front bench, was a powerful underlining of the plain fact that it was only because Jenkins was Home Secretary that these proposed measures were being given the parliamentary time to succeed.

Roy Jenkins was, from the start, determined to use his office to drive forward a programme of social liberalism, but that did not mean that he could not be tough so far as law and order were concerned. As he told the House of Commons: "I am happy to accept the libertarian label. But it would be a great mistake to believe that there is any connection between such an approach to matters of individual conduct and a soft or defeated approach to the organised criminal conspiracies or more isolated acts of brutal violence which at present disfigure our society."[11]

In the last weeks of 1966 Jenkins introduced a substantial reform of the criminal justice system. His

_____

[*] Strictly speaking the Medical Termination of Pregnancy Bill.

Criminal Justice Bill, which ran to 72 clauses, was an overhaul of court procedures, courtroom practice and aspects of sentencing, including parole and the opportunity for early release. It included many reforms which are now so taken-for-granted that it is almost hard to recognise that they date only from this time in the 1960s - for example, that judges should be able to impose suspended sentences or that juries should be able to reach a majority verdict. It also comes as something of a surprise that it was Jenkins' bill that required, for the first time, that a certificate would be needed to own a shotgun. The Bill overall combined measures to improve efficiency in the system with measures that attempted to avoid prison sentences where other penalties would be a more measured response. As Jenkins told listeners to the BBC in a talk on 1st December 1966, his Bill was "a concerted attack on crime which, by assisting the police and the courts, should enable us to bring criminals to justice and at the same time send to prison only those for whom prison is necessary in the interests of society".

This Bill received Royal Assent on 27th July 1967. Unknown to Jenkins the next few months would be his last at the Home Office. He had by now established himself not just as an outstanding Home Secretary but as an outstanding member of the Government. He had successfully weathered some awkward storms, involving variously a series of murders of police officers and the sensational prison escape of the convicted Soviet spy, George Blake. But Jenkins' reputation remained high. There were some who suggested not only that he was a future Prime Minister but that the realisation of this might be imminent. As Barbara Castle, not a great fan of Jenkins, had recorded in her diary on Monday 21st November 1966: "Sunday's papers are full of Roy Jenkins again. There is obviously a campaign on to run him as Harold's successor."[12]

The announcement of devaluation on 18th November 1967 opened the door to what would be Roy Jenkins' final post in that first Wilson government. Callaghan's determination that he must resign as Chancellor was not accompanied by any serious inclination to return to the backbenches. Callaghan had some time earlier indicated to Jenkins that he favoured a job swap between them and although Wilson was generally disinclined to give people what they wanted, he had in this case little alternative. He knew that Jenkins was a masterly performer in Parliament and that, post-devaluation, it was essential to have a Chancellor who could command confidence in the House. On 29th November, just eleven days after devaluation, Wilson saw Jenkins and offered him the post of Chancellor of the Exchequer. Jenkins accepted and the seals of office were duly exchanged with Callaghan on the following day.

Up to this point, Jenkins' ministerial advancement had always played to a strength of background knowledge and preparation. At both the Ministry of Aviation and the Home Office he arrived with a confidence that was built on personal history. At the Treasury the context was very different. Jenkins had for years written and spoken about economic matters, but, as he admitted in his memoirs, he could not properly be described as an economist.[13] An additional handicap was that he had been previously excluded from the Cabinet's economic committee. For the first time he depended on senior officials for guidance and direction and, paradoxically, his officials were – so unlike Sir Charles at the Home Office - reluctant to provide a lead. They knew that Jenkins had for a considerable time previously believed that devaluation was necessary and perhaps this convinced them that their new Chancellor was gifted with a deeper insight and understanding than he really had. This impression is likely to have been reinforced by the almost film-star treatment given to Jenkins' appointment in the press. On the Sunday following his appointment, for example, the *Observer* carried a front-page splash about the Chancellor's plans, then on page 8, alongside the paper's leading articles, it carried an open letter to Jenkins from Professor Alan Day of the London School of Economics. Further-on in the paper there was a full-page interview with Jenkins, conducted by Kenneth Harris, and finally on the back page there was even a gossipy piece headlined 'The Jenkins Secret': "How does Jenkins maintain his air of effortless superiority and relaxation?" the piece asked, before concluding that the answer was that "A large part of his secret is Mrs Jenkins".

Glossy publicity of this kind is unlikely to have helped Jenkins' senior officials to adjust to their new Chancellor. Perhaps they felt in two minds as to whether he should be deferred to as omniscient or left out to dry as a salutary reward for "effortless superiority". Certainly Jenkins subsequently blamed his officials for what he saw as a lack of helpfulness that contributed to what he later characterised as a fundamental oversight in his first actions at the Treasury. Following devaluation, the key priority had to be to increase exports and reduce imports. It was only by balancing the trade accounts – or at least by reducing the imbalance – that the pound could recover in strength and take the heat out of the currency market. Jenkins was, however, not shown guidance which had been prepared for Callaghan on the immediate need to cut demand at home. The consequence was that Jenkins decided that, because the new value of the pound would take time before it resulted in improved export orders, he needed to avoid short-term employment by keeping home demand at its current level.

So while Jenkins fully grasped that higher taxation would be needed to reduce imports he fell into the error of thinking that he could – in fact should – delay those rises to protect employment in the short term, until the hoped-for flood of export orders enabled him to safely deflate at home. His mistake, unchecked by any demur by his officials, had two consequences. The first was to trigger a domestic boom in spending and the second a failure to demonstrate beyond argument that the potential rebalancing of the economy, following devaluation, was being urgently pursued.

Devaluation had not provided Jenkins with an immediate solution to Britain's economic problems. November's trade figures revealed a deficit of £158 million. The pound remained under great pressure and the country's reserves were now so low that an exceptionally heavy run on the pound could have exhausted those reserves in a single day. A second devaluation was at least a possibility – and some thought it likely. In mid-December Barbara Castle recorded for her diary Wilson's judgment that the economic situation was "menacing".

Jenkins' immediate response was that the balance of payments deficit must be tackled by further and massive cuts to public spending. He agreed with Wilson that his proposed cuts should be put to the full Cabinet in January and the Prime Minister decided that the best course of action would be to share the details of those cuts with an 'inner-Cabinet' group (around 10 ministers including Wilson and Jenkins) whose early involvement would help to build support for the new measures when the package of cuts was put to the full Cabinet. At this meeting, held a few days after Christmas, Jenkins informed his colleagues of an intention to make cuts amounting to £850 million. But he added that none of these cuts could take place within the last few months of the current financial year and in the coming year the reduction would amount to only £100 million.

Jenkins was able to provide some details of where these cuts would fall though he was careful not to provide his colleagues with a paper setting out his intentions in detail. Among the proposals that he did disclose were cuts in defence, education, roads and a small amount of additional revenue-raising from the introduction of some NHS charges.

Barbara Castle, who was excluded from this inner-cabinet committee, characterised it as a "special group of Ministers, hand-picked by Harold to supervise this latest exercise in slashing". But in fact the disparate range of the cuts Jenkins had in mind meant that almost everyone even in this core group was bound to find there at least one item or another to which to object. To Jenkins' irritation, the strongest resistance of all came from James Callaghan who came to the meeting determined to make life as difficult as possible for his successor. The meeting ended inconclusively and certainly without achieving Wilson's intention of building an advance consensus for Jenkins' proposals.

It took six sessions of the full Cabinet to argue through Jenkins' cuts. Each of his proposals was fiercely contested, though the group of critics was fluid with alliances being formed and broken according to the target of any particular cut. Only Callaghan was more or less consistently in the corner arguing against Jenkins. Eventually the Chancellor, who, according to Barbara Castle, consistently demonstrated "courteous but steely inflexibility", was driven to point out icily that "The Home Secretary and I have a fundamentally different approach. He wants us to continue as we have done for the past three years. I don't believe we can afford to do so."[14]

The package of cuts was finally agreed at a meeting on 12th January. On the defence side it included the bringing forward to the end of 1971 the withdrawal of troops from the Far East and the Persian Gulf, the phasing-out of the existing aircraft carrier fleet, a scaling-back in planned naval construction and a cancellation of the order for F111 aircraft from the US. Cuts at home included postponing the raising of the school leaving age, introducing a two shillings and sixpence charge for each item on an NHS prescription and a reduction in approvals for new council house-building. The list of measures included what appeared as a particularly egregious example of giving with one hand and taking away with the other - the forthcoming planned rise of seven shillings in family allowance would go ahead but would effectively be clawed-back by an equivalent increase in tax at the standard rate and above.

The complete package was announced to the House on January 16th, not by Jenkins but by Wilson, who concluded his speech with the stark warning that these cuts were "only part of a continuing process which will dominate national financial and economic management for the next two years. Other measures including budgetary decisions will be required." These grim words were presumably framed to send a clear signal to the currency market that Britain was now determined to 'hang tough' with regard to its financial problems. The downside to Wilson's words was the risk of encouraging an immediate rise in domestic consumption as people brought forward their spending plans to get ahead of any future tax rises.

Jenkins was well aware of this risk and he had originally wanted to delay the announcement of the public expenditure cuts until they could be combined with an early budget speech in February. His permanent secretary at the Treasury had advised him against this, on the grounds that the economic forecast would at that stage not be ready to inform budget decisions. Once again, Jenkins retrospectively believed that he had been given bad advice and that he should have insisted on both spending cuts and tax changes being announced early and as a single package.

As Jenkins worked on the preparation of his March budget another economic storm blew up – this one not a consequence of UK weakness but a clear lesson that the economy at home was vulnerable to weaknesses elsewhere in the world. The United States had for years been running a budget deficit. This had steadily increased during the 1960s and then dramatically soared as a result of the costs of the Vietnam War. The deficit in 1967 was nine billion dollars, more than twice that of the year before and by 1968 the deficit had ballooned to a massive twenty-five billion. The result was an international nervousness about the stability of the dollar and an increasing trend to convert currency holdings into gold. This demand for gold added to the financial pressures in the US which was committed, as a result of an international agreement made in 1961, to use dollars to keep the price of gold down to a fixed level of 35$ an ounce – support which in recent years had cost the US billions of dollars.

The market's increasing lack of confidence in the dollar inevitably increased the appetite to get out of sterling and into gold. Downward pressure on the pound intensified to within a hairsbreadth of the point where, under the

1944 Bretton Woods Agreement, a second devaluation would have been required. Jenkins described this period, towards the end of February 1968, as a "nerve-wracking" crisis. Once again the Bank of England was forced in defence of the pound to expend vast sums from its rapidly-diminishing reserves.

The United States was meanwhile scrambling to defend its own currency and had come up with a way of decoupling the association between gold and the dollar. Their plan was to create a two-tier trading system for gold – the former price of 35 dollars an ounce would apply only to sales of gold to governments that did not buy gold in any other way. Outside of that restricted market gold was to be left to find its own price-level. But as a preliminary to introducing that change – and to buy the time to gain the co-operation of the other countries that were part of the original gold-price-fixing agreement – the United States asked the British government to close for one day the London Gold Market, the home of international gold sales.

It was the investment banker Sir Siegmund Warburg, called-in by Jenkins for advice at this point, who came up with the idea that Britain should not only close the London Gold Market on the day the US had requested (Friday 15th March) but also use the opportunity to close the currency market on the same day, thus buying an additional day of respite for the pound. Jenkins immediately saw the strength of this suggestion and took it to Wilson, who immediately agreed. The only remaining obstacle was that to declare an additional Bank Holiday required an Order-in-Council, which in turn entailed getting together a group of privy councillors to meet with the Queen. The required number of senior ministers was scratched together at short notice and the Order-in-Council was duly signed in the early hours of the Saturday morning. It was Wilson's failure (more likely deliberate than accidental) to include George Brown in the group that went to the Palace that led to Brown's explosive exit from the government.

Just three days later Jenkins rose in the House of Commons to deliver his first budget. Reflecting the events of the last few days he began by acknowledging that he spoke "in the wake of a weekend of world monetary upheaval" and he warned the House that "we must have a stiff Budget followed by two years of hard slog". The budget was indeed stiff – Jenkins had decided to raise an additional £923 million in tax, making it the most deflationary budget since the Second World War. Purchase tax was raised in a series of bands, ranging from 27.5% at the lower end to, at the top end, a rate of 50% which was to be applied to luxury goods – fur coats, cameras, perfumes and so on. Road tax also went up, as did taxes on gaming, petrol, wines and spirits (though beer duty was left unchanged). The focus of these increases was on indirect taxes but an exception was his announcement of an increase in Selective Employment Tax, which had been introduced by Callaghan as an attempt to wash-out employment from service industries into manufacturing jobs.

All this amounted to deflation with a vengeance.

Jenkins' overall intention was that as a result of his increased taxation, the next eighteen months' projected growth of 3% in private consumption could be reversed into a 1% fall. It was, according to the Economics Editor of the *Guardian*, a case of intentional "overkill" – designed to send a clear message about the country's intention to defend the new value of the pound. The speech was nonetheless surprisingly well-received on the Government benches. Sir Alec Cairncross, then head of the Government's Economic Service, recorded in his diary that Jenkins was "cheered by his supporters more loudly at the end than I can recall in other recent budgets".[15] Even Edmund Dell, an excoriating critic of all Chancellors from Hugh Dalton to John Major, paid tribute to Jenkins' skill at the despatch box that day: "The Budget speech was a masterpiece. Never has pain been inflicted with greater elegance. There has been no finer Budget speech since the war."[16]

The economic situation following the budget was subjected to more stress as a result of external factors. Germany's strong surplus position was leading to some expectation that its currency would have to be revalued upwards and France's corresponding weakness was thought to be likely to end in a devaluation of the franc. The pound was dragged into the frenzy of speculation and on one particularly frantic trading day in mid-November the Bank of England expended nearly one-eighth of its remaining reserves to keep the pound above the point which would have triggered a further devaluation.

In his Budget speech Jenkins had announced – almost

as a throwaway line – that the government intended to extend its power to make further changes to tax by the use of the 'regulator' This was a device first introduced in 1961 and gave the government the power to vary indirect taxes by up to 10% without prior parliamentary approval. It would be only five months before the regulator was needed. On 22nd November Jenkins had to stand up in the House to announce an increase in purchase tax and a 10% rise of the duty on beer, wine, spirits, petrol and tobacco. Although these fresh increases were set by Jenkins in the context of the speculation around the values of the Deutsche Mark and the franc it was clear that the need for the regulator was not solely due to these external factors. Despite the tax rises in the spring budget consumer spending had reached a level that was £500 million higher than the Treasury had predicted and this inevitably impacted negatively on imports and absorbed some capacity for exports. The immediate effect of this use of the regulator was to inject a further dose of deflation, putting about 1% on the cost of living.

Despite all this additional pain there were, at last, some indicators of hope. An inspection team from the International Monetary Fund (which, at the time of devaluation, had provided $1400 million of standby credit, attached to strict conditions) had departed declaring themselves completely satisfied with the measures taken so far, including the use of the regulator. There was further reassurance from the Governor of the Bank of England who allowed himself to say that the Government's economic policy was proceeding on the right lines and encouraging news too from the National Institute of Social and Economic Affairs which forecast that the balance of payments would shortly go into surplus.

Of course in the past other visionaries had seen light at the end of the tunnel only for it to be revealed as a false dawn. But these reasons for hope glimpsed in late 1968 turned out to be justified. There were still difficult days to come and in his 1969 budget Jenkins had to deflate by a further £340 million of additional taxation. But the balance of payments was, despite occasional setbacks, now moving towards positive territory – movement assisted by the discovery that Board of Trade statisticians had for years been under-recording UK exports. By August 1969 the balance of trade had, at last, moved into a sustainable surplus.

In the previous year's budget Jenkins had announced the government's intention to legislate for further controls over prices and incomes – in particular he indicated that wages, salaries and dividends were to be held to increases of no more than 3.5% and that the Prices and Incomes Board would have the powers to delay increases above this level or rises unjustified by productivity. In the event Jenkins' extension of wage controls produced only four new claims with which the Board had to deal, but that did not mean that wage inflation was no longer an underlying concern at the Treasury. In his 1969 Budget, Jenkins stressed the need for what he called "more orderly arrangements" in industrial relations, by which he meant smoother processes of collective bargaining that would avoid the economic damage caused by industrial action. "The Government", Jenkins informed that House, "have, therefore, decided to implement without delay, during the present Session, some of the more important provisions incorporated in the White Paper 'In Place of Strife'."

This budgetary commitment to Wilson and Castle's plans for the reform of industrial relations was carefully phrased – it notably occurs in the context of a passage about smoothing the process of wage bargaining, delicately stepping around any hint that *In Place of Strife* was in part a means of managing pay restraint. The reality behind Jenkins' support for Barbara Castle's proposals was that he was deeply concerned about the threat of wage inflation. Just a few weeks before the Budget he had admitted to Crossman that this was a "grave danger" and he had been keen to press ahead with a new Prices and Incomes Bill as an insurance against any delay in implementing *In Place of Strife*.

In January 1969 Jenkins had privately told Crossman that "I promised my support to Barbara…whether it was right or wrong I gave her my support". But over time the apparently interminably slow progress of her plans cost Barbara the Chancellor's support. In his memoirs Jenkins asserts that the delay was not only mistaken, it was dangerous; because trade union reform was so sensitive for a Labour Government that success could only occur if the reform was taken "on the run". By mid-June 1969, however, Jenkins had given-up any hope that Barbara's plans could or should survive and so he arranged to see her privately. "There he told me," she wrote in her diary, "with that evasive look he has been developing lately, that I would have gathered that he no longer thought the fight worth the cost."[17] Jenkins acknowledged in his autobiography that reneging on his promise of support was discreditable; his part in the execution of *In Place of Strife* was to say the least ignoble.

The humiliating abandonment of Barbara's flagship policy essentially signalled an open season for wage demands, backed by actual or threatened industrial action. On 23 October 1969 - against a multi-headed background of disputes that included a strike at the Standard-Triumph car factory in Liverpool, an unofficial strike by 121,000 miners and a threatened Bonfire Night strike by firemen – the Cabinet had a lengthy discussion about the industrial situation. In his diary description of the meeting Crossman recorded that Barbara Castle "had to admit that the whole industrial field is in complete anarchy". More soberly, the official record of the meeting noted that "general concern was expressed at the deteriorating condition of industrial relations, which amounted in some industries to a total abdication of responsibility on the part of industrial workers".[18]

It was against this background – with its high risk of accelerating wage inflation – that Jenkins set about preparing what would be his last Budget. An additional challenge to his preparations was that 1970 was widely expected to be the year in which Wilson would decide to hold another General Election. His party clearly hoped that Jenkins would deliver a budget that would be a vote-winner. In a rather prim passage in his memoirs Jenkins explained that he would have regarded a give-away budget as "a vulgar piece of economic management below the level of sophistication of the British electorate". The reality is, as Jenkins acknowledged, that, despite an enormous improvement in the economic picture, he had very little room to play with. In fact, the commodity of which he had the most to give away was good news.

And there was good news in plenty. The balance of payments – the Wilson government's Calvary since 1964 – was at last in surplus, by a predicted £550 million. Exports were up by 4%. Bank of England reserves had grown by £76 million. External debt was massively reduced. What had been a deficit of £1956 million in the public accounts in the previous year had now been turned into a £600 million surplus.

Jenkins was, however, in no mood to risk these gains with a reflationary budget. His main handout was to adjust tax thresholds with the effect of exempting an additional two million people from liability for income tax. The tone of his speech was celebratory in terms of achievement to date, but so far as any loosening of the reins was concerned it was, the *Guardian* judged, "a 'no-change' Budget". Its reception in the House was one of general dissatisfaction on all sides. On the Labour benches there was a sense of disappointment that an election-winning budget had not been produced from the hat. On the Conservative side there was frustration that Jenkins' caution had denied them the ammunition to accuse him of an electioneering budget.

The General Election was called for June 18th. The campaign seemed favourable to Labour until, just before polling day, the government had to reveal a £31 million deficit in the last month's trading figures. In fact this was an anomaly – due to the purchase of two jumbo jets by the state international airline BOAC – but after the fanfare of the Budget, it was not only highly embarrassing for Jenkins, but inevitably damaging for Labour. The Conservative margin of victory was not great – just 30 seats – but Jenkins, who had been promised the post of Foreign Secretary if Labour won, was suddenly out of office. He was just 49.

Roy Jenkins was in some ways a slow starter. He entered Parliament later than any of the others in the 'Big Six'. He did not enter the Cabinet until he became Home Secretary at the very end of 1965. But, in the long run, his active career outlasted by far any of his contemporaries in that first Wilson government. He was still a national figure when he died in January 2003. In the intervening years he had effectively four careers – as Shadow Foreign Secretary and Deputy Leader of the Labour Party, as President of the European Commission, as the founding-father of the Social Democratic Party (as well as its leader and a potential Prime Minister) and finally as a distinguished and highly successful political biographer.

From almost his first days in Parliament he had acquired a reputation as a politician who was never afraid to dare. His support from the backbenches of the Obscene Publications Bill in the early sixties and, as Home

Secretary, his active backing for reform of the law on abortion and on homosexuality were clear markers that here was a man who was never going to be confined to issues and positions that were uncontroversial, or within politically safe lines. In 1971, as Deputy Leader of the Labour Party, he was widely tipped to become Wilson's successor and on course to be a future Prime Minister. But he deliberately sacrificed this advantage and prospect when Wilson's reversal of his previous support for entry to the European Union propelled Jenkins, together with 68 other Labour MPs, to vote with the Heath Government in a motion that committed the UK to an application to join the Common Market. The number of Conservative MPs who voted against the motion meant that but for the act of defiance by Jenkins and other Labour members, the motion would not have passed.

Jenkins' principled act of disloyalty cost him considerable support within his own party, which eventually decided that if Britain had joined Europe before it returned to power it would then hold a referendum so that the electorate could decide whether to remain or leave. This was for Jenkins the last straw. He resigned from the deputy leadership and made it clear that he no longer wished to serve in the Shadow Cabinet.

But, in the autumn of 1973, Jenkins decided to return to the fold and he stood again for election to the Shadow Cabinet. In his memoirs he distances himself from any suggestion that this move was a marker to keep his hat in the ring for any future leadership election. But those who encouraged him to stand in the Shadow Cabinet election were in no doubt that a renewed place for Jenkins on the opposition front bench would provide a springboard to propel him into the leadership. Given the animosity generated by his vote on the government side over Europe, Jenkins did surprisingly well. He came fifth in the poll, only six votes below Callaghan, who topped the list. Wilson, after some delay, asked him to shadow the Home Office which he accepted, but when a decision had to be made over who should wind-up in a debate on the government's economic policy Jenkins suggested himself. The following day the *Times* wrote of his speech "here was the voice of authority that the Labour Party has so sadly lacked in the long months since Mr Jenkins retired to the back benches". It would, however, turn out to be, as Jenkins was later to reflect, the last parliamentary triumph of his career.

The following year Edward Heath called his *Who Governs Britain?* election and received a dusty answer. After a few days of delay (while Heath desperately courted the leader of the Liberal Party in the forlorn hope of scratching together some kind of pact) Wilson was at last back in Downing Street. Jenkins, without any great enthusiasm, accepted the offer of the Home Office – it was nearly forty years since any politician had been given a second stint as Home Secretary. Jenkins' second term at the Home Office was more turbulent than the first. He did bring about significant reforms – a Sex Discrimination Act, a Race Relations Act (tightening up an earlier and somewhat toothless reform), a Theatres Act which abolished the statutory censorship of any plays put on for public performance and the establishment of a board to consider complaints against the police. These reforms – all of them initiated by Jenkins, though some only passed into law shortly after he had left the Home Office – were persisting evidence of the commitment to social reform argued in his 1959 book *The Labour Case*.

But, beyond these reforms, Jenkins' work was dominated by issues of law and order and in particular the eruption of mainland terrorism carried out by the IRA. In the space of six weeks in the autumn of 1974, pub bombings in first Guildford and then Birmingham left nearly thirty dead and over 250 injured. In an immediate reaction, Jenkins was able, within days of the Birmingham attack, to introduce a Prevention of Terrorism Act that passed through Parliament in little more than twenty-four hours. Jenkins admitted to the House of Commons that the measure was "draconian" but, he believed, justified by events. In later life, Jenkins regarded the measures as necessary at the time, but regretted that they had still remained on the statute book nearly twenty years later.

Labour was meanwhile continuing to contort itself over its relationship with Europe. The proposal to hold a referendum to decide whether or not to continue membership of the community had gained irresistible force within the Party and the decision to proceed with the necessary legislation put Jenkins in a near-impossible situation. He was completely opposed to the principle of a referendum on this issue and yet the Home Office had to be involved in the legal steps necessary to make it happen. The solution was that the legislation was seen through the Commons not by Jenkins but by Edward Short, whose role included oversight of that part of the Cabinet Office that handled constitutional matters.

Harold Wilson, only too aware of the disagreement within his Cabinet over the issue of 'leave or remain', artfully decided that he would suspend the usual rule of Cabinet unity and allow his ministers to choose for themselves on which side of the debate to campaign. It was a foregone conclusion that Jenkins would side with the campaign to stay in Europe, but he went further than that and actually became President of the 'Britain in Europe' movement as well as a leading member of the separate 'Labour Campaign for Europe'.

The ensuing vote was a victory for Jenkins – 67% of the votes were for remaining in Europe – and also for Wilson who, despite his double-dealing prior to the referendum, had campaigned on the same side, though outside any of the front organisations. The battle over the issue had, however, left Jenkins distinctly jaded and when, in January 1976, Wilson spoke to him in general terms about the upcoming appointment of a new President of the European Commission, Jenkins found himself in two minds as to whether he should stay in UK politics, in the hope of becoming Prime Minister, or allow his name to go forward for the Presidency.

His havering over the matter was accentuated by his inside knowledge of Wilson's otherwise secret plan to shortly resign. Jenkins decided to wait for this resignation and then to make a bid to become Wilson's successor. When Wilson announced his surprise resignation, in

March 1976, Jenkins joined the race alongside five other contenders. But after the first ballot left him in third place he decided to withdraw from the contest and, after a run-off between just two of the original six, James Callaghan became the new Prime Minister.

Jenkins' first hope was that Callaghan would appoint him as Foreign Secretary (which would have completed a hat-trick of the three 'Great Offices of State'). But Callaghan had been warned-off putting Jenkins into the Foreign Office by Michael Foot – whose own failure in the recent leadership election had not deterred him from the vainglorious assumption that he was the best person to determine Cabinet appointments.

The best that Callaghan was prepared to offer was a continuation of his term as Home Secretary. Jenkins found this prospect unappetising and he made up his mind to have his name submitted for the European Presidency. His success in that appointment meant that in December 1976 he left the House of Commons and, just two weeks later, was installed as President of the European Commission.

His four-year term as President was a time of expansion and increasing ambition for the EU – he presided over the implementation of the European Monetary System and paved the way for the introduction of the Euro and the establishment of the European Central Bank. Expansion and ambition may have been the watchwords at the European Commission but they were very much not the national keynotes in Britain, where Callaghan's government was plunged into a succession of crises and in time a dark period of industrial chaos. In November 1979, just six months after Callaghan had lost the General Election to Margaret Thatcher, Jenkins gave the annual BBC Dimbleby Lecture. "Britain" he told his audience, "has been sluggish, uninventive and resistant to voluntary change, not merely economically but socially and politically as well...Politicians cannot cling defensively to their present somewhat ossified party and political system while convincingly advocating the acceptance of change elsewhere...".

This analysis was correctly interpreted as a platform from which to launch a new political grouping. The launch countdown began ticking in January 1981 when Jenkins, alongside Shirley Williams, David Owen and Bill Rodgers (the 'Gang of Four') issued a statement of principles that became known as the *Limehouse Declaration* and which was followed, just a few weeks later, by the establishment of a new centre-left party, the Social Democratic Party. In July that year Jenkins stood as an SDP candidate in a by-election in Warrington and was only narrowly defeated. He stood again the following year – this time in the Scottish constituency of Glasgow Hillhead – and won by a margin of more than two thousand votes.

For a time the SDP (which formed an alliance with the Liberal Party) seemed to have gained irresistible momentum and since Jenkins was its leader there was widespread expectation that he could become the next Prime Minister. But gradually the juggernaut started to lose the air in its tyres. Internal squabbling within the new party and the rising stock of the Prime Minister, Margaret Thatcher, (boosted by the Falklands War) combined with the disadvantages of the traditional first past-the-post system to result in just six SDP members (including Jenkins) being returned at the 1983 General Election. Jenkins was then replaced as leader of the SDP by David Owen and after he lost his Glasgow Hillhead seat in the 1987 General Election, he entered the House of Lords as Baron Jenkins of Hillhead.

In September 1964, on the eve of the election that had brought Wilson's first government to power, Jenkins saw the publication of his biography of the Liberal Prime Minister Herbert Asquith. It was well-received and many decades later it remains the standard Asquith biography. After his retirement from active politics Jenkins wrote many articles and books, including notable biographies. His life of Gladstone, published in 1995 won the Whitbread Prize for Biography of the Year. His 2001 biography of Churchill was a bestseller, though it received mixed reviews from professional historians. Professor Andrew Roberts described it as a "masterpiece of biography", while Dr Piers Brendon dismissed it as "absurdly over-praised".

Roy Jenkins died on the morning of 5 January 2003, devotedly cared for till the end by his wife Jennifer – who all those years before had been described by the *Observer* as the key to 'The Jenkins Secret'. Jennifer Jenkins had her own secret - her willingness to tolerate her husband's serial infidelity. His extra-marital relationships were well-known to her but seemed to have done nothing to diminish the strength of their relationship which had endured since their days as students

If Harold Wilson read the *Guardian* on 16 January 1968, just a few weeks after Jenkins had become Chancellor of the Exchequer, he would have been less than pleased to read an assessment by the paper's political correspondent, Peter Jenkins: "What Mr Wilson now needs from his Chancellor is not powerful economic expertise, but the powerful assistance of an ambitious, resourceful, confidence-inspiring politician to pull the Government, the Labour Party, and the country together." This implication that the Prime Minister was now vitally dependent on Jenkins to pull the Government's chestnuts out of the fire was echoed just two days later in the *Times* when the journalist-broadcaster Ian Trethowan wrote that "Mr Wilson's loss of credibility has been tacitly acknowledged and for the time being Roy is very much the boy".

But while Roy was "very much the boy" he was also very much his own man. His political instincts were free-ranging and frequently found him working against the common grain. When he took up causes such as the reform of the obscenity laws, or spoke from the front bench in favour of abortion law reform, he was openly signalling a disregard for safe and conventional opinion.

This independence of mind was insistently stubborn. When he was urged to give-in to demands from IRA hunger-strikers, he declined to make concessions as long as they refused food. When in 1970 his Cabinet colleagues wanted a pre-election budget bonanza he refused to budge. In opposition in the 1970s he defiantly voted for the government's side over entry into Europe. In the 1980s he struck out to 'break the mould' of politics with the formation of the Social Democratic Party. He was, throughout his career, a consummate politician who atypically refused to be confined by considerations of tactical advantage or political convenience.

Unsurprisingly he was frequently misjudged. Barbara Castle dismissed Jenkins as "essentially a political dilettante", a comment which tells us less about Jenkins and more about Castle's ability to misunderstand any position which did not exactly correspond with her own. What the *Observer* had characterised as his "air of effortless superiority and relaxation" was a misinterpretation of a different kind. The reality was that his outer confidence and projected sense of ease were built on a habit of careful analysis and energetic preparation.

In his short time at the Ministry of Aviation he initiated a complete reform of the previously chaotic way in which aircraft design and production had been managed. At the Home Office, as well as sweeping away antediluvian social laws, he instituted a rationalisation of police organisation that replaced a large number of small and inefficient independent police authorities with larger, more efficient units that could be modernised and made more effective. As Chancellor, after a less than confident start, he imposed order and discipline on the economy and – unlike Callaghan who was always predicting good times just around the corner – he never offered false hope or promised more than he could deliver.

The title of his autobiography, *A Life At The Centre*, was chosen both to reflect a career that had always been close to main events and a stance that was positioned somewhere close to the middle ground in politics. But the political centre was for Jenkins a wide-ranging space. His political instincts were never closely territorial and at times he seemed less a party politician and, in an entirely positive sense, more a political adventurer. In politics he never preferred the fixed menu to the options that were available *à la carte*.

8

Harold Wilson:
Hope Without Glory

When Harold Wilson became Leader of the Opposition in January 1963 his party had not been in government since 1951. His over-riding aim was to ensure that Labour would, under his leadership, break the Conservative grip on power. There were promising signs to Labour's advantage. The Prime Minister, Harold Macmillan, was looking tired and out-of-touch. When he retired in October 1963, after being given what turned out to be an unnecessarily gloomy verdict on his health, his replacement, Alec Douglas-Home, seemed perfectly cast to symbolise an endurance of the old-fashioned ruling class. As the Earl of Home it was clearly unacceptable for him to serve as Prime Minister, so he resigned his peerage and, after a hastily-engineered by-election, became the new MP for Kinross and West Perthshire. This sixty-year-old ex-Etonian with his aristocratic background, his ancestral estate and his taste for grouse-shooting seemed a gift to Labour.

But Wilson knew only too well the perils of over-confidence. He could recall that Labour had achieved a

12-point lead in the opinion polls before the 1959 election – and had still lost. And Wilson was right not to assume that Home's succession as Prime Minister would be an automatic vote-winner for Labour. At the time Wilson had become party leader he had enjoyed an opinion poll lead of 21 points, but that had dropped to 9 ½ points even before Home had taken over as Prime Minister. At the start of 1964, although almost one in two people expected Labour to win the next election, there was still considerable confidence across the country in the Conservative Party – Labour were 12 points behind in terms of the party considered best at handling the economic situation and 20 points behind in terms of their perceived ability to handle foreign affairs.

So, in the final months before the General Election, Wilson knew that victory for Labour was anything but a done deal. He knew that he had to throw everything into convincing people to vote for Labour and that if he lost a fourth General Election in a row his party would inevitably be characterised going forward as the party of permanent losers. It is this conviction that inspired the style and the almost over-the-top vigour of Wilson's election campaign. Seen in hindsight his rhetoric is undeniably over-blown, his assertive confidence comes across as exaggerated and his promises of a 'New Britain' are clearly fanciful. But the style belongs to a man who was driven by a conviction that he had to go full tilt to win. Of course his campaign took on the style of a personal promotion, but Wilson's motives were not self-centred. His self confidence and his deliberate placing of himself centre-stage emerged from his belief that he was Labour's greatest electoral asset.

In the early months of 1964 he undertook a nationwide pre-election speaking tour. In Birmingham he declared it time for a "breakthrough to an exciting and wonderful period in our history". In Swansea he offered a future with a "firm basis of economic power". In Edinburgh he condemned the Conservative government for selling Britain short economically and promised instead a "dynamic, purposeful alternative". By the time he reached the Royal Albert Hall the rhetoric setting was turned-up to maximum. Labour's policies were, he declared, "dynamic, urgent, up-to-date, worthy of a great people...We shall restore a sense of economic purpose".

Wilson had chosen to go all-out with a personal branding for Labour. He styled and projected himself as representing a complete break with a stuffy, out-moded past and a breakthrough to a "New Britain" achieved by fresh thinking that would, by a major change in economic and fiscal policy, create, in the words of the Labour manifesto, "a go-ahead Britain with the strength to stand on her own feet". Through this kind of talk, Wilson had gone out of his way not just to establish a particular identify for his party in general, but in particular for himself as Prime Minister.

To some extent, of course, these speeches and the optimistic words of the manifesto were just the stuff of which electioneering is always made. But a point can be reached at which pre-election confidence can be seen to be 'over-promise'. And beyond that there is another point, when over-promise is revealed as extravagant over-selling. And the flamboyance of Wilson's image-making in the run-up to the election ran a considerable risk: the danger of serious damage - not just presentational, but personal - when things went wrong.

In the end it always comes down to money. And in October 1964 that is where it also began. Wilson's first government is ultimately defined by its handling of the economy. One of Wilson's first decisions (in reality a foregone conclusion) was to appoint Callaghan as Chancellor and Brown as the head of the new Department of Economic Affairs. This was the first manifestation of a balancing act. The division of the Treasury's hitherto monolithic control was an act of fission which, with all its potential for rivalry, might seem an odd way of seeking 'balance'. But Wilson was sufficiently wily (and realistic) to understand that balance is not an absence of conflict but an equilibrium between tensions.

This desire to neutralise rivals – by keeping them preoccupied or setting one against the other – is not uncommon in government leaders. Most Prime Ministers try to protect themselves from potential usurpers or replacements. But in Wilson's case his behaviour was about more than just personal protection. In Wilson's mind safeguarding his position was not just in his own interest, it was in the interests of the Party. He was haunted by memories of past splits – particularly when so many in the Party abandoned their own leader Ramsay

MacDonald in 1931 and, a generation later, the fierce inter-party civil war prompted by the Bevanite split in the 1950s. In Wilson's mind his road to success had been based on his ability to draw support from both the left and the right of his party. Any threat to his personal position was a threat to party stability.

Both appointments were, of course, risky. Callaghan, despite his crash course at Ruskin College, was scarcely economically literate and, in Wilson's view, not particularly bright. The Prime Minister made a more favourable assessment of Brown in terms of intellect, but he was well-aware of George's volatility. Given the weight Wilson attached to the concept of national planning it was a gamble to appoint Brown to the DEA with responsibility for preparing a show-case National Plan. Creating such a plan from scratch might seem to call for a cool head and stable thinking – not exactly Brown's forte. But in practice Brown was probably the only Minister with enough gutsy energy to drive the Plan through (particularly if, as was to be the case, the actual detail of the Plan was safely delegated into the hands of others). With these two appointments Wilson, at a stroke, ensured that his leading political rivals would have their hands full. Brown would be absorbed in his Plan and Callaghan preoccupied with mastering his brief at the Treasury. Neither man would have space or time to go on manoeuvres against Wilson.

But this device came with a risk. And this risk – of splitting economic management into two and appointing as the two heads men who had little or no economic expertise – was magnified when it became understood in the first hours of the new Government that it was facing an economic crisis. Devaluation had inevitably to be considered as a response but Callaghan, supported by Treasury advice, was against it, as was Brown. But there can be no doubt that it was Wilson's judgement that settled the matter. If Wilson had insisted at the outset that devaluation was necessary, neither Callaghan nor Brown would have been able to resist.

But Wilson's thinking was over-shadowed by the historical association between Labour and devaluation. The devaluations of 1929 and 1949 had both happened under a Labour Prime Minister. Wilson was determined to avoid the risk of his party being tagged as the party of devaluation and convinced that it was down to him to protect Labour from the charge that when in power it always devalued. So when Wilson was given his incoming briefing with its dire figures of deficit it was inevitable that he would unhesitatingly rule out devaluation and determine that at all costs he must maintain confidence in the pound internationally and at the same time secure for Labour a reputation for economic stability. His fear of being forever tagged the Prime Minister who sold out on the pound was a decisive deterrent.

The question of whether Wilson made the right call has been the subject of shifting opinion in the years since. For most of that time it has been held that Wilson was wrong and that his failure of nerve at the start was the cause of, or at least a principal factor in, the economic troubles that ensued. But in more recent years a contrary judgement has occasionally emerged. But while this newly emergent revisionist view – that Wilson's instinct was economically correct – has been closely argued by a number of economic historians it is a feature of their arguments that they often turn on sophisticated analysis of complex financial data. The economic statistics used are undoubtedly correct, but they are figures that were not available at the time and so policy has to be judged in the light of what was known or understood by the participants at the time the decision not to devalue was made.

Wilson, Callaghan and Brown reached their decision without any advisers present. But in any event the Permanent Secretary to the Treasury and other senior officials would have advised against devaluation. This does not however provide much supportive cover because the Treasury's opposition to immediate devaluation was at least in part tactical. Wilson's predisposition to rule out devaluation was widely recognised in the Treasury and a view was held there by senior advisers that, as one of them later put it, "Devaluation might yet be necessary; but it was preferable to wait until the government had learnt its lesson".[1]

Perhaps the greater of Wilson's mistakes was, once the decision had been taken, to rule out any future mention of the subject.[*] Devaluation became the 'Great Unmentionable' and this proscription stifled discussion

---

[*] Though behind the scenes a committee of Treasury, DEA and Bank of England officials continued to meet to prepare devaluation contingency plans.

and suppressed any advice that threatened to re-open what was ruled to be a subject officially closed – a constraint that Crossman later described as "real intellectual censorship from No. 10. He (Wilson) doesn't want to face the possibility of devaluation...".[2]

In time the unmentionable would become unavoidable, but it might have been different if, once devaluation had been rejected, there had been a willingness to grasp an alternative – radical deflation. But, in the run-up to the election, Wilson had created a hostage to fortune by condemning the strategy of deflation as a red-light intended to bring the economy to a stop. Worse still, he had in a pre-election speech, in Swansea early in 1964, anticipated a balance of payments crisis as the inheritance of an incoming Labour government but had promised his audience that this would be dealt with not by deflation but by the use of the reserves and overseas borrowing.

So in its first days the Wilson Government was in a bind of its Prime Minister's own making – devaluation denied and deflation defied. When papers were prepared by the Treasury's advisers that set out to analyse the choice between devaluation and drastic deflation* the authors of the papers were ordered to destroy them. The solution to this self-imposed dilemma was for Callaghan to bring in a budget that managed to face both ways – deflationary increases in tax and duty, counter-balanced with reflationary increases in state pensions.

Unsurprisingly the markets were unconvinced and

---

* The choice was not completely either/or. Devaluation would also have to be accompanied by deflation – as Roy Jenkins proved.

sterling came under renewed pressure. Less than a week later Wilson had to use a speech at the Guildhall to insist that the government was "determined to keep sterling strong and see it riding high". The *Sunday Times* journalist Henry Brandon thought that this speech had a "Churchillian ring". A more apt parallel is with an entirely different character from our island story – King Canute. Sure enough, despite Wilson's determination, the tide insisted on rolling-in. Just five days after his speech the Saturday edition of the *Financial Times* led with the headline GOVERNMENT FACED BY FINANCIAL CRISIS. In his Mansion House speech Wilson had declared that his government had no intention of solving its economic problems by the use of deflationary measures, which he dismissed as a "defeatist doctrine". Only a week would pass before the Chancellor had to announce a deflationary rise in Bank Rate.

There is no reason to suppose that a Conservative Government would have handled things any better – in fact the most immediate of the new Government's responses had been to implement a package already-prepared pre-election by the outgoing Conservative Chancellor, Reginald Maudling. It is also true that the central challenge faced by Wilson's government was an inheritance from the Conservatives, stretching back to the Macmillan years. Essentially the problem was that the economy was in a state of disequilibrium – the domestic economy was running too hot to be supported by its adverse balance of payments (exacerbated by the UK's massive overseas defence spending). The problem was not new – the trouble was that Wilson had promised something completely different by way of response, a new style of economic competence, and, away from the giddy atmosphere of the pre-election meeting halls, the new thinking on the economy turned out to look remarkably like more of the old. The danger in all this for Wilson was that having identified himself so directly with this vision of a 'New Britain' any failings could be seen as tantamount to a devaluation in his personal currency.

Wilson understood that a presentational problem called for a presentational solution. His tactic was to create a diversion – to focus the blame not on economic management but on the sabotaging of the economy by bad agents. The good work of the government was, in this story, being subversively undermined by speculators. Wilson took any and every opportunity to point the finger of blame at the "wreckers" who were "making a private killing". Even when devaluation finally became inevitable Wilson could not resist directing the blame in the same direction. In a post-devaluation television interview he insisted that his government's chief mistake had been to under-rate the power of speculators.

A curious feature of some of Wilson's finger-pointing was that it regularly included accusations that the speculation was "unpatriotic". The plain implication of this was that the speculators (or at least some of them) were British. It is hard to understand why Wilson thought this could possibly be true. Wilson was either engaged in unjustified mud-slinging or he was basically ignorant of the way the law acted to prevent home-based speculation.

Short-selling of sterling through British banks was illegal (forbidden under Exchange Control regulations) and within the UK at the time it would have been impossible for British citizens to have used overseas banks instead. So Wilson's accusation of unpatriotic behaviour was completely groundless.

The short-selling of the pound was taking place on international markets. But while overseas betting against the pound was aggravating Britain's problems, it was those very problems that made speculation worthwhile or at least prudential. Given the extent of those problems, speculators expected the pound to be devalued. And, in the long run, they were right. But in the early years of the Wilson Government the speculators may never have thought it reasonable that devaluation could be avoided for so long.

The currency markets were, in any event, also acutely aware of Wilson's pre-election promises – and his assurances that the economic situation would not act as a brake on his government's other policy promises. But this inevitably provoked the question as to whether the Labour Government had the means to pay for its ambitions. In any tug-of-war between policy and the pound, a flight from the latter could seem less like cynical speculation and more like prudent foresight.

It was of course not just currency dealers who wondered just how feasible it was for Britain to maintain sterling at its current value and still pay for its manifesto commitment to full employment, stable prices, up-rated benefits, better education (including a raising of the school leaving age), a modernised health service, increased council-house building and, for the private sector, the introduction of local-authority-backed 100% mortgages. The Wilson Government's answer to how all that was possible was to point to the National Plan, with its growth target of a "25% increase in national output between 1964 and 1970".

No one can deny that Wilson was a believer in planning - but did he believe in the Plan? In his memoir of his 1964-70 government Wilson described the National Plan as a "remarkable and thorough piece of work…It was a brave effort." This is a rather limp endorsement of what was show-cased at the time as a flagship policy – to sum it up retrospectively as a "brave effort" is a rather bathetic tribute.

It seems doubtful that Wilson had much confidence in the National Plan from the start. Even the man who was mainly responsible for constructing the Plan – Donald MacDougall, Director-General of the Department of Economic Affairs – knew that it was built on shaky ground. Years later, MacDougall described how on the Plan's publication it received in the Press "probably more favourable comment than it deserved". Shortly after publication MacDougall visited the United States where he gave a number of talks about the Plan. One of his difficulties in giving those talks, he remembered, was that he "almost began to believe that everything – yes everything – I was saying was one hundred per cent true".[3]

What The National Plan offered Wilson was cover – a breathing space during which something could be seen to be being done. And, beyond that, something good might turn up. And at the start of 1966 there were signs of hope – trade figures had improved and the pressure on sterling had eased. Wilson seized the opportunity to call a General Election. The Labour Party manifesto, *Time For Decision*, managed to achieve a tone combining sober statesmanship with self-congratulation: "During the past 18 months, Britain has faced, fought and overcome its toughest crisis since the War. More, it has in the teeth of adversity fashioned the new instruments of policy with which, under the guidance of the National Plan, a new and better Britain can be built....During the next five years we intend to carry through a massive programme for modernising and strengthening British industry. That is the prime purpose of the National Plan."

Readers of *Time for Decision* would never at the time have guessed that within weeks of the publication of the manifesto, the National Plan would be officially consigned to the waste-paper basket. They might too have been surprised to know that, despite the manifesto's boast of a commitment to full employment, there was behind the scenes governmental concern that unemployment was too low. The deflationary measures used so far had failed to make much impact on the high employment rate – much to the concern of James Callaghan who believed that unemployment needed to rise. "How else can we make the economy work?" he complained to his Cabinet colleagues.[4]

But Wilson's timing was perfect, resulting in a Labour landslide that gave Wilson a majority of nearly a hundred.

But the election had been called in the nick of time. The crisis that, according to the manifesto, had been vanquished was soon back with a vengeance. Within weeks the country was plunged into a fresh currency crisis and the Governor of the Bank of England had to warn Wilson that the drain on reserves was now so heavy that devaluation might be unavoidable. The immediate response was to increase Bank Rate by 1% and banks were required to double the amount given over to the Bank of England to be held as special deposits. But these initial touches on the brake were too late and too light to stem the tide.

In the face of a dangerously deteriorating position, the Government had seemed to dither. On Sunday July 10 the leading article in the *Observer* had judged that "The Government is facing the complete breakdown of its economic policies". The following day the *Times* pointedly questioned whether the Government knew how to handle the crisis. By Tuesday, provoked by these and similar comments, Wilson was obliged to make one of his now-traditional 'firmness of purpose' speeches: "We shall not shrink from any further measures, however severe or unpopular, that may be necessary now or at any other time".

Behind the scenes the Cabinet was at odds over what was to be done. Wilson had up to this point managed to keep key economic decisions close to home – decided essentially by himself with input from Callaghan and Brown. But the magnitude of this latest crisis made rule from the centre – or at least by inner cabinet – too risky.

A broader consensus was now needed around the critical decisions that would have to be made. Wilson not only had to open-up the economic debate more widely within the cabinet, he even had to admit discussion of the 'great unmentionable'. Devaluation could at last be openly discussed in Cabinet and with Brown now converted to the idea – and Callaghan wobbling between for and against – Wilson had to demonstrate some flexibility. In private conversation with Crossman he even went so far as to say that "I'm not adamant against devaluation, but we shall have to get the pound stabilized first so that we can float from strength not from weakness". The strategy Wilson dangled before Crossman was to take immediate measures to secure the pound at its current parity, then introduce import restrictions to ease the balance of payments and then, in a year's time, not devalue but allow the pound to float.

The idea of flotation had come up before; Wilson had threatened the Governor of the Bank of England with the possibility in 1964. The threat had worked but the Governor must have known, as must Wilson, that the suggestion was highly problematic. The Bretton Woods agreement of 1944 excluded the option of flotation and a breach of that agreement might well have prevented Britain getting access to further bailout loans from the International Monetary Fund. Wilson's apparent interest in this scheme may have been genuine at the time, or it may just have been a strategy to encourage Crossman to believe that Wilson was prepared to consider radical approaches to the new crisis. In any event, although

Wilson was obliged to let the possibility of devaluation or flotation be at last openly discussed, he soon deftly shunted the issue into a siding, by ruling that the matter should be referred to a special Cabinet committee.

The devaluers/floaters in the Cabinet had at least been allowed to voice their opinion, but in the end they were outnumbered by what Barbara Castle described as the "do nothing yet brigade". But doing nothing about devaluation did not mean doing nothing at all. On 20th July, Wilson got up in the House to announce a massively deflationary package that aimed to reduce current demand by £500 million. The next day's *Guardian* declared that "the Labour government has given Britain the biggest dose of deflation we have seen". It was less than four months since Labour had won a massive election victory on the back of confident assurances that the adverse economic tide had been turned.

It had been a humiliating volte-face for the Government, but by the time of the next Budget – in April 1967 – breezy optimism was back in style. "The freeze and squeeze have been worth it", Callaghan told the House as he reported an improvement in the balance of payments, the repayment of some loans and an upturn in the international confidence in sterling. "We are back on course," he concluded, "The ship is picking up speed. Every seaman knows the command at such a moment: 'Steady as she goes'." There would be just 221 days to go before the ship was on the rocks of devaluation.

The announcement of devaluation, on Saturday 18th November 1967, was in retrospect a real turning-point.

Roy Jenkins' eventual grasp of the importance of securing the benefits of devaluation by combining it with measures of deflation, finally achieved the economic stability that the government had, through its own failings, thwarted since coming to power.

Whatever had been gained initially in political terms – by insulating Labour from being labelled as the 'devaluation party' – had been squandered in economic terms. Not least in the cost of the vast sums of money that had been spent on defending the pound – not to mention the debts that had been incurred in order to finance that defence. But in the end the years of devaluation deferred had also had an enormous cost politically and, however skilfully Wilson tried to cover the reversal, he had now had the shine taken off his public image.

One criticism of Wilson is not entirely just. The day after devaluation he made a television broadcast in the course of which he explained that the change in parity "doesn't mean, of course, that the pound here in Britain, in your pocket or purse or in your bank, has been devalued." This explanation led to wide criticism that Wilson was misleading viewers by giving the impression that devaluation would not affect them personally. But the reason why Wilson made this point is that the Treasury's briefing manual on how to handle a devaluation (guidance which had been originally drafted in 1964 and occasionally updated since) specifically warned that in 1949 some people had mistakenly understood that the devaluation of that year had reduced the face value of the money they held. The 'pound in your pocket' section of Wilson's television broadcast was actually drafted by a very senior Treasury official – William Ryrie, Assistant Secretary for International Monetary Affairs – who agreed the controversial wording of that section with Marcia Williams, Wilson's private secretary. Wilson's intention was to avoid popular misconceptions about devaluation, not to conceal its real implications. In fact, his broadcast made perfectly plain that people would be affected by devaluation's upward impact on prices. If the clumsiness of the wording in that broadcast was misleading, it was innocently so.

His manner during that broadcast was a masterclass in grave statesmanship. It is too easy – and unjust – to dismiss this as play-acting. One of Wilson's great strengths was to absorb significant reversals with reassuring calm. This was an enormous asset to his leadership. He had a remarkable ability to reposition and move forward after a setback and this was backed by considerable self-possession and reserves of personal courage.

The reputational damage from devaluation extended to Wilson's two most senior colleagues. George Brown had to move to the Foreign Office from the Department of Economic Affairs, bitterly aware that his National Plan was now nothing more than an exhibit in the Museum of Abandoned Ideas. James Callaghan, the humiliated Chancellor, moved to the Home Office having to endure, as a final insult, that Wilson preferred to replace him with Roy Jenkins, rather than accept Callaghan's recommendation that he should appoint Anthony Crosland.

But for all that there was now an opportunity for a fresh start. And Jenkins, after some initial missteps, did exhibit a compelling picture of both grasp and grip. Wilson, who could not in any case afford to lose a second Chancellor, did not attempt to thwart Jenkins' deflationary strategy. And, to his considerable credit, he did not press his Chancellor to deliver a give-away budget in the election year. It is a fair criticism that for the first three years of his Government Wilson really had only one economic aim – to defend the pound. But once that defence had failed Wilson faced-up to its consequences and fully committed his authority to endorsing Jenkins' economic policy. The Labour Party's manifesto for the 1970 election was able to point out that the deficit of £800 million it had inherited in 1964 had by the financial year 1969/70 been turned into a surplus of £550 million. This was thanks to Roy Jenkins – but also a credit to Wilson who had provided Jenkins with unqualified backing.

It had been Wilson's bad luck that on finally getting Labour over the electoral line, he came to power at a time of acute economic crisis. His misfortune was increased by the smallness of his majority in the Commons. He knew from the moment that he entered Number 10 that he would not have much time before he would have to call another election. Inevitably he knew that a devaluation at the start would provide the Conservative Party with the central charge in its next election campaign. His defence – that he had to protect Labour from being branded as the party of devaluation – may not be the whole truth. It seems probable that Wilson was sufficient of a realist to know that devaluation might in the long run be inevitable, but that a combination of massive overseas loans and a modest tightening on expenditure would in the meantime give his Government enough breathing space until he could call another election with the hope of this time winning a substantial majority. If devaluation was then unavoidable, he would at least have another five years before he had to go to the country again.

The principal reason why Wilson's 1964-70 government is to be judged a failure is because it loudly pre-advertised its own test of its future success – and failed it. In the run-up to the 1964 General Election, Jim Northcott - a member of the Labour Party's research staff – wrote for Penguin a small book, *Why Labour?*, setting out the case for a Labour vote. With the dangers of the Maudling boom already in view, Northcott warned his readers that "once again we face the prospect of yet another post-election payments crisis, followed by the same old round of cuts, squeezes, freezes and all – unless we have a major change to economic policy". This seemed clear enough. But, of course, once the inevitable post-election payments crisis arrived, Britain did not get a major change to economic policy – it got a continuation of the same old one as before.

The lesson of hubris was not learned. Before the 1966 election the Labour Party manifesto boasted that "This is a Government that governs: it does not flop along from crisis to crisis as the Tories did, for so much of their 13 years". Perhaps the most fitting comment on this comes from Harold Wilson himself: "The situation we are debating today is painfully familiar. Once again, within a few months of a General Election which was fought on prosperity, the magic has gone and we have to face economic realities…champagne only a few months ago, and now we have the morning after". These words are, however, not a candid reflection on his own government's over-sold promises but words spoken by Wilson in the House of Commons in 1960 the year after the Conservatives had won their third General Election in a row. "A week is a long time in politics," Wilson once said – but perhaps it is easier to keep track of time when the weeks (and the opportunities for hostages to fortune) keep repeating themselves.

The record of the 1964-70 government is not a history of great achievements. But it is not a story devoid of successes or positive improvements. Many features of everyday life, now taken for granted, owe their start in life to Wilson's first Government. Amongst them are the reduction of the age of majority to 18 (including the right to vote); the introduction of the roadside breathalyser, backed by a scientific definition of intoxication; the establishment of the Open University; decimal currency; the legal principle of equality of pay for men and women; majority verdicts in trials; suspended sentences; the installation of car seat-belts as a factory-fitted standard and the original Trades Description Act that established consumer-protection against misleading information.

Another success – though at the time some considered it a failing – was the decision to cut-back on Britain's military commitment overseas, particularly its commitment to a presence at the furthest reaches from home. The withdrawal from 'East of Suez' was, at the time, a retreat forced-on a reluctant government by the overall cost of the overseas deployment and its financially-draining impact on the balance of payments. But in scaling-back at least the outer fringes of these overseas commitments, the decision had in retrospect some claim to being the most tangible sign of a move towards achieving, on the world stage at least, the status that Wilson had promised in the very title of his 1964 manifesto – a "New Britain".

The changes often cited as the most significant achievements of the 1964-70 government are the number of social reforms. A good example is *The National Health Service (Family Planning) Act 1967,* which made contraception more widely and more easily obtainable. Until this became law, family doctors could prescribe the contraceptive pill to married women only and local authority 'family planning' clinics were permitted to provide help only to married women whose health was deemed at risk from further pregnancy. This change in the law was one of a number of advances that although technically not government measures, would never have reached the statute book without government support. Other highly significant examples of social reform during 1964-70 include the Abortion Act, the Divorce Act (which amongst other improvements introduced the concept of 'no-fault' divorce and the unilateral right to divorce after two years of separation) and the Sexual Offences Act (that legalised homosexual activities between consenting adults in private).

Wilson has been given credit for allowing the liberal-minded Roy Jenkins to throw his weight (and in consequence the gift of the necessary parliamentary time) behind these progressive measures. But while there were positive advances in legislation of this kind there were also reversals that suggest at least inconsistency in Wilson's social conscience. In May 1966, Roy Jenkins, speaking as Home Secretary, had trailed his intention to reform current race relations legislation. He declared "I define integration not as a flattening process of assimilation, but as equal opportunity, accompanied by cultural diversity, in an atmosphere of tolerance. This is the goal."[5] But the goal posts were abruptly moved under James Callaghan, Jenkins' successor as Home Secretary, who introduced a new law specifically targeted at restricting non-white immigration. Wilson seems to have been as content with Callaghan's hard-line position as he had earlier been with the libertarian aspirations of Roy Jenkins. In this regard, as in too many others, it suggested that there might be no fixed points in his ethical compass. The ultimate illustration of this would appear post-1970, when, for reasons no stronger than political convenience, Wilson came out against the basis of Heath's entry into Europe, even though it was clearly on terms that he would have accepted when he had attempted to join during his own time in government.

Wilson was repeatedly suspicious of his colleagues' ambitions, with at times an almost paranoid conviction that others were plotting to replace him. But this mistrust had not inhibited him from bringing into his Cabinet hugely talented people who could achieve the status of rivals. But once Wilson had packed his Cabinet with big talents, he then used a range of tricks to keep them under control. He shuffled his ministers around; he insulated key decisions by confining their discussions to small, inner groups; he played one minister off against another and he allowed discussion to ramble-on in order to postpone or even avoid a controversial decision.

These tactics were admittedly underhand, but the key ministers in his cabinet were powerful horses – and, in any event, not naturally inclined on their own to pull as a team. Had Wilson been a less confident Prime Minister he might have insulated himself against rivalry and resistance by filling his cabinet with low-fliers incapable of gaining the height to offer any serious disagreement or challenge. He chose not to do this, but instead picked people whom he knew to pack serious political challenge. His Cabinet was all the better for it. The failings of Wilson's government were in no way due to a shortage of intellectual capacity or a lack of big ideas. Brown, Castle, Crossman, Healey and Jenkins were not only big thinkers, but also hard-hitters. Out of the 'Big Six' only Callaghan had an undistinguished mind - though, as events would later turn out, he had the firmest grip on the greasy pole of ambition.

Perhaps Wilson's most critical weakness, so far as his

management of the Cabinet was concerned, was that he kept his cards close to his chest at times when what was actually needed was direct leadership. But direct leadership requires, amongst other things, a longer-term view. And, as Tony Benn noted in his diary, "Harold Wilson simply doesn't like forward thinking".[6] Wilson was strong on political tactics, much less at home with political strategy. He could usually be relied on to know what to do 'in the moment' but repeatedly struggled to see beyond the immediate. He had a capacity for detail, but little interest in – or feeling for – the big picture. This short-sightedness would frequently lead to difficulties, even to embarrassment – for example, when he decided on the use of sanctions against Rhodesia because of its illegal act of unilateral independence, Wilson assured the world that these sanctions would work "in weeks rather than months". This assurance was, to say the least, incautious, and failed to foresee that the blockade on trade with Rhodesia would be circumvented by South Africa and Portugal and willingly ignored by other countries, including France, Germany and Japan.

Despite so much accumulating political and economic wreckage, Wilson retained a remarkable degree of popular confidence, much of it built on his personal image. Late in the day of the 1966 General Election, Wilson left the Adelphi Hotel in Liverpool to travel to the count in his Huyton constituency. As he came out onto the street he was greeted by a waiting crowd with cheers and shouts of "Good Old Harold!"[7] And that public display of local affection does illustrate something remarkable about Wilson's popularity. He possessed the dignified gravity of a Prime Minister, but he also came across as someone homely and unaffected. A Prime Minister who was – to use in an entirely different way a phrase usually attached to a later leader – "one of us". What is even more remarkable is that much of that public affection – and to a degree confidence – endured, no matter what.

Heath's victory at the 1970 General Election almost certainly owed nothing directly to the devaluation of the pound – the effect was indirect, with people withholding their vote from Labour out of resentment over the wage-freeze that had been part of the devaluation package. But although Heath had won the people's vote he could never match Wilson in everyday popularity. His stiff awkwardness was a stark contrast to Wilson's 'man of the people' image (as evidenced by his pipe-smoking, his suits from Burton's, and his declared preference for tinned salmon and alleged taste for HP sauce).

Despite the enormous energy and intellectual capacity for big ideas around the Cabinet table – not to mention all the reserves of political energy accumulated during the long years in Opposition – it is impossible to characterise the 1964-70 government as a success. One hostile critic dismissed its record as a "breach of promise".[6] Another commentator, more favourably inclined, judged it to be "the light that failed".[9] Perhaps the most ingeniously-perceptive characterisation was to describe the story of Wilson's government as like "an old Hollywood film run backwards, in which the happy ending is at the beginning, and everything thereafter goes wrong".[10]

In the run-up to the 1964 election Harold Wilson did not just offer a 'happy ending', he promoted it with a personal guarantee. On the face of it, the Conservative victory in 1970 was a damning verdict on his credibility. But when Heath got into trouble with the trade unions and called another General Election, it was to 'Good old Harold' that the country turned again – even though Wilson had been notoriously unsuccessful in his own showdown with the unions. In 1959, after Labour's third election defeat in a row, the Conservatives had seemed to have established an invincible place as the natural party of government; Labour appeared doomed to a political life confined exclusively to the opposition benches. It was Wilson's leadership that triumphantly reversed the Party's fortunes, to the extent that in 1976 he became the first Labour leader to win four terms as Prime Minister.

There is a fine statue of Harold Wilson on the forecourt of Huddersfield Station. The sculptor, Ian Walters, has magnificently captured Wilson's likeness and posture, but the statue has a resemblance that is also strongly metaphorical. The statue shows Wilson in full-stride, dressed in a seriously-crumpled suit, indicated by heavy creases to the jacket and the trousers. The entire figure is pure Wilson. The purposeful step and the firm set of the head reference Wilson's promise of a better tomorrow, while the bedraggled suit seems to hint at the shop-worn record. It is hard to imagine a more striking visual interpretation of what seems to be the most fitting epitaph for Wilson's 1964-70 government. Hope without glory.

NOTES AND REFERENCES

CHAPTER ONE: - Introduction

[1] Party Political Broadcast, 15 July 1964
[2] Tony Benn, Out of the Wilderness: Diaries 1963-67, p 131

CHAPTER TWO: - George Brown: Drunk With Power

[1] Quoted in Brian Brivati, Hugh Gaitskell, p72

[2] Roy Jenkins, The Chancellors, p 454

[3] Quoted in Alan Bullock, Ernest Bevin, Foreign Secretary, p 441

[4] Richard Crossman, The Backbench Diaries of Richard Crossman, p482

[5] See John Brunner, What use is the National Plan? New Society, 25th March 1965

[6] Barbara Castle, The Castle Diaries, p 165

[7] Barbara Castle, *op cit*, p165

[8] George Brown, In My Way, p205

[9] Paul Gore-Booth, quoted by Peter Paterson, Tired and Emotional: The Life of Lord George Brown, p237

[10] Yoshihiko Mizumoto, Harold Wilson's Efforts at a Negotiated Settlement of the Vietnam War 1965-67, Journal of International History, March 2005, p31. See also, Sylvia Ellis, Britain, America and the Vietnam War, p220

[11] Oral history transcript, Chester L Cooper, interview 3(iii), 8/7/1969 LBJ Library Oral Histories, LBJ Presidential Library

[12] Denis Healey, The Time Of My Life, p335

[13] Barbara Castle, *op cit*, p 339

[14] George Brown, In My Time, p174

[15] Barbara Castle, *op cit*, p 398

[16] Richard Crossman, Diary of a Cabinet Minister, Volume 1, p 161

[17] Barbara Castle, *op cit*, p 167

[18] Eric Roll, Crowded Hours, p 171

[19] See Obituary, Sir Donald MacDougall, Daily Telegraph, 29 March 2004

[20] Nick Fenn, Of Shreds and Patches, p 58

[21] See Richard Toye, The Labour Party's External Economic Policy in the 1940s, The Historical Journal, 43, 1 pp 212

[22] James Callaghan, Time and Chance, p 184

[23] Richard Crossman, Diaries of a Cabinet Minister, Vol 1, p 300

CHAPTER THREE: - Richard Crossman: The Politics of Disruption

[1] Anthony Howard, Crossman: The pursuit of power, p266

[2] Quoted by David Marquand, The Progressive Dilemma, p139

[3] Anthony Howard, *op cit*, p85

[4] Alan Watkins, Brief Lives, p37

[5] Richard Crossman, The Backbench Diaries, p 326

[6] Andrew Roth, The Yorkshire Walter Mitty, p 140

[7] Richard Crossman, The Backbench Diaries, p 47

[8] Richard Crossman, *ibid*, p 409

[9] Richard Crossman, *ibid*, p787

[10] Richard Crossman, *ibid*, p 969

[11] Quoted in Dominic Sandbrook, White Heat, p 59

[12] Hansard, 22 July 1963

[13] Richard Crossman, Diary of a Cabinet Minister Vol 1, p 45

[14] Alan Watkins, The Academic in Office, Spectator, 29 October 1965

[15] Anthony Howard, Crossman, p 273

[16] Hansard, 10 March 1971

[17] James Callaghan, Time and Chance, p 167

[18] Richard Crossman, Diary of a Cabinet Minister, Vol 1, p 153

[19] Richard Crossman, *ibid*, p 81

[20] Report of the enquiry into the collapse of flats at Ronan Point, Canning Town, HMSO 1968, Para 183

[21] Andrew Cox, Adversarial Politics and Land, p 134

[22] Quoted in Michael Tichelar, The Failure of Land Reform in Twentieth Century England, p 165 (where however the date of the broadcast is incorrectly attributed to 1965).

[23] Sunday Times, 5 October 1975

[24] Alan Watkins, The Academic in Office, Spectator, 29 October 1965

[25] Richard Crossman, Diary of a Cabinet Minister, Vol 1, p 470

[26] Richard Crossman, Diary of a Cabinet Minister, Volume 2, p 17

[27] Bernard Crick, The Reform of Parliament, Preface *(unpaginated)*

[28] Richard Crossman, Diaries of a Cabinet Minister, Vol 2, p 118

[29] Richard Crossman, *ibid*, p 236

[30] Richard Crossman, *ibid*, p 347

[31] Richard Crossman, Diaries of a Cabinet Minister, Vol 3, p 412

[32] Richard Crossman, *ibid*, p 784

[33] Christopher Moran, Classified: Secrecy and the State in Modern Britain, p 248

[34] Harold Evans, Good Times, Bad Times, p 17

[35] Richard Crossman, Diary of a Cabinet Minister, Vol 1, p 98

[36] Richard Crossman, Diary of a Cabinet Minister, Vol 3, p 459

[37] Quoted in Philip Zeigler, Wilson, The Authorised Life, p 454

[38] Roy Jenkins, Portraits and Miniatures, p254

[39] Tam Dalyell, Dick Crossman, p 183

CHAPTER FOUR: - James Callaghan: Point-to-Point Navigation

[1] James Callaghan, Time and Chance, p167

[2] Samuel Brittan, Inside the DEA, p 59

[3] Kenneth O Morgan, Callaghan A Life, p 186

[4] Hansard, 4 April 1963

[5] Bank of England Report for the Year ended 28th February 1965

[6] Bank of England Report for the Year ended 28th February 1966

[7] Hansard, 1 March, 1966

[8] Callaghan, Time and Chance, p 193

[9] Harold Wilson, The Labour Government 1964-70, p249

[10] Richard Crossman, Diary of a Cabinet Minister, Volume 1, p 557

[11] Crossman, Diaries of a Cabinet Minister, Vol 1, p568

[12] Samuel Brittan, Steering the Economy, p335

[13] Barbara Castle, The Castle Diaries, p280

[14] Quoted in Edward Pearce, Denis Healey, p339

[15] Hansard, 20 February 1968

[16] Richard Crossman, Diary of a Cabinet Minister, Volume 2, p 636

[17] Bill Smithies and Peter Fiddick, Enoch Powell on Immigration, p 20

[18] CAB/128/43

[19] Tony Benn, Office Without Power, p320. Cf. "Callaghan could not possibly have been accused of racial prejudice". Morgan, Callaghan A Life, p 30

[20] The Downing Street Declaration, Cmnd. 4158

[21] Harold Wilson, The Labour Government, 1964-70, p. 697

[22] Richard Crossman, The Diaries of a Cabinet Minister, Vol. 3, p. 516

[23] Barbara Castle, The Castle Diaries 1964-70, p. 686

[24] Kenneth O Morgan, Callaghan A Life, p. 714

CHAPTER FIVE: - Barbara Castle: Driving on the Left

[1] William Mellor, What we stand for in the struggle for socialism, Tribune, 1 January 1937

[2] Barbara Castle, The Castle Diaries, p. 51

[3] The National Plan, p. 6

[4] Harold Wilson, The Labour Government 1964-70, p 11

[5] Quoted in Fifty Years of the Breathalyser, Parliamentary Advisory Council for Transport Safety, 2017, p. 2

[6] Richard Crossman, Diaries of a Cabinet Minister, Vol 2, p. 531

[7] Richard Crossman, Diaries of a Cabinet Minister, Vol 1, p. 428

[8] Clive Jenkins, 'We Haven't Got Enough!' in The Incompatibles: Trade Union Militancy and the Consensus, ed. Robin Blackburn & Alexander Cockburn, Penguin 1967

[9] Barbara Castle, Fighting All The Way, p. 413

[10] Ben Pimlott, Harold Wilson, p. 527. See also Austen Morgan, Harold Wilson, p. 355. Pimlott's and Morgan's accounts are based on interviews with Healey. But Healey gave a slighty different version in his autobiography, see Healey, The Time of My Life, p. 341.

[11] The Times, 15/11/68

[12] Barbara Castle, The Castle Diaries, p566

[13] The Guardian, 31 December 1968

[14] Richard Crossman, Diaries of a Cabinet Minister, Vol 3, p303

[15] The Times, 29 May 1968

[16] The Guardian, 29 May 1968

[17] Hansard, 26 June 1968

[18] The Guardian, 4 May 2002

[19] Roy Hattersley, Who Goes Home? p69

[20] Roy Jenkins, Life at the Centre, p 290

CHAPTER SIX: - Denis Healey: Politics as a Martial Art

[1] Geoffrey Williams & Bruce Reed, Denis Healey, p. 31

[2] *ibid*

[3] Denis Healey, Time of My Life, p. 169

[4] Hansard, 2 August 1956

[5] Denis Healey, Time of My Life, p. 174

[6] Ian Mikardo, Back-Bencher, p. 202

[7] The Times, 19 October 1964

[8] Geoffrey Williams & Bruce Reed, Denis Healey, p. 169

[9] Denis Healey, Time of My Life, p. 251

[10] Quoted in Edward Pearce, Denis Healey, p. 260

[11] Hansard, 23 November 1964

[12] Richard Crossman, Diaries of a Cabinet Minister, Volume 2, p. 85

[13] The Guardian, 17 February 1967

[14] Hansard, 24 July 1967

[15] Tony Benn, Office Without Power, p. 3

[16] The Times, 30 December 1967

[17] Cecil King, The Cecil King Diary, 1965-70, p. 204

[18] Hansard, 26 March 1974

[19] Quoted in Edward Pearce, Denis Healey, p. 577

CHAPTER SEVEN: Roy Jenkins: Politics à la Carte

[1] Roy Jenkins, A Life at the Centre, p. 41

[2] Roy Jenkins, Asquith, 1964, p. 20

[3] Woodrow Wyatt, Confessions of an Optimist, p. 175

[4] PREM 11/4612

[5] Anthony Shrimsley, The First Hundred Days of Harold Wilson, p. 68. See also Jenkins, A Life at the Centre, p. 162

[6] Richard Wiggs, The Case Against Supersonic Transport, p. 95

[7] AF/CMS/329/64

[8] Hansard, 9 February 1965

[9] Cecil King, The Cecil King Diary 1965-1970, p. 19

[10] Hansard, 22 July 1966

[11] Hansard 2 February 1966

[12] The Barbara Castle Diaries, p187

[13] Roy Jenkins, A Life at the Centre, p. 60

[14] Barbara Castle, The Castle Diaries, p355

[15] Alec Cairncross, The Wilson Years, A Treasury Diary, p. 290

[16] Edmund Dell, The Chancellors, p. 357

[17] Barbara Castle, The Castle Diaries, p. 674

[18] CAB/128/44

CHAPTER EIGHT: Harold Wilson: Hope without Glory

[1] Alec Cairncross, Managing the British Economy in the 1960s, p. 92

   Richard Crossman, Diaries of a Cabinet Minister, Volume Two, p. 42

[3] Donald MacDougall, Don and Mandarin p. 165-166

[4] Barbara Castle, The Castle Diaries, p. 58

[5] The Guardian, 24 May 1965

[6] Tony Benn, Office Without Power, p. 228

[7] Eyewitness account provided to the author by Roger Willis.

[8] Clive Ponting, Breach of Promise

[9] Michael Stewart, The Jekyll and Hyde Years

[10] See Robert Rhodes James, Ambitions and Realities, p 211

SELECT BIBLIOGRAPHY

Annan, Noel, *Our Age*, 1990

Arnison, Jim, *The Million Pound Strike* 1971

Beckerman, Wilfred (Ed) *The Labour Government's Economic Record 1964-1970* 1972

Benn, Tony, *Out of the Wilderness, Diaries 1963-67* 1987

——, *Office Without Power, Diaries 1968-72* 1988

Blackaby, F T (ed) *British Economic Policy 1960-74* 1979

Brandon, Henry, *In the Red* 1966

Brittan, Samuel, *Steering the Economy* 1971

——, *Inside the Department of Economic Affairs* 2012

Brivati, Brian, *Hugh Gaitskell* 1996

Brown, George, *In My Way* 1971

Brown, Neville, *Arms Without Empire* 1967

Bullock, Alan, *Ernest Bevin, Foreign Secretary* 1983

Cairncross, Alec, *Managing the British Economy in the 1960s* 1996

——, *The Wilson Years* 1997

Cairncross, Alec & Eichengreen, Barry, *Sterling in Decline* 2003

Callaghan, James, *Time and Chance* 1987

Campbell, John, *A Well-Rounded Life* 2014

Castle, Barbara, *The Castle Diaries, 1964-70* 1984

Castle, Barbara, *Fighting all the Way* 1993

Clegg, Hugh, *How to Run an Incomes Policy* 1971

Conservative Political Centre, *Fair Deal At Work* 1968

Crosland, Susan, *Tony Crosland* 1982

Crossman, Richard *The Diaries of a Cabinet* Minister, *Volume One* 1975

——, *The Diaries of a Cabinet Minister, Volume Two* 1976

——, *The Diaries of a Cabinet Minister, Volume Three* 1977

Dalyell, Tam, *Dick Crossman, A Portrait* 1989

Davis, William, *Three Years Hard Labour* 1968

Dell, Edmund, *The Chancellors*, 1996

——, *A Hard Pounding* 1991

——, *A Strange Eventful History* 1999

Dorfman, Gerald A, *Government vs Trade Unionism in British Politics Since 1968* 1979

Evans, Harold, *Good Times, Bad Times* 1983

Foot, Paul, *The Politics of Harold Wilson*, 1968

Hattersley, Roy, *Who Goes Home?* 1996

Healey, Denis, *A Labour Britain and the World* 1964

——*The Time Of My Life* 1990

Hennessy, Peter, *The Prime Minister* 2000

Hill, Andrew & Whichelow, Anthony, *What's Wrong With Parliament?* 1964

HMSO, *The National Plan* 1965

HMSO, *Royal Commission on Trade Unions and Employers' Associations, Report* 1968

Howard, Anthony, Crossman, *The Pursuit of Power*, 1990

Hunter, Leslie, *The Road to Brighton Pier* 1959

James, Robert Rhodes, *Ambitions and Realities* 1972

Jenkins, Peter, *The Battle of Downing Street* 1970

Jenkins, Roy, *Pursuit of Progress* 1953

——, *Essays and Speeches* 1967

——, *European Diary* 1989

——, *A Life at the Centre* 1991

——, *A Life at the Center* 1991 (US)

——, *Portraits and Miniatures* 1994

Kellner, Peter & Hitchens, Christopher, *Callaghan, The Road to Number Ten* 1976

King, Cecil, *The Cecil King Diary 1965-1970* 1973

Lapping, Brian, *The Labour Government 1964-70* 1970

MacDougall, Donald, *Don and Mandarin*, 1987

Manser, W, *Britain in Balance* 1971

Mikardo, Ian, *Back-Bencher* 1988

Mitchell, Joan, *Groundwork to Economic Planning* 1966

——, *The National Board for Prices and Incomes* 1972

Morgan, Austen, *Harold Wilson* 1992

Morgan, Kenneth O, *Callaghan, A Life* 1997

Northcott, Jim, *Why Labour?* 1964

Paterson, Peter, *Tired and Emotional, The Life of Lord George Brown* 1993

Pearce, Edward, *Denis Healey* 2002

Perkins, Anne, *Red Queen* 2003

Pimlott, Ben, *Harold Wilson* 1992

Ponting, Clive, *Breach of Promise, Labour in Power 1964-70* 1989

Radice, Giles, *Friends & Rivals* 2002

Roll, Eric, *Crowded Hours* 1985

Roth, Andrew, *Sir Harold Wilson, Yorkshire Walter Mitty* 1977

Sandbrook, Dominic, *White Heat,* 2006

Shrimsley, Anthony, *The First Hundred Days of Harold Wilson* 1965

Smithies, Bill & Fiddick, Peter, *Enoch Powell on Immigration,* 1969

Stewart, Michael, *The Jekyll and Hyde Years* 1977

Taylor, Robert, *The Trade Union Question in British Politics* 1993

Thomas, Elizabeth, *Tribune 21* 1958

Tomlinson, Jim, *The Labour Governments 1964-1970, Economic Policy* 2004

Williams, Geoffrey & Reed, Bruce, *Denis Healey and the Politics of Power* 1971

Wiggs, Richard, *The Case Against Supersonic Transport* 1971

Wilson, Harold, *Purpose in Politics* 1964

——, *The New Britain* 1964

——, *The Labour Government 1964-70* 1971

Wyatt, Woodrow, *Confessions of an Optimist* 1985

Wybrow, Robert J, *Britain Speaks Out, 1937-87* 1989

Ziegler, Philip *Wilson* 1993

INDEX

K

L

Land Commission, 73, 80, 81, 82
London Gold Pool, 47

M

MacDonald, Ramsay, 307
Mackintosh, John, 99
Macmillan, Harold, 63, 224, 259, 303
majority verdicts, 323
Marples, Ernest, 162, 166
Maudling, Reginald
   dash for growth, 29
McDougall, Donald, 34, 52
Mellor, William, 149
Ministry of Transport, 111, 160, 164, 196, 204
Morrison, Herbert, 67
Mortimer, Jim, 180
Mountbatten, Lord Louis, 225

N

National Board for Prices and Incomes, 33, 40, 339
National Executive, 6, 13, 20, 67, 107, 153, 154, 171, 188, 251
National Plan, 31, 33, 34, 35, 36, 38, 53, 54, 55, 56, 57, 122, 159, 307, 314, 315, 320, 330, 333, 338
   published, 34
National Union of Seamen, 124, 170

Neal, Len, 180
Neild, Robert, 113
Northcott, Jim, 322

O

O'Neill, Terence, 136, 139
Open University, 323
Owen, David, 298, 299

P

Paisley, Ian, 139
Passmore, Sir Thomas, 161
Plowden, Sir Edwin, 269
Political Warfare Executive, 62

R

R A Butler,, 220, 273
Race Relations Act, 132, 294
Rachman, Peter, 74
Reginald Maudling, 29, 113, 114, 116, 220, 311
Rent Act, 73, 74, 75, 76, 101
Roberts-Arundel strike, 177
Robin Day, 28, 86
Rodgers, Bill, 298
Ronan Point, 79
Roy Hattersley, 203
Royal Ulster Constabulary, 134
Ryrie, William, 320

S

Scanlon, Hugh, 171
Sexual Offences Act, 274, 325

348

Printed in Great Britain
by Amazon